The Future of Anthropological

Anthropology is no longer a single discipline, but rather a range of different practices carried out in a variety of social contexts. Important new questions have been posed by the sustained challenge which third world, black and feminist scholars have provided to the established agenda of the social sciences and humanities in recent years. It is in this context that the nature and purpose of social knowledge, and in particular anthropological knowledge, comes into particular focus.

By examining the changing nature of anthropological knowledge and of the production of that knowledge, this book challenges the notion that only western societies have produced social theories of modernity and of global scope. Knowledge of society can no longer be restricted to a knowledge of face-to-face social relations but must encompass the effect of technology, global consumption patterns and changing geopolitical configurations.

The question 'what is social knowledge for?' is not intended to provoke an answer, but rather a series of interrogations. In *The Future of Anthropological Knowledge* contributors explore the nature of social knowledge from a variety of perspectives and examine the manner in which anthropological knowledge is changing and will be reformulated further in the future. In raising questions about who produces knowledge and theory, they map out an innovative agenda for the discipline in the twenty-first century.

Henrietta L. Moore is Reader in Social Anthropology and Director of the Gender Institute at the London School of Economics and Political Science.

ASA Decennial Conference Series
The Uses of Knowledge: Global and Local Relations
Series editor: Marilyn Strathern

The Future of Anthropological Knowledge

Edited by Henrietta L. Moore

London and New York

First published 1996
by Routledge
11 New Fetter Lane, London EC4P 4EE

Simultaneously published in the USA and Canada
by Routledge
29 West 35th Street, New York, NY 10001

Typeset in Times by
Florencetype Ltd, Stoodleigh, Nr Tiverton, Devon
Printed and Bound in Great Britain by
TJ Press (Padstow) Ltd, Padstow, Cornwall

British Library Cataloguing in Publication Data
A catalogue record for this book is available from the British Library

Library of Congress Cataloguing in Publication Data
A catalogue record for this book has been requested

ISBN   0–415–10786–5 (hbk)
ISBN   0–415–10787–3 (pbk)

Contents

Contributors

Peter Harries-Jones received his first degree in anthropology from Rhodes University, South Africa. He later studied under Evans-Pritchard and received his senior degree from Oxford University. He was the last research appointee of the Colonial Office to the Rhodes-Livingstone Institute in Zambia. His research in Zambia resulted in several publications, including a book about the urban organization of the independence movement. He later taught at University College, Swansea, and University of Khartoum before moving to York University in Ontario, Canada. His more recent work has been on the joint themes of social advocacy, social movements, communication and epistemology related to these themes. His particular interest has been in the environmental movement, both as a global and local phenomenon. His books include *Making Knowledge Count: Advocacy and Social Science* (McGill, 1991), which explores epistemology and method relating to the study of new social movements; and *A Recursive Vision: Ecological Understanding and Gregory Bateson* (University of Toronto Press, 1995) is a detailed study of Bateson's ecological epistemology. Based on archival research of letters and unpublished manuscripts, it presents the matrix of ideas from which Bateson draws his holistic perspectives about our ecological predicament. Forthcoming articles discuss the difficulties of relating environmental epistemology to social movement practice.

Wazir Jahan Karim is an anthropologist and Professor of anthropology at the School of Social Sciences, Universiti Sains Malaysia. She is also Chairperson of Graduate Studies at the School of Social Sciences, Universiti Sains Malaysia and Protem President of the proposed Malaysian Academy of Social Sciences (MASS). She obtained her Masters and Doctorate in anthropology at the London School of Economics and Political Sciences and has conducted extensive research on Malaysian indigenous minorities and women in politics, culture and religion, more specifically adat and Islam and the rights of Muslim women under Syariah Law. She has written and edited several books on minorities and women including *Ma' Betise' Concepts of Living Things* (London: Athlone, 1981); *Emotions of Culture: A Malay Perspective* (Singapore: Oxford University Press, 1990); *Women and Culture: Between Malay Adat and Islam* (Boulder: Westview, 1991); *Gendered Fields: Women, Men, Ethnography* (with D. Bell and P. Caplan (eds), London: Routledge, 1992) and *Male and Female in Developing Southeast Asia* (Oxford: Berg, 1994). She is currently conducting research on the impact of changes in environment and technology on minorities and coastal communities and the development of models of consumption in class and gender. Another forthcoming book is entitled *Sexuality and Domination* (1996).

Norman Long is Professor of social studies at the University of Bath. His publications include *Encounters at the Interface: A Perspective on Social Discontinuities in Rural Development* (The Agricultural University, Wageningen, 1989) and (with A. Long) *Battlefields of Knowledge: The Interlocking of Theory and Practice in Social Research and Development* (Routledge, 1992).

Emily Martin is Professor of anthropology at Princeton University. Her recent publications include *The Woman in the Body: A Cultural Analysis of Reproduction* (Beacon Press, 1987) and *Flexible Bodies: Tracking Immunity in America from the Days of Polio to the Age of AIDS* (Beacon Press, 1994). She is currently writing a book on the changing meanings of work in the USA.

Henrietta L. Moore is Reader in social anthropology and Director of the Gender Institute at the London School of Economics. Her books include *Feminism and Anthropology* (Polity Press, 1988) and *A Passion for Difference* (Polity Press, 1994).

Aihwa Ong, an Associate Professor of anthropology at Berkeley, is the author of *Spirits of Resistance and Capitalist Discipline: Factory Women in Malaysia* (State University of New York Press, 1987). She is the co-editor (with Michael G. Peletz) of *Bewitching Women, Pious Men: Gender and Body Politics in Southeast Asia* (University of California Press, 1995), and (with Don Nonini) of *On the Edge of Empires: Capitalism and Identity in Modern Chinese Transnationalism* (Routledge, 1996).

Paul Richards currently holds a joint appointment at the Agricultural University Wageningen (the Netherlands) and the Department of Anthropology, University College London (UK). He is the author of *Indigenous Agricultural Revolution* (1985), *Coping with Hunger* (1986) and *Fighting for the Rain Forest* (1996).

Mayfair Yang was born in Taiwan and received her Ph.D. in anthropology at the University of California, Berkeley. She is now Associate Professor of anthropology at UC Santa Barbara, teaching courses on Anthropology of Gender, Traditional Chinese Culture, Contemporary Chinese Society, Interpretive Anthropological Theory, and Anthropology of Mass Media. She received a five-year National Science Foundation grant, which allows her to go to China frequently for fieldwork. Her publications include *Gifts, Favors, and Banquets: The Art of Social Relationships in China* (Cornell University Press, 1994). She has also published many articles.

Series editor's preface

This book is one of five to have been produced from the Fourth Decennial Conference of the Association of Social Anthropologists of the Commonwealth held at St Catherine's College, Oxford, in July 1993. Sections were organized by Richard Fardon, Wendy James, Daniel Miller and Henrietta Moore, each of whom has edited their proceedings. In addition Wendy James acted as Oxford Co-ordinator, and it is principally due to her untiring efforts that the conference took place at all. As Convenor, I take the opportunity of acknowledging our debt to her, and of registering gratitude to Priscilla Frost for her organizational assistance and to Jonathan Webber for acting as conference Treasurer.

The Institute of Social and Cultural Anthropology at Oxford gave material as well as moral support. The following bodies are to be thanked for their generous financial assistance: the Wenner–Gren Foundation for Anthropological Research, the British Council, the Oxford University Hulme Trust Fund, the Royal Anthropological Institute and the Association of Social Anthropologists itself.

To suppose anthropological analysis can shift between global and local perspectives may well imply that the two coexist as broader and narrower horizons or contexts of knowledge. Indeed, the relationship seems familiar from the ethnographic record: in cosmologies that set a transcendent or encompassing realm against the details of everyday life; or in systems of value that aggrandize this feature while trivializing that; or in shifts between what pertains to the general or the particular, the collective or the individual. And if knowledge consists in the awareness of context shift, then such scaling may well seem routine. However, this book does not take scale for granted. It examines certain contexts in which people (including anthropologists) make different orders of knowledge for themselves as a prelude to questioning assumptions about the 'size' of knowledge implied in the contrast between global and local perspectives.

Marilyn Strathern
University of Cambridge

Chapter 1

The changing nature of anthropological knowledge
An introduction

Henrietta L. Moore

What role can anthropology play in the multipolar, globalized, post-colonial world we all now inhabit? How should anthropology respond to the shifting political determinations of representation and knowledge production? Anthropology is no longer a singular discipline, if it ever was, but rather a multiplicity of practices engaged in a wide variety of social contexts. A whole series of new questions has been posed by the sustained challenge which third world, black and feminist scholars have provided to the established agenda of the social sciences and humanities in recent years. The world of the academy has begun to tilt on its axis and to revolve in a slightly different manner. Such changes have been paralleled by significant shifts in the geopolitics of the world economy. It is in this context that the nature and purpose of social knowledge, and in particular anthropological knowledge, comes into particular focus.

The question 'what is social knowledge for?' cannot be answered; at least, not in the singular or the definitive. In any event, such a question is not intended to provoke an answer, but rather a series of interrogations. From the moment the process of interrogation gets under way, the terms themselves begin to present problems: whose knowledge; what sort of knowledge; what constitutes the social? These problems are emblematic rather than representative of a series of particularly pressing intellectual and political difficulties, all of which bear in some way or other on the highly charged relationships between knowledge, identity and power. The chapters in this volume work over the question of the nature of social knowledge from a variety of perspectives, and they examine the manner in which anthropological knowledge is changing and will be reformulated further in the future. In raising questions about who produces knowledge and theory, they map out an innovative set of understandings about the nature and politics of the anthropology of the twenty-first century. In this introduction, I examine some of the main themes raised in the rest of the book and provide my own suggestions for the future of anthropology.

WHO ARE THE PRODUCERS OF KNOWLEDGE?

We have all been aware in the social sciences of the impact of the critique of the Cartesian *cogito* and the unravelling of grand narratives and totalizing theories, variously labelled post-modernism, post-structuralism and/or deconstructionism. The debates sparked by these critiques have led to a revision of the role of the academic and/or the expert practitioner. One consequence has been a call for a revaluation of the actor's or community's point of view, as part of a more general call to specificity, to the local. The clear demand is that the politics of positionality and location should be recognized and addressed.

The anthropological response to this move has been ambiguous and driven by uncertainty. The call to the local and the specific was hardly radical. Anthropologists have long prided themselves on their valorization of the 'actor's point of view' and on their grasp of local circumstance and local perspectives. What was new was the questioning of the interpretative authority of the anthropologist and the focus on writing rather than fieldwork as the domain of knowledge production. Paradoxically, some hostile critics felt that what was being threatened was not only the anthropologist's experience of personal interaction and her collection of systematic data, but also the emphasis on local specificities. While supporters held that the post-modern turn revealed the dialogic and shared nature of cross-cultural interpretation and representation, detractors argued that anthropological texts were now more about the anthropologists than the people they were studying. In other words, both sides claimed the more authentic connection with local people and their specificities. At its most uninteresting, the debate collapsed into an unenlightened scuffle between the self-declared supporters of empiricism on the one hand and interpretation on the other. What is strange is that all this discord should have left so many important questions untouched.

For one thing, the anthropological definition of knowledge remained curiously divided. Anthropologists had always been happy to see local people as producers of local knowledge about for example, agricultural experimentation, cosmological theories, and medical cures, but there was very little question of such knowledge being valorized outside the local domain. This was true both for supporters and detractors of the so-called post-modernist turn. In other words, local people produce local theories and such theories are, almost by definition, not comparative ones. The implicit assumption was therefore that the theories of non-western peoples have no scope outside their context.

This unwitting parochialization of all theories other than those produced by western science and social science was paradoxically reinforced by the deconstructive/post-modernist turn which makes all theories partial and local. It thus never seemed to occur to the anthropological supporters of this move that it might be necessary to consider the comparative pretensions of local theories as part of the process of reanalysing knowledge production rather than simply revealing the partial nature of anthropological truths.

Deconstructionism argues, of course, that all theories are partial, and there is thus no distinction between the local theories of anthropologists masquerading as comparative social science and those of the people being studied. However, this position occludes the point about the production of knowledge and of how that production is valorized. Anthropologists, for all their concern with local understandings and specificities, do not habitually view the people they work with as producers of social science theory as opposed to producers of local knowledge.

This assumption is connected to the lack of politicization of knowledge production within the discipline of anthropology as a whole (see Ong, Chapter 4, this volume). The major issue here is one about how anthropologists treat each other and about how that treatment is predicated on the geopolitics of resource allocation (see Karim, Chapter 6, this volume). This problem is not confined to anthropology, but is rather a feature of the dominance of western theorizing in a variety of disciplines and of the structuring of the academy along the fracture lines of centre–periphery politico–economic relations. Anthropologists from the developing world, for example, may produce theoretically innovative work, but if they claim that it draws on theoretical traditions outside mainstream western social science, they are likely to find that it will be denigrated as partial and/or localized. If they are critical of western social science, they may find that they are sidelined. Western social science consistently repositions itself as the originary point of comparative and generalizing theory.

THE GENEALOGY OF DISCOURSE

It is in the context of the post-modernist debate in the social sciences and the humanities, and the resulting theoretical elaboration of notions of difference, that we can see this point amplified most clearly. Black and third world scholars, post-colonial theorists and feminists have pointed out how the analogical figure 'same-as'/'different-from' which underpins western philosophical thinking works in a pervasive and discriminatory manner to structure forms of representation and knowledge in specific contexts.[1] Several black and third world scholars in a variety of disciplines have developed specific theories of signifying, and methods for reworking the relationship between the same, the other and the analogue that function outside the Cartesian model of the knowing subject. I am thinking here of the work of various African philosophers and theologians, including Jean Kinyongo, Oleko Nkombe, Vincent Mulago, John Mbiti, Alexis Kagame of Henry Louis Gates and Gerald Vizenor, amongst others (Masolo 1994; Mudimbe 1988: chapters 2 and 3; 1991: Chapter 2; Gates

1988; Vizenor 1988, 1989). These theories, while dependent for their current intelligibility within western academia on the rise of post-modernism, are not post-modernist and are not derived from or intellectually dependent on post-modernism. This is not an attempt to develop an origins theory, but simply to point out that post-modernism shares some characterisitics with ways of philosophizing or thinking that have existed in other times and other places.[2] This point should not need making, but there is a purpose in the politics of the moment in empha-sizing that the critique of the Cartesian *cogito*, like Picasso's modernism, did not simply originate in Paris. The mutually informing nature of critical frameworks and analytical categories developed in apparently diverse intellectual milieux and geographical locations is only one of the reasons why claiming the originary nature of western philosophy and theory is misleading.

The critique of the subject–object relations based on the Cartesian *cogito* is one way of trying to rethink alterity, and by extension subjectivity and collectivity. Africa has a long history as the defining trope of an alterity which grounds western subjectivity, reason and identity. It is not surprising then that various African scholars should have sought to transcend this dualism and to establish alternative frameworks for the relationship between subject and object. The fact that these efforts began in the 1930s and were explicitly linked to the political projects of liberation and nationalism is something barely known about and almost completely unrecognized by the vast majority of social scientists and humanities scholars. The revaluation of some of this work, and the sudden mainstream respectability of black scholars like Henry Louis Gates and Gerald Vizenor, is the consequence of the modishness of post-modernism in the duck pond of western theory. In other words, their intellectual per-spectives have suddenly become valorized by the development of post-modernist thought in the West with its clearly parallel concerns, giving rise to a relatively comfortable situation where they can be safely understood as derivative. Feminist theory has experienced a similar problem, moving from being 'overstated' to being an 'offshoot' of post-modernism/deconstructionism. What this all amounts to is a testament to the continuing failure to recognize some groups of people in the world as producers of knowledge.

In seeking to link together a number of critiques of alterity, I am not suggesting that African, native American and Afro-American scholars are all making exactly the same kinds of argument. This would be crass, and besides, I am not interested in erecting an alternative totalizing theory. The more general point is really one about exclusion and about the genealogy of discourses. For example, one of the reasons for the general neglect of African philosophy by the western academy is that in the period since the 1950s a good many African philosophers have been writing on the borderline, or rather in the borderlands, between theology and anthropology (Mudimbe 1988, 1991; Masolo 1994). Their distinctive contribution has been in trying to link African religious beliefs to Christian theology. It is this very engagement with faith, both on the practical and the intellectual level – many of these scholars are actually Catholic priests and not practising anthropologists – which has permitted their reclassification and relocation as theologians rather than as secular scientists of culture. The scope of their enterprise, while located in specifics, is both comparative and global, just as it was for those African scholars writing about negritude.

The discourses of African philosophy cannot be understood outside the contexts of anthropology as a generalizing science and colonialism as a specific historical and political project. This is a point made most forcefully by African scholars from a variety of perspectives. There are those who make a claim for a specifically African philosophy based on African concepts and beliefs, sometimes known as ethno-philosophers, for example, Kagame (1956), Mbiti (1969) and Nkombe (1977), and their work seeks to revalorize African philosophy in the face of a colonial dialectic which consistently refigures what is African as the inferior of what is European. Other African scholars, for example, Towa (1979), Hountondji (1983) and Bodunrin (1984), are extremely critical of the ethno-philosophers whose work they see as a form of descriptive ethnography which fails to escape the terms of alterity dictated by a colonized and colonial mentality. Both sets of positions are thus underpinned, albeit in very different ways, by a recognition of the historical and political project of philosophy in Africa. This point is ignored to a significant degree by many non-African scholars, including anthropologists, who consistently fail to realize that the search for identity and authenticity which is essential to this work is part of a project of modernity; that is, a project for the future, and it is in this sense that the aspirations of the work are global. There are supporters and detractors for a complex array of ideas about subjectivity, nationalist identity, regional autonomy and Africanization within the communities of African scholars involved, but one dominant trend which Mudimbe (1988: Chapter 5) identifies involves a critical rereading of African and western theories and interpretations in order to expand the possibilities for knowledge production in the future. The relationships between knowledge and power remain very much bound up with questions of individual subjectivity and collective identity, as it does for the rest of the world. However, it would be a mistake to imagine that a privileging of the local and the specific, as well as a repudiation of certain kinds of totalizing theory, must necessarily entail a prohibition on comparative thinking, if not the end of knowledge itself.

When it comes to looking at the practices of western academic anthropology, it is often an incomplete and rather inchoate set of anxieties about comparison, authenticity and identity which seem to have served to rule much anthropology written by African scholars out of court. If we read Evans-Pritchard on the Nuer, why do we not read Francis Deng on the Dinka; and if we refer to Evans-Pritchard on the Luo, why do we not defer to Ogot; why do we not in fact use any of the major anthropology texts written by African scholars in the 1930s, 1940s and 1950s as teaching texts? One response is that these authors are not anthropologists, they are theologians or historians. Another response is that these texts are not anthropological because they are culturally specific and partisan. This is the kind of criticism regularly levelled, for example, at Jomo Kenyatta's book on the Kikuyu. 'Culturally specific, partisan', why should that be grounds for disqualification? Such characteristics do not, after all, necessarily distinguish these texts from any other anthropology text. The argument is surely one about who can be said to produce true knowledge.

There is a particular danger in discussing situated knowledges: in acknowledging the importance of alterity and diffraction in their constitution and conceptualization, one slips too easily into an unthought dialectic of opposition which is the negativity of difference. Mudimbe has said that one of the failings of anthropology is that it begins by measuring the distance from the same to the other (1988:81). What has to be avoided is any tendency to construct African knowledge(s), for example, as simple reversals of Euro-American ones. Processes of radical othering are merely methods of exclusion and hierarchization by another route. Indigenization of knowledge(s), while potentially powerfully creative for individuals and collectivities within specific contexts, runs the risk of defining certain kinds of knowledge as absolutely local, without comparative scope or wider application. It is imperative that anthropology should recognize that local knowledge, including local technical knowledge, can be part of a set of knowledges properly pertaining to political economy and the social sciences, and can thus be comparative in scope, as well as international in outlook (Richards, Chapter 7, this volume). What is sometimes implied in anthropological writing about local knowledges is that they constitute closed systems, in the sense that they are incapable of self-reflection and auto-critique. Indeed, this has long been thought to be one of the criteria which distinguishes traditional societies from modern ones. In the debate over whether African philosophy can be properly said to be a philosophy, one of the disputes has been about the existence or non-existence of an ongoing auto-critique of concepts, notions and forms of argument. It is reflexivity which is thought to be characteristic both of philosophy and of modern knowledge; without such auto-critique there is no knowledge, merely belief.

THE TECHNOLOGIZATION OF ANTHROPOLOGICAL KNOWLEDGE

This point raises the question of what constitutes knowledge. So far, I have been using the term knowledge(s) to encompass the theoretical in the broadest sense: philosophy, political economy, the social sciences, the humanities. I have not been speaking in the strict sense of those most modern forms of knowledge: science and technology. I want to turn now to the way in which science and technology are transforming anthropological knowledge through a transformation of its objects of enquiry.

The idea of the world as a very small pond linked together by the massive power of communication media and international capitalism is one of the background principles informing a great deal of intellectual endeavour, commercial activity, and techniques of government at the present time. One of the things that technology has really revolutionized is the scale or scales at which social relations operate. Face-to-face interaction, as many scholars have pointed out, is no longer the only basis for society, and this point alone revolutionizes anthropology's object of study. The shift that has taken place, and one which has been reflected in the language in which we teach and write, has been between social relations and sociality. The concept of sociality tries to embrace human/human and human/non-human relations. Writing that employs the notion of sociality is dependent on a decentring of the Cartesian subject, but most of it is not derived from nor even inspired by post-structuralism or post-modernism.[3]

One problem here concerns the mediation of our understanding of our bodies and of our self-understandings via technology (see Martin, Chapter 2, this volume). This includes everything from modern medicine's ability to represent the interior of bodies, and even our cells, to the transformation of intimate relations brought about by globalized soap operas and patterns of commodification. We are all now technologized selves in some very important sense. One consequence of this is that the boundaries of the self are expanded, and often breached. The self is no longer, if it ever was, a singular, self-contained entity, but a participating, relational one; and one which is no longer simply human.

However, selves, as we tend to forget, have probably never been simply human. They have in many times and many places been part divine, part animal, part vegetable and part machine. The new cosmologies of the hyper-real provided by computer games and the cinema may have much more to do with Dogon ancestors and the Ramayana than anthropologists, with their traditional and modern societies, have had time to comprehend. This is not to deny the interventionist power of modern science and technology, nor the massive asymmetries of power which sustain technological diffusion. But the imagined cosmologies of contemporary societies are proper objects for anthropological enquiry; and the availability and the speed with which technological productions diffuse makes everyone a producer of knowledge about technology to some degree or other. Perhaps more importantly, technology touches everyone's sense of self, all individual and collective identities. To a certain extent, it could be argued that this is not particularly new; perhaps it is only now that technology seems so pervasive and so intrusive that we, as ordinary observers of the contemporary condition, can see the degree to which selves are technologized.

The kind of thing I have in mind when I speak of the relationship between technology and identity is the way in which, earlier this century, blood transfusions in Central Africa produced stories of vampires and of children being stolen for their blood. These tales, which were reworkings of old themes and stories, were often aimed at Christian missionaries whose celebration of the Eucharist must have made them vulnerable to such accusations (White 1993a, 1993b). However, these stories were as much about colonial wealth extraction and exploitation as about anything else. Their modern counterparts are many, but in the 1970s when Malawi's new capital Lilongwe was built with South African money (and remember, Malawi was the only state in the region to support South Africa), people often refused to work on water installation schemes, particularly when the pipelines were to run close to hospitals. The story was a simple one: the purpose of such pipes was to pump blood from Malawi to South Africa to pay for Lilongwe. Debts must after all be paid. Technology transforms social relations.

These examples of technologized selves and identities do not feed on the hyper-real, on the kind of images purveyed by computer games and videos, but perhaps the part-turtle, part-human, part-machine actors who people the hyper-real are continuous, as well as discontinuous, with earlier forms of technologized selves. The idea that the modern world is producing individuals who are no longer fully human, that modernity attacks the completeness of the person, is misleading if we are trying to suggest that people in other times and places have been simply fully human.

What a particular perspective on technology opens us to as anthropologists, and as individuals, is not just the problems and potentialities of the contemporary moment, but a different way of thinking about selves and identities, an emergent auto-critique of our own knowledge constructions, a genealogy of our own discourse. And we arrive there by acknowledging other people as producers of knowledge about technology – knowledge which has a comparative and an international perspective – and by recognizing transformations in ourselves, as well as in our domains of enquiry.

If the boundaries of selves, subjectivities and collectivities are expanded by technology, and if what is breached in the process is the singular,

Cartesian subject and its binary economy of same/not same, then we should also be aware that other kinds of entities are put in question by a reformulation of the anthropological object of enquiry. Once again, this reformulation is forced by a recognition of others as producers of knowledge. Attention to local practices and discourses of knowledge entails a recognition of the global not as a monolithic entity sustained by grand narratives of progress, but as a set of situated and interrelated knowledges and practices, all of which are simultaneously local and global. Once again, we could say that post-structuralism and post-modernism have enabled an acknowledgement of diversity and plurality, and thereby of alternative accounts by others. However, a more critical perspective here would suggest that the alternatives preferred by much post-modernist theory are those that it produces itself, rather than those produced by others, hence the many accusations of exclusion and depoliticization levelled at post-modernist theorizing.

The formerly unquestioned entities of social science thinking, like system, subject and society, have come under attack from inside and outside anthropology, and over many years. At issue here are questions of fixity and closure. The bounded is being replaced, at least in academic discourse if nowhere else, by the relational. We are now no longer looking for ontological categories, but for interwoven patterns; what was once systemic is now mobile. What I have in mind here is Marilyn Strathern's analysis of body parts and social relations (1988), Gille Deleuze's desiring machines and nomadic knowledge (Deleuze and Guattari 1987, 1994), and Edward Said's (1983: Chapter 10) travelling theory (see also Yang, Chapter 5, this volume). These theories draw on rather different intellectual traditions, but what they share is a particular kind of critical practice.

POWER AT THE MARGINS

Both Deleuze and Said are concerned with the role of the intellectual which is, as they see it, to unmask power and thereby limit its affects.[4] This they consider should be the ethical relationship of academic knowledge to power (see Karim, Chapter 6, this volume). In addition, Deleuze emphasizes the violence of modern systems that use order as a form of domination, and his notion of ideas as mobile strategies that are resistant to systemization is congruent with his understanding of the role of the intellectual in modern society. Both Deleuze and Said stress the importance of knowledge production at the margins, of being in exile from the centre; and this decentring of the subject, which is both metaphorical and physical, has much in common with the independently developed theories of third world, feminist and black scholars which have long emphasized the analytical and critical power of the excentric perspective. I do not want to emphasize the commonalities between these theories because I am not interested in subsuming their differences. However, it is hard to overplay the value of these emerging discourses which seek to establish a space and a locale in the borderlands for knowledge production. Part of the significance of focusing on borderlands and margins has to do with questions about how knowledge works in different places, how it gets transformed, but also with borderlands and margins as spaces of transition, transformation and reformulation. What is new about such conceptualizations is that centres, borders and margins are no longer fixed locales, and the economy of exchange between centre and periphery is disrupted.

On another level, the replacement of fixed centre–periphery relations by a multicentred political economy has had clear consequences for the arts, social and political sciences, philosophy and technology. The manner in which we theorize our world is changing, as are the power relations constitutive of theory. The knowledges now produced are simultaneously local and global, but they are not universal. This is perhaps nowhere more apparent than in the rise of social movements and social interest groups. Such groups empower themselves by creating and/or amassing, and then transmitting, specialist knowledge. Anthropology has played a role here, through what is termed advocacy anthropology and participatory research, as other academic disciplines have done (see Harries-Jones, Afterword, this volume). What is particularly interesting about the specifically local or located knowledge generated by the activities of interest groups is that it is generalizable as a technique of knowledge, or, if you prefer, as a kind of analytics.

THE ANTHROPOLOGY OF GOVERNANCE

This methodologization of knowledge and of its link with power is, according to Foucault, one of the defining features of a modern world. If one takes Foucault's genealogy of the subject and subjectification in the European context as one genealogy amongst others, then the argument is a convincing one. However, to rewrite Foucault's genealogy as a progressive narrative of the relationship between the traditional and the modern does not, in my view, make a convincing argument. For example, the nineteenth-century Bemba polity of Central Africa was, for the most part, unable to secure political control of its citizens via direct means because of the vastness of the terrain, the sparse population, the fluidity of residence and the lack of technology. What the Paramount Chief did do was to mark upon people's bodies, through amputation and blinding, the prerogatives of the chief. As the paramountcy established itself more firmly in the early decades of the twentieth century, the nature of citizenship altered, and with it the modes of subjectification.[5] The chief's control of production processes through the strict ritual timing of the burning of the fields was, amongst other things, the operationalization both of a technique of power and of a technique of subjectification. The power of the Bemba chiefs depended on this ritual political economy which, in its turn, marked local people's experience of the cycles of the year, of the climate and the landscape, of the gendered division of labour, of eating and sexual relations, and of the comings and goings of labour migrants.

Anthropology's recognition of the importance of such techniques of power, subjectification and knowledge has had little to do with Foucault traditionally, largely because anthropology developed this method of analysis in the context of so-called traditional or stateless societies. An implicit division between traditional and modern societies, and a rather specific view of the domain of anthropological enquiry may also explain why so few anthropologists have attempted to develop an eclectic Foucauldian approach in the context of a contemporary anthropology.[6] This is particularly surprising given the trend in anthropology towards critical reflexivity and the analysis of knowledge/power relations. In spite of the assumed popularity of Foucault within the discipline in recent years, we still lack a sustained genealogy of anthropological discourse. Perhaps, more importantly, there has been little attempt to use Foucault to engage with a debate on intellectual ethics, the grounds for a moral anthropology, and questions of doubt, care and solidarity.

Let me begin with the first point and address the question of how a neo-Foucauldian perspective might enrich a reformulation of anthropology's subject of enquiry. Foucault attempted to enlarge on his 'microphysics of power' concerned with bodies and individuals, and laid out in *Discipline and Punish*, by developing a 'macrophysics of power' concerned with populations.[7] What interested Foucault here was the art and/or practices of government, the means of managing populations. In his essay on governmentality, he attempts to show how entities, such as society and the economy, which are essential for modern governance, emerged in Europe between the sixteenth and eighteenth centuries. The emergence of such entities required particular material and conceptual conditions, including the development of specific techniques, knowledges and expertise (Foucault 1991). During this time, Foucault argues, the family disappeared as the model for government and was replaced by a perspective based on the population. The notion of a population produced new problems, such as birth and death rates, epidemics, circulations of labour and wealth, which had to be recognized and managed. And out of this management came statistics, the science of the state (Foucault 1991: 99). The purpose of government evolved, not as the exercise of sovereignty, but as the welfare of the population, the increase of its wealth, health and longevity. Thus government becomes inseparable from the knowledge of all the processes related to the population from what has come to be called the political economy of the state (Foucault 1991: 100).

Foucault's concept of governmentality is an aid to understanding and analysing all the mechanisms (techniques of knowledge, power and subjectification) through which social authorities seek to administer the lives of individuals and collectivities, and the way in which individuals and collectivities respond. This analytical perspective can be used to analyse the state, but it is not state-focused. Crucially, it also involves what Foucault called 'bio-politics'; that is the indirect mechanisms and the forms of self-government that are part of disciplinary regimes, and which exist to align personal behaviour and self-management with political and economic objectives. This is one of the traditional domains of anthropological enquiry, as I mentioned earlier, and includes everything from the organization of household space and eating habits to the regulation of production cycles and the ritual enactment of cosmological principles. All anthropologists are now engaged with working in populations that are part of nation states, but I am not proposing a study of the state. As Foucault said, the modern state does not have that degree of functionality we tend to attribute to it; it is really 'no more than a composite reality and a mythicized abstraction' (Foucault 1991: 103). It is not the impact of the state on society which is of interest, but the impact of governmentality on ways of living and on social institutions, including the state.

Foucault uses the notion of governmentality to indicate a certain mentality, a particular way of thinking about the sorts of problems which can and should be addressed by particular authorities and through particular strategies. Governmentality is concerned with specific discourses and practices, and with the particular rationalities which sustain them in the context of a given set of material and historical conditions.[8] Such rationalities will always be local, developed in specific contexts by politicians, academics, the media and ordinary people (see Long, Chapter 3, this volume). However, these rationalities will also be international in their perspective and global in their scope. They are forms and techniques of knowledge which tie people into those processes of modern living which are beyond their control but in which they are forced to participate, directly or indirectly.

A modern anthropology would surely have as one of its major objectives the critical analysis of these forms of rationality. Governmentality involves background assumptions about divisions of labour, domains of enquiry and means of procedure which give rise to analyses, reflections and strategies that presuppose the development of specialist forms of knowledge. Modern government thus involves a mass of intellectual labour which seeks to develop new methods of documentation, analysis and evaluation. Amongst these new methods are all the social science disciplines, including social anthropology. Social anthropology is therefore part of the rationality of governmentality, and this is the case whether you teach in Peking, Detroit, Kano, Rio or Delhi.

Modern government also involves moral questions and ethical debate about, for example, the circumstances under which it is legitimate or feasible for certain kinds of authorities to intervene in people's lives, and about the boundaries between the public and the private. There is a huge range of issues here, but I would like to suggest that governmentality is a proper object of anthropological enquiry, both in its local manifestations and in its comparative scope. While the specific case history which Foucault provides for Europe is not a universal model, and thus we could agree that specific forms of governmentality exist in specific places, it could also be argued that certain forms of governmentality are global in their scope, if not necessarily in their effects. There are economic rationalities imposed by international bodies, and sometimes welcomed by individual governments, such as structural adjustment, which have very specific local effects in terms of household composition, urban living standards, agricultural labour and asymmetries of power between women and men. These economic structures, developed through expert debate and based on philosophical assumptions, are engaged with global asymmetries of power and forms of domination. Local responses, however, are far from passive, and new forms of knowledge and self-government are evolved at the local level, inside ministerial offices, shanty dwellings, neighbourhood bars and maize depot stores. These are discourses on governmentality. The international community's attempt to promote good governance in Africa, while sending UN troops to oversee the breakup of nation states in various parts of the globe has produced a bitter debate on human rights, ethnic identity and issues of self-determination and self-government. These are also discourses on governmentality, sometimes viciously fought out through bio-politics which involve torture, killing, dismemberment, dislocation and dispersal. Governmentality involves techniques of knowledge and power which touch all individuals and collectivities, whether directly or indirectly. Health care, family planning programmes, irrigation schemes and educational provision are all part of these disciplinary techniques, and they are all intermeshed with expert knowledges, including those of the social sciences. Many anthropologists in universities all around the globe, whether or not they are working in anthropology departments, are involved in the techniques of government. This concerns not only those who engage in development work and consultancy, but also those who provide the ethnographic information on which plans and policies depend, those who investigate the effects on local populations of regional and national decisions, and enquire into changing marital strategies and livelihood options, and demonstrate the interconnections between witchcraft and wealth, and engage in dialogue with local people and other anthropologists on these issues (see Long, Chapter 3, this volume). But most importantly, we are involved because we teach, because education is part of this process of governmentality. It is one of the major ways in which individuals come to align themselves with moral, ethical, economic and political objectives, and because we teach we all have a hand in this process, wherever we work and whatever we actually teach. Critical reflection on our practices would suggest that there are compelling moral and ethical reasons for trying to develop a modern range of anthropologies which do actually take account of the complexities and techniques of knowledge production within and between societies, groups and regions.

NOTES

1 These classificatory terms are most problematic, but they work to identify self-declared positions and locations, not to define categories.
2 This is a quite unsurprising point, especially since many of the African philosophers and theologians involved in the early debates about 'the existence and nature of an African philosophy' were influenced by the Harlem Renaissance and negritude movements, as well as by phenomenology, existentialism and surrealism.
3 See, for example, the work of Ingold and Carrithers.
4 See Deleuze 1983; Deleuze and Guattari 1987, 1994 and Said 1983, as well as his Reith lectures for 1993.
5 See Moore and Vaughan 1994, for an extended discussion of the impact of colonial rule on the Bemba polity and its effects on the nature of chiefly power.
6 Major exceptions here include the work of Ong (1987) and Rabinow (1989).
7 For an extended discussion of this and other issues concerned with rationality, modernity and governmentality, see Gordon 1987, 1991; Miller and Rose 1990.
8 Sandy Robertson's book *People and the State* (1984) is one of the few anthropological texts to try and tackle these issues.

REFERENCES

Bodunrin, P. O. (1984) 'The question of African philosophy'. In R. Wright (ed.) *African Philosophy: An Introduction*. University Press of America: Lanham.
Deleuze, G. (1983) *Nietzsche and Philosophy*. London: Athlone.
Deleuze, G. and Guattari, F. (1987) *A Thousand Plateaus: Capitalism and Schizophrenia*. Minneapolis: University of Minnesota Press.
—— (1994) *Nomadology: The War Machine*. New York: Semiotext(e).
Foucault, M. (1991) 'On Governmentality'. In G. Burchell, C. Gordon and P. Miller (eds) *The Foucault Effect*. London: Harvester Wheatsheaf.
Gates, H. (1988) *The Signifying Monkey: A Theory of Afro-American Literary Criticism*. New York: Oxford University Press.
Gordon, C. (1987) 'The soul of the citizen: Max Weber and Michel Foucault on rationality and government'. In S. Lash and S. Whimster (eds) *Max Weber, Rationality and Modernity*. London: Allen & Unwin.
—— (1991) 'Governmental rationality: an introduction'. In G. Burchell, C. Gordon and P. Miller (eds) *The Foucault Effect*. London: Harvester Wheatsheaf.
Hountondji, P. (1983) *African Philosophy: Myth and Reality*. London: Hutchinson.
Kagame, A. (1956) *La Philosophie Bantu-Rwandaise de L'Etre*. Bruxelles: Academie Royale des Sciences Coloniales.

Masolo, D. A. (1994) *African Philosophy in Search of Identity*. Bloomington: Indiana University Press.

Mbiti, J. S. (1969) *African Religions and Philosophy*. London: Heinemann.

Miller, P. and Rose, N. (1990) 'Governing economic life', *Economy and Society* 19(1): 1–31.

Moore, H. L. and Vaughan, M. (1994) *Cutting Down Trees: Gender, Nutrition and Agricultural Change in the Northern Province of Zambia, 1890-1990*. NJ: Heinemann.

Mudimbe, V. Y. (1988) *The Invention of Africa*. Bloomington: Indiana University Press.

—— (1991) *Parables and Fables: Exegenesis, Textuality, and Politics in Central Africa*. Bloomington: Indiana University Press.

Nkombe, O. (1977) 'Methode et point de départ en philosophie africaine: authenticité et libération. In *La Philosophie Africaine*. Kinshasa: Faculté de Théologie Catholique.

Ong, A. (1987) *Spirits of Resistance and Capitalist Discipline: Factory Women in Malaysia*. Albany: State University of New York Press.

Rabinow, P. (1989) *French Modern: Norms and Forms of the Social Environment*. Massachusetts: MIT Press.

Robertson, A. F. (1984) *People and The State: An Anthropology of Planned Development*. Cambridge: Cambridge University Press.

Said, E. (1983) *The World, the Text and the Critic*. London: Faber & Faber.

Strathern, M. (1988) *The Gender of the Gift*. Berkeley: University of California Press.

Towa, M. (1979) *L'Idee d'une Philosophy Africaine*. Yaounde: Clé.

Vizenor, G. (1988) *The Trickster of Liberty: Tribal Heirs to a Wild Baronage*. Minneapolis: University of Minnesota Press.

—— (1989) *Narrative Chance: Post-Modern Essays to Native American Indian Literature*. Albuquerque: University of New Mexico Press.

White, L. (1993a) 'Vampire priests of central Africa or African debates about labour and religion in colonial northern Zambia', *Comparative Studies in Society and History* 35(4): 744–70.

—— (1993b) 'Cars out of place: vampires, technology and labour in East and Central Africa', *Representations* 43: 27–50.

Chapter 2

Interpreting electron micrographs[1]

Emily Martin

I think I felt as I would if a doctor had held an X-ray to the light showing a star-shaped hole at the center of one of my vital organs. Death has entered. It is inside you. You are said to be dying and yet are separate from the dying, can ponder it at your leisure, literally see on the X-ray photograph or computer screen the horrible alien logic of it all. It is when death is rendered graphically, is televised so to speak, that you sense an eerie separation between your condition and yourself. A network of symbols has been introduced, an entire awesome technology wrested from the gods. It makes you feel like a stranger in your own dying.

(DeLillo 1984)

One theme in the social study of science relates closely to the theme of this book: global and local uses of knowledge. In a recent book by a biologist, Richard Lewontin, *Biology as Ideology*, the author argues (though his book is intended to put a stop to it) that 'science has replaced religion as the chief legitimating force in modern society'. Science claims that its method is objective and untouched by politics, true for all and for all time. Science claims that its product is universal truth: 'the secrets of nature are unlocked. Once the truth about nature is revealed, one must accept the facts of life' (Lewontin 1991: 8). On the one hand, to capture the force of these universal truths, the term 'global' hardly seems large enough. On the other hand, would not such universal truths blot out the 'local' entirely? There is a strong normative injunction in science that strives to disallow the views of non-scientists:

the layman and the non-specialist are posited in the natural sciences as ones whose interpretation of, and opinion about, the works of science *ought* not intrude into the relevant discussion at all. Their views are culturally fixed as being in principle irrational, or at least irrelevant.

(Markus 1987: 22)

The natural sciences might be a kind of limiting case in their insistence on the global – nay, universal – applicability of their findings, and their simultaneous insistence that no point of view outside the natural sciences ought to affect their findings. In the face of this insistence, anthropology is in a position to play an important role. Anthropologists are beginning to take up the ethnographic study of science's global system of knowledge, much as they earlier took up the study of other systems of knowledge with universalistic claims, such as world religions (Hess 1992). But anthropologists have been slower to explore carefully the role of non-scientists in the formation of scientific knowledge in the West or the developing world.[2] Important ethnographic questions in such an exploration, ones that will guide this chapter, are whether people outside science will interpret the works of science, given the opportunity, despite the strong sanctions against doing so, and whether they do so in terms that are primarily local and particular rather than global and universal.[3]

In order to examine these questions, I focus on micrographs, hugely magnified visual representations of microscopic biological entities and processes that play an important role both in the ongoing activities of research scientists, and in the media that is meant to carry the works of science to the public.[4] The use of technology to effect scale changes will be central to my discussion. The powerful operations of many technologies – photography, microscopy and tissue preparation – are brought into play to lift tiny molecules and cells within the body into a scale large enough for visibility by means of the naked eye. The power inherent in the scale changes made by these operations could serve both as an emphatic demonstration of the amazing ability of science and to silence the voices of laymen and non-specialists when confronted with their results. As we will see, no such silencing occurs. For scientists and non-specialists alike, micrographs provide a lively field for the play of imagination.

USING AND ENCOUNTERING MICROGRAPHS

My recent research was designed as a social history and ethnography of the immune system. The research was carried out over three years in diverse settings: an immunology research laboratory, several HIV clinical settings, workplaces, and a variety of urban neighbourhoods. As part of the fieldwork, I worked as a technician in the laboratory, became a member of the local chapter of ACT UP, and served as a volunteer 'buddy' to several people with HIV/AIDS. Together with a team of graduate students, I carried out over two hundred extended interviews in urban neighbourhoods and workplaces.[5] In the laboratory setting, I frequently attended lectures on immunology in classrooms and lecture halls. Almost inevitably, the lecturer would illustrate his or her statements with slides and transparencies. The slide would frequently depict a microscopic view of the cell or process being described. Various minute participants in the immune system (T cells, antibodies, tissue stricken by auto-immune reactions) would suddenly loom huge on the screen in the lecture room, dwarfing us all. The rhetorical flow of the lecture was often timed to produce these images at a moment of closure and proof: this is what I say we found, and *here is a picture of it*! In one striking case, where the lecturer was able to illustrate a process he had discovered experimentally with a video tape of the cells actually engaged in the process, the audience audibly gasped in appreciation.[6]

As well as a sense of drama, there is certainly a lively aesthetic involved when scientists produce, choose and display these images. After many a lecture, I heard people commenting to each other about the 'beautiful', 'incredible', 'stunning', 'technically perfect' micrographs that were shown. The standards are so high, researchers told me, that one would never dare (for fear of ridicule) use an image that was imperfect: one that showed extraneous dirt, one that was blurred, one that showed any degradation from the tissue-fixing process. But aside from this (a topic about which a great deal more could be said), the main thrust of the pictures in science is to clinch an argument by revealing visual evidence of what one is claiming.[7] In the immunology laboratory where I carried out fieldwork, this was impressed upon me in many ways. One researcher lamented that the photographs accompanying his articles could not be as convincing as those of his colleagues who used micrographs of cells: his findings depended on the western blot, a technique he was teaching me, and however well it was done, it could only result in fuzzy and indistinct bands in vague shades of grey. Another recalled a turning point in immunology, when Gerald Edelman, a Nobel Prize recipient, saw for the first time a micrograph of an antibody, showing that it had the shape of a Y. The visual clarity of the photograph forced Edelman to revise his own calculations, which had wrongly led him to believe that antibody molecules were structured in the shape of a T. This moment serves as a model of how photographs, especially electron micrographs, are used to achieve closure and finality in a scientific argument.[8]

Outside research science, I noticed that electron micrographs illustrating biological processes appear in a great variety of popular publications.[9] Whole books are devoted to revealing the invisible world of microbes and micro-organisms that live among us (see e.g. *Microcosmos* (Burgess *et al.* 1987); *The Secret House* (Bodanis 1986)). Ordinary household appliances have been redesigned specifically to rid our homes of these (once seen) unwanted guests. Advertisements for vacuum cleaners with special filters are now commonly accompanied by electron micrographs of the dust mite, which is a common cause of allergies. Films and textbooks on biology for schools covering topics from asthma to reproduction frequently include many micrographs illustrating cells, viruses, etc. and their activities.[10]

Electron microscopy plays the role of medical sleuth in a popular article about a potentially disastrous outbreak of an infectious virus brought into the USA by way of African monkeys intended for scientific research. Electron micrographs of cells from one of the monkey's liver provide 'definite confirmation' that the cells are infected with a filovirus, a type of virus that includes Ebola virus, known to have been lethal to almost nine out of ten humans who contracted it in previous outbreaks in Africa (Preston 1992: 71). In the end, the filovirus in the USA turned out to be a variant of the deadly Ebola which was not harmful to humans. But the four Hollywood film studios which wanted to offer Richard Preston a contract for the film rights to the story apparently intended to make the electron microscope as sleuth a central feature of the plot.[11] (We will have to wait and see whether Twentieth-Century Fox, who won the contract, follows through.)

Because of all this, we built a series of interactions with electron micrographs into the general interviews on health that we were conducting in urban neighbourhoods. Once a conversation with someone was well under way, we would show him or her a series of micrographs of cells involving the immune system. We would say that these were enlarged photographs of inner parts of the body and ask in one way or another, 'What do you make of this?' If the person hesitated to say anything, wanting more specific information from us, the interviewer would read aloud the brief caption that appeared with the photograph in the original publication.

One of our goals was to see how familiar people were with these images perambulating out from science into the society, in what Latour calls the 'irruption of objects into the human collective' (1990: 152). Another goal was to see whether, even though the images were usually taken to have been produced by science and scientists, the quintessential domain of the rational, people would dare to speak about them imaginatively. We would often ask, 'do these pictures bring any thoughts to mind?' or 'how do you react to these pictures?' We were interested in whether people would have anything to say at all, given the strong authority with which science speaks in our culture, and given the strong antithesis between the taken-for-granted rationality and certainty of scientific knowledge and what we were asking for: imaginatively produced meanings.

In due course, we would also ask whether having seen the images that we introduced or other similar ones might change the way the person thought about his or her body or self. Obviously, asking such a question so bluntly and in such a confined context has limited utility. The results presented below should be taken only as an initial indication of what kind of impact these images might be having on society in general.

MICROGRAPHS AS OBLIGATORY PASSAGE POINTS

Considerable attention has been paid in social studies of science to ways in which scientific machines and their operations and tests can become 'obligatory passage points' for the conduct of science (Latour 1983, 1987; Cambrosio and Keating 1992: 370). Like foot soldiers who must cross a river by only one bridge, scientists come to regard certain procedures or tests as obligatory in order for their research to be considered valid. For example, Cambrosio and Keating detail how new entities, monoclonal antibodies, and an associated machine, a fluorescent activated cell sorter (FACS), came into standard usage in contemporary immunology. These tools led to the development of new techniques that quickly became 'obligatory passage points': once they became a standard part of research practice, scientists working in relevant areas had to use these techniques in order to have their work accepted as valid (1992: 365).

In the history of science, Steven Shapin and Simon Schaffer trace the process by which Robert Boyle in the seventeenth century was able to make witnesses' observations of his air pump such an obligatory passage point: 'discussions about the Body Politic, God and His miracles, Matter and its power, could be *made to go* through the air pump' (Latour 1990: 152; see also Shapin and Schaffer 1985). Latour often argues that the force of these scientific tools that become obligatory passage points resides in their ability to effect a change in scale:

> Boyle modifies the *relative scale* of phenomena: macro-factors about matter and God's powers may be made amenable to an experimental solution and this solution will be a partial modest one . . . [Boyle] refines his experiment to show the effect on a detector – a feather! – of the aether wind postulated by Hobbes thus hoping to disprove his contradictor. How ridiculous! Hobbes raises a big problem and he is rebutted by a feather inside a transparent glass inside a laboratory inside Boyle's mansion! . . . [Hobbes] denies the possibility of what is becoming the essential feature of modern power: change of scale and displacement through workshop and laboratories.
>
> (Latour 1990: 153)

Among the non-scientists in our research, micrographs were what might be called *weakly obligatory* passage points. People who are not scientists do not face the demands of the laboratory setting in which scientists obligatorily illustrate results with beautifully clear micrographs whenever possible. But non-scientists do live in a world filled with print and video media which are saturated with micrographs. From *Time* and *Newsweek* to science teaching films in secondary schools, the simple ubiquity of micrographs means that almost everyone has bumped into them before. But in one context of our fieldwork, contact with images and knowledge about cellular entities were *strongly obligatory*: a college class on cancer and AIDS taught by a molecular biologist in a large state university. One member of our ethnographic research group took the course and interviewed the professor and a selection of the students who took the course. I begin with a discussion of this context, because unlike the people in our general interviews, these students were literally being tested on how well they absorbed the professor's view of what makes up the body.

The professor, who I will call Peter Keller, had a clear message he wanted to convey to students:[12]

> I think one's attitude towards one's health is enormously important to determining one's health. So without really trying, just by studying the immune system ... you have this stuff. Your B lymphocytes are incredible. I think they're saying 'Oh!' and you almost stand up a little taller and you walk around and say 'I'm powerful', which I think is extremely useful in being powerful and being healthy. So I just in some sense, consciously identify with powerful things in me. ... So I mean people presumably less educated, who may never have really thought about their immune system. ... So I would picture, if you went in there and got a group of twenty people together and said, 'You know what you have in you? You have this immune system. You know what it can do? I mean you know why a vaccine works? You know why you only get a cold, a disease only once?' And 'Wow, really? I have that in me?' It seems to me, I just take that for very granted that that is empowering, and makes people stronger.

But in spite of his strong agenda and the power imbalance between the professor and his students, those students had a wide range of different responses to images of cells of the immune system. One student echoes the professor's message:

> I don't think the average person realizes, you know, what your body does. I mean, it's such a gigantic task to take care of these things, all this stuff's going on, so much all the time. I think we just take a lot for granted, but it really is kind of neat.
> [Yeah, that it can do that without your knowledge?]
> Yeah, right, I mean for all I know it can be, you know, combatting a disease, or something.
>
> (Drew Stratton)

Another reflects back on how much he was influenced by the class which he had attended two years before, but rejects altogether the link Professor Keller takes for granted between the biological details and feeling empowered.

With all the lingo that was going on, the technical, the different types of cells, all the interaction within the system. I don't know if that just turned me off, or. . . .

[The technical language?]

Yeah . . . I just lost interest, or I thought of it as something physical, and I didn't really see any connection, just because whenever you're going over something like that, it's very objective, and this happens here and then this, this, then this happens, then this step, and this type of cell invades here, and I just found a separation between the cells and that, and I just threw that into more of a physical area, you understand?

[I see. You didn't like the cell separation?]

Yeah. And just how definite everything was.

[What do you mean?]

Just the concept, what was presented in the biology of it all. It just seemed like too much was known, or not that a lot was known, but maybe since I couldn't relate to that, I felt that that couldn't help me, so I didn't take anything from it? I mean just all the names and all the different processes involved. I didn't really care about it.

[Really, that's interesting.]

Just maybe it's because if someone comes and names all the different processes and explains how they work, but as far as using that for my own good, or. . . . And I think that's one of the reasons why I got a C. [Laughter]

It's true. I barely got a C at that . . . I got a lot out of the course, but just not as far as the technical lingo and all the different processes involved.

(Mike Franzini)

Other students acknowledged the impact of knowledge about cells of the immune system but felt it *reduced* their sense of empowerment and control.

I could think, like, I have more control, because, you know, there are things you can do to affect something that's going on in your body, but then you think you could be in less control because there's so many other things in your body that, maybe, you don't know about. And they just go on constantly without even you thinking about them, so, I mean. So that, I guess that could make you think that I was like, in less control, too. Like, a whole, like, other world, like. All those things, you know. I mean.

(Martha Novick)

Others find it difficult to feel the enlarged images are really part of them, much less that they are empowered by knowledge about them.

It's actually hard for me to picture these things in my body. I mean I'm sure they're there, but you know, seeing them so, so big, I mean this is really scary. And, I mean this up close is ... I mean they're so microscopic, you know what I mean? That when you magnify it by a certain amount, it's scary. But I mean, I can't really associate these things inside my body. It's kind of hard for me to. Like when the pictures go away, I won't really, you know, I'll see them, but I won't really still –
[You won't identify with them?]
Not really.

(Cary Lennox)

EFFLORESCENCE OF IMAGERY

This brief discussion indicates that there is a wide latitude of reactions, even in circumstances where an authority figure is suggesting a particular interpretation. Given this, we might expect people we have interviewed in various neighbourhoods to offer many different interpretations of micrographs. Taken as a whole, the things people said can only be described as a profusion, an extravagance, an excess of images. Sometimes they tumble out one on top of another. Here is one example: 'Sort of like a landscape, perhaps coralish, maybe a seascape or something. ... Sort of a crystal quality ... the cancer cell looks sort of like a puff pastry, doesn't it and this looks like a Dunkin' Donut hole with coconut on it' (Bill Scott). Here are some more: 'Those remind me like a plant, it looks like a plant, these look like somebody being at sea, you know what I'm saying? Like they call those jellyfish and stuff like that – plants that be in the sea' (Tyrone Walker). 'This looks like something's shooting out of it, trying to kill the other one, kind of almost Star Wars-ish ... almost like a frog or a toad or whatever, it has a long tongue that shoots out and gets flies. ... Sputnik! a satellite would be the other thing that it conjures up ... or something under sea, Jacques Cousteau-ish ... something like an alien. ... I like this one better because it takes it inside, it's a little more like some sort of knight being the champion and engulfing it and killing it as opposed to the other one being almost like a leech and attaching itself and then killing it, killing it, more like a tick, I don't like ticks, of course' (Charles Kingsley).

Sometimes specific photographs elicited extended commentary.

On a picture of how arthritis affects the bone:
[Could you explain to me again what you think is happening with the arthritis?]
It looked like a desert that collects sand through here and then this rock, and this right here kind of like a little eye and an ear, like an

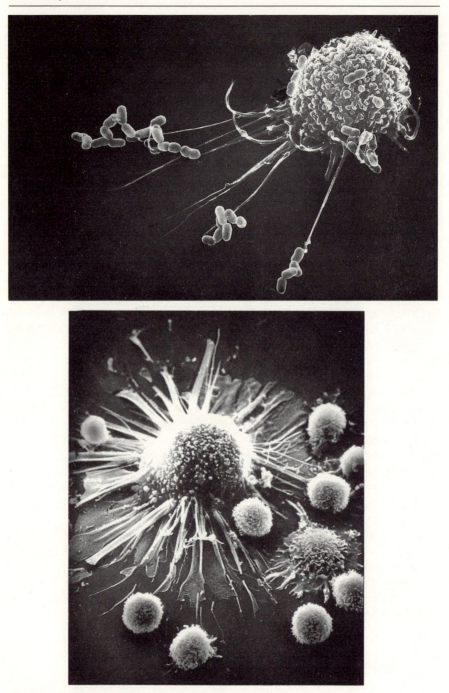

Electron micrographs of immune system cells
Source: Boehringer Ingerheim International GmbH, with permission.

animal that's fighting for its life. Or maybe like a little baby animal, the eye and the nose right here, that can't do too much for himself, or like fossils of what used to be. A monster through here. This look like wasted land, maybe something after maybe a bomb hits.

(Tara Holcolm)

On a picture of a white blood cell and a tumour cell:
Yeah, you can look at a picture like this and just get a feeling for almost the psychology of these things, tumour cells just like gobbling up nutrients and taking over from healthy tissue. I mean this reflects a sort of malevolence that, I don't know, I just think of tumours in that way, and you know, this poor little white cell here, it's like, the sucker doesn't stand a chance.
[This is bacteria and, let me see, this is the explanation, *this* is *this* enlarged.]
It's almost evocative of like patriarchal notions of conquest. This is like the United States invading Panama, right here. Except in this case, the little suckers really do need to be kept in check.

(Sally Feldman)

On a picture of a white blood cell and bacteria:
[So what do they make you feel, or think of? What do they remind you of? If it brings any thoughts to you! Maybe it doesn't.]
I guess that's what cells would look like inside your body. Looks like it's trying to do something, get away from something, or something. . . .
They look like spiders trying to catch flies on a web, or something.
[A spider? Oh, yeah.]
Trying to catch an ant or something. . . . This one looks like it's getting bigger or whatever . . . so does this one.
[What?]
I say it's trying to grow.

(Horace Miller)

It is evident that many people do not hesitate to exercise their imaginations when confronted by the tracings of scientific knowledge. This is so in spite of the overt awareness that the photographs themselves (however they were produced) are often taken as prima facie evidence that scientists have amazing powers. Many people commented on how extraordinary it is that scientists have the ability to make pictures like these: 'It makes me marvel at what we are, not only . . . that this exists inside our bodies, but that we as humans have been able to photograph these. I think that's kind of neat' (George Miller).

When we look in more detail at the reflections inspired by micrographs, we see clearly their potential to mobilize a great variety of emotional and conceptual positions.

They encourage empathy with the pain of illnesses they depict:
[Do you think when you look at pictures like this, do you think that's changed at all, how you see your body?]
I think so. First of all the pictures of the arthritis make my understanding of that and of what Linda's fighting off a lot more graphic. It makes that more real, what arthritis is. And gives me a better sense of understanding the kind of pain that she can have with it . . . seeing that. It looks painful.

(Cindy Radlaw)

They elicit awe at the incredible processes going on within:
[When you see these kind of photos, I mean at the really micro, micro level, and you think about them in terms like this, does it change the way you think about your body?]
Yeah. I think you forget what's really going on in there. What really you're made up of, it's awesome, I mean it's fascinating to me. It's awesome, it makes me realize how incredible the human body is, you know, what's really going on in there. You walk around every day, you exist, but what's really happening to you?

(Elizabeth Houlihan)

They inspire appreciation of how actively the body is always working . . .
[Does it make you think differently about your own body when you see pictures like that?]
Like this picture, what it makes me feel like is that my body is very active, in what it can do. And, because I feel my body functioning at times, I feel like yeah, we're doing all right. If I have a bruise, if I've bumped myself or something, and I see a bruise and then the next day I notice that it's faded, that does make me feel good about my body, because I feel as though things are working.
[So you can sort of imagine these things going on?]
Going ZAP! Space invaders.

(Lisa Demarco)

. . . so much that the body is like a 'little city'.
Wow, that's bizarre. It's really wonderful, that's really quite amazing to think that they all look, they have shapes like nature, you know? These are like flowers. Don't you think?
[Yeah. Why do you think that's bizarre?]
Well, because they're all inside you, and you know, and they're all covered with fluids and you just, you think about the body as being, if you think about it, and you don't do it that often, unless it's acting up, and you really don't think about it, you just take for granted that all these things are working, the heart is pumping and the blood's flowing.

You take it for granted, till something goes wrong. But to think that there is so much activity, it's like a city, like a little city, you know?

(Judy Lockard)

They show us the body keeps on working even when we 'as a human' do not help things along:
This white blood cell is shooting off the bacteria, trying to repel it? I think that our body knows what to do, you know. Sometimes our mind, sometimes we as a human will do things that aren't so good for us. Smoking a cigarette, drinking too much, eating too much, you know, but internally, thank God, our body functions to the degree of, you know, just unbeknownst to our mind, our body is repelling the bacteria. It's forming a shell against the bad stuff, you know, and trying to ward off, bring in the good stuff.

(Carol Neilson)

The images help us create 'myths' to promote an active sense of being healthy:
[With the microphotos, when you look at that scale of health and illness, does it change the way you think about your body?]
Sure it does ... it's important to have a sense I think of your body fighting off disease, rather than of disease overwhelming your body, or your body being ravaged by diseases and of knowing that the army is inside you and trying to take care of you and nasty little invaders. I think myth is extremely important in that way, and these pictures are very important for scientists of course, but they're also important in creating myths about the body, about how the body works.

(Geoff Peters)

For some, to 'actually see these things' adds credibility to scientific claims concerning health:
[How do these photos sort of compare to how you imagine the virus, or the bacteria to be? Like let's take the photo of HIV. Does this make any impression on you?]
Yes, I think it does. I think it does to the population at large. Until you see it, until you can identify it, unless you can put a visual to it, I think it's just something that somebody's telling you is inside your body. ... Maybe it's just something that's happening inside your body. I think once you give somebody a picture, and say this is what it looks like, this is what's in your body, this is it, I mean, it hits home a lot quicker. Actually it does to me, just looking at these pictures, because as far as visualizing what the virus looks like, I mean, I never even attempted because who knows.

(Daryl Huff)

It's very interesting to see, you know, to actually see these things. It makes it much more concrete and real to me. . . . There's part of me that feels like well none of this is really happening because I can't see it.

(Joan Breslau)

The images can satisfy curiosity about the processes that lead to specific, personally experienced illness:
[Well I was just wondering if looking at this gives you any impressions?] This one don't, but the first one would give me more impression than this.
[What kind of impression?]
I don't know . . . to see how the cancer forms, I guess.
[So you mean it's more interesting to look at that?]
Yes. To see, I guess, how it starts. I would like to know how it starts. You know, I've had cancer, and I had a mastectomy. Now, in my other breast, there are calcium deposits, and they're just tiny little white things that show up on a mammogram or X-ray, and that's all right as long as they stay away from one another. But if they start to come together, four or five of them come together, and make I guess, a mass or little round ball or whatever you might call it, then that is when they get worried, you know, and they try to find out then if there is cancer starting in the other breast. . . .
[And so when you were saying you look at this photo, does it give you some ideas then about what happens, or . . . ?]
Yeah, it just kind of shows me that, you know, if this one little cell starts and then, you know, it just keeps like spreading I guess you call it, and another little cell forms.
[So if you look at a picture like this, can you associate it with what's going on in your own body then? Like do you . . . ?]
Yeah, I often wonder if anything else is going on in my body. Yeah, I do. I wonder about it, but I don't worry about it.

(Beverly Samuels)

And they can suggest links between the body's interior and the external environment:
[Looking at a picture of an asbestos fibre inside a cell.]
William: Every [construction] job I'd go [to] and they were spraying it, I would leave. I'd just get out of there, you know? 'Cos I could see what was happening. You had to be breathing it in. Looked like icicles floating, shining when the sun hit it. You know, I'd get off the job in a minute, walk off.
[What do you think about pictures like this?]
Well that's what's happening to our bodies, and somebody. . . .
Mildred: Gives you a realistic idea of what's happening.

William: That's right, and somebody's going to come up with a cure, which I think they have taken enough of our money now, they should have something by now.

(Mildred and William Cosgrove)

ALIENATION AND DECONTEXTUALIZATION

In the midst of so much delight and admiration, many people could also see another side of the effect of these images. Sometimes the lability of the images, the very fact that they could be anything at all, overwhelms the instructions they come with – that they depict what is really happening inside us.

[When you see these kind of photos, does it change the way that you think about your body? Seeing, sort of, these little minuscule operations.] Does it change the way I think about it?
[Yeah.]
Seeing it, at this magnification, it takes on almost a surreal look to it so that it doesn't seem quite real. So much so that even though it exists, it looks like something otherworldly. . . . A photograph of this nature doesn't have as much effect as seeing someone with a full-blown case of AIDS, or something like that. Show a before and after picture. But make sure that the before is a happy picture. . . . These, you know, there's nothing that anyone could look at and say, 'Yeah, I've seen that before', or 'That's me'.

(George Miller)

Here, George Miller asserts that a representation of a whole person's body with a full-blown case of AIDS would connect with him more power-fully than a 'surreal, otherworldly' micrograph of HIV.

Philip Monroe was probably the most verbally enthusiastic when looking at the micrographs. He repeated over and over again that they were 'phenomenal', 'fascinating', 'incredible'. Even so, he also experi-enced a sense of unreality about his connection to the processes they illustrated:

It's like being in two different worlds.
[Really?]
Yeah, I mean, even though I've seen all these kinds of things before and I realize that these are the exact same kinds of things that are in my body, it's still distanced somehow, and I think it's because . . . these cells act on their own, you know, there's no connection between . . . me being a conscious human being and this cell that's inside me.

In Latour's terms we might describe this as a failure of the reversal of scale, which has already been accomplished in the laboratory, to be understood by everyone in society at large. In other people, the scale reversal is so successful that they carry it one step further:

> Maybe we're a part of something so big that it doesn't know that we exist. You know, and we're just going along, just like these cells are going along. . . . And so, you know, it's just like maybe these cells don't even know that they're a part of a body, which is weird, but maybe they don't, you know? Maybe they're just doing this function, because it's what's programmed into them, but they don't know, you know, oh, I'm part of Bob or, you know, whatever. They don't know this. So like that, we don't know that we're part of something bigger. We're just going along doing what we believe to be what we're supposed to do or whatever.
>
> (Brackette Thompson)

Whether the scale reversal is relished or rejected, the ability of the images to create and sustain distance from one's own body is palpable. Shot through many of the comments above is the theme of distance: the images involve 'separation', one 'can't relate' to them, they are 'like a whole other world', it is 'hard to picture' these things in one's body, they are 'distanced', they, and we, are in 'two different worlds', they are 'surreal, otherworldly'.

In speaking of the creation of distance between the colonial British and the inhabitants of India, Bernard Cohn refers to the role of *depiction* in establishing and maintaining a power differential:

> Indians [are depicted] as isolated, *decontextualized objects* whose meaning can only be inferred from their special dress or the presence of the tools of their trades, and displaying the markers of the services which they were to provide to the sahibs and memsahibs.
>
> (Quoted in Corrigan 1988: 267)

As depictions, micrographs show microscopic entities radically decontextualized from the context of the body. They are so decontextualized that, like ink blots, they can be anything at all, from jellyfish in the ocean to star wars in outer space. Of course the images emerge from the laboratory into public media complete with written directions for their interpretation; scientific labels tell us what they 'really' depict. In practice, it is perhaps the extent to which the visual images are denuded of context that allows the written labels to be ignored, instead giving rise to the role of the images as mediators of the imagination.

POWER AND SCALE

I have so far treated the neighbourhood interviews as a kind of collective text produced by non-scientists. Although there were obviously many individual differences, there was no grouping based on gender, age, ethnicity, class or residence in the near two hundred interviews that did not show involvement in the micrographs in the intense ways I described above. We also found similarly intense involvement among those we interviewed who were political activists, AIDS/HIV activists and community leaders. There was, however, one exceptional case in which a man rejected the micrographs roundly, finding them irrelevant to his and his community's life. When John Marcellino, a community leader in Mercerville, a neigh- bourhood with high unemployment and pervasive poverty, first saw the photographs, he said,

> That's disgusting ... [laughing] that's very mystical ... I mean I know that's really amazing, it's like looking up into the sky at night, you know what I mean, and really thinking about it. I mean, I know that's really amazing. ... You don't learn about this kind of stuff, you know, in school or anything like that, they don't teach you about this kind of stuff, so I don't understand it. But I know it's pretty amazing.

But in spite of his amazement, Tom goes on to assert the distance that separates him and his community from the scientists who have produced these images.

> See, we don't talk to many scientists.
> [No.]
> You know, so I don't get to hear that much stuff. This is not a conversation that includes us. I tell you that most of our people don't.
> [No.]
> You show these pictures, somebody's going to think that it's some spaced out artist, you know what I mean? People have no idea what this conversation is about. You know what I'm saying?
> [Yeah, but you watched a National Geographic (film called *The Miracle of Life*)?]
> Yeah.
> [So, what I was wondering is that, after watching that or after seeing pictures like this, does that change in any way the way you think about your body, or about yourself?]
> For a little while, probably. But not permanent I don't think.
> [In what way would it be very little?]
> Because it's too much to comprehend I guess, because I didn't get enough information to really understand it. Though I understood it more than, when we started talking. [Laughing.] But I mean, probably because I don't really understand it, I understand it in different terms, you know.

Faced with the social realities of the poverty and ill-health that are pervasive in Mercerville, Tom finds the esoteric knowledge of the interior of the body irrelevant: 'it's really interesting, but it's not important at all.'

I've had people die of cancer, I guess I'm still more concerned with how they feel, and their part in life and how they're going to go into death than I am about what is going on with this disease inside of your body or their body. You know? I don't know if that makes sense, but how this thing works is kind of, it's really interesting, but it's not, it's not important at all. You know what I mean?
[Yeah, I know what you mean.]
I mean, what's important is all this stuff out here we're trying to deal with. And if I didn't have anything else to do, I mean I could just watch videos about it for a long time, you know, I would love to talk to people about it. I'd like to learn more.

Biological science relentlessly pushes the level of its analysis down to a scale below the level of human lived experience, to the level of microbes, cells or genes. Marcellino is able both to feel the attraction and force of knowledge about events happening at that level ('It's interesting . . . I'd like to know more . . .'), and to articulate the irrelevance of this level to human lived reality. To do this he has to *constantly pull the level of discussion up from the microscopic scale to the human scale*. The flow of knowledge coming from science is 'not a conversation we are part of'. For the people in his community who 'have no idea what this conversation is about', he is 'more concerned with their part in life and how they are going into death' than with what is going on with the cells inside their bodies.

The predicament affecting even Tom Marcellino with his particularly adroit ability to confront the knowledge produced by science is that even the most energetic effort to 'pull' the scale of knowledge up above the microscopic cannot cancel out the impact of having seen things at the microscopic level. The impact may be the greater for taking the form of hugely magnified images of the very tiny, an experience that we have seen can be as disorienting as it is exciting. Once the body has been seen in that way, I suspect the experience is not easily forgotten. The experience is also frequently re-evoked by the 'saturation' of the visual field in media and teaching materials with micrographs; and by processes like testing (whether a college examination or a T cell count) that increasingly make knowledge of the microscopic biological entities inside us an inescapable point of passage.

These encounters with micrographs show us that the scientific questions impelling production of these images are not necessarily the questions that grip people as they marvel at them, reject their relevance or integrate them creatively into ordinary life. These images are used to produce closure in arguments among scientists; when people outside science respond to them they result in anything *but* closure. Instead there is a kind of efflorescence, a constant recreation, of the local: what for one person is a dreadful prospect – like DeLillo's 'horrible alien logic', 'an entire awesome technology wrested from the gods' that makes you 'a stranger in your own dying' – is, for another, a spectacle filled with awe, and, for another, simply a mildly interesting by-product of a scientific conversation that ignores what is most important: the social and economic conditions that are producing suffering and illness in one particular poor urban neighbourhood.

The focus of the scientific conversation is to assert the importance of and depict substances and processes that are universal, globally human (we all have these cells in our bodies, we are all threatened by these cellular abnormalities). A process or an entity that was observed in only one test tube at only one time would have little scientific significance. Non-specialist witnesses to the universal entities shown in micrographs, while not denying their universality, stress, in an opposite manner, what gives them local significance. The arthritis that Linda suffered, the asbestos William Cosgrove could see glinting in the sun on the construction site, and the poverty in John Marcellino's community: these kinds of factors, moving in a myriad particular and local ways to inflect the universal with difference, are taken to matter most.

APPENDIX

(Personal names are pseudonyms; names of neighbourhoods, e.g. Franklin, are pseudonyms of neighbourhoods in Baltimore in which we did fieldwork.)

Breslau, Joan, F, twenties, Euro-American, Franklin, translator.
Cosgrove, William, M, sixties, African-American, Montclair, retired.
Cosgrove, Mildred, F, sixties, African-American, Montclair, retired.
Demarco, Lisa, F, twenties, Euro-American, Franklin, counsellor.
Feldman, Sally, F, twenties, Euro-American, Franklin, secretary.
Franzini, Mike, M, twenties, Euro-American, Newcomb, engineering major, college senior.
Holcolm, Tara, F, twenties, African-American, Franklin, unemployed.
Houlihan, Elizabeth, F, twenties, Euro-American, Montgomery, pre-school teacher.
Huff, Daryl, M, twenties, Euro-American, Montgomery, salesman.
Keller, Peter, M, forties, Euro-American, Newcomb, professor.
Kingsley, Charles, M, thirties, Euro-American, Montgomery, state government worker.
Lennox, Cary, F, twenties, Euro-American, Newcomb, management, college sophomore.
Lockard, Judy, F, forties, Euro-American, Hamilton, state government worker.
Marcellino, John, M, forties, Euro-American, community organizer.

Marshall, Abby, F, twenties, Euro-American, Montgomery, financial officer.

Miller, George, M, twenties, Euro-American, Montgomery, insurance agent.

Miller, Horace, M, thirties, African-American, Bristol, unemployed.

Monroe, Philip, M, twenties, Euro-American, Montgomery, student/accountant.

Neilson, Carol, F, thirties, Euro-American, Montgomery, bartender.

Novick, Martha, F, twenties, Euro-American, Newcomb, college sophomore.

Peters, Geoff, M, thirties, Euro-American, Montgomery, graduate student.

Samuels, Beverly, F, seventies, Euro-American, Franklin, retired.

Scott, Bill, M, twenties, Euro-American, Franklin, architect.

Stratton, Drew, F, twenties, Euro-American, Newcomb, finance major, college senior.

Thompson, Brackette, F, 17, African-American, Montclair, high school student.

Walker, Tyrone, M, twenties, African-American, Bristol, unemployed.

NOTES

1 Some of this material appears in another form in *Flexible Bodies: Tracking Immunity in America from the Days of Polio to the Age of AIDS* (Martin 1994).

2 A notable exception includes Hess 1992.

3 See Markus 1987 for discussion of how these sanctions operate.

4 On the coverage of science in the media see Goldsmith 1986; Nelkin 1987; LaFollette 1990.

5 Graduate students who assisted in the fieldwork were: Bjorn Claeson, Monica Shoch-Spana, Karen-Sue Taussig, Wendy Richardson and Ariane van der Straten. The research was funded by the Spencer Foundation.

6 See Traweek 1992: 429, for a description of high energy physicists' use of slides in lectures; see Rasmussen 1992, for a description of how scientists use electron microscopy to convince their colleagues.

7 See Fox-Keller and Grontkowski 1983; Latour 1986 for different views of the primacy of visual evidence in science.

8 See Lynch 1985 on how electron micrographs are made into 'docile objects' in the laboratory.

9 For a few of the many instances, see micrographs that appear in *The Economist* ('A decoy for AIDS?' 1988: 306, 81), *Nutrition Action* (Barone 1988); *Healthsharing* (Elliott 1989); *The New Yorker* (Preston 1992).

10 For the most part, electron micrographs occur in the domain of the 'media' rather than in clinical contexts. Hence, although they often depict biological processes that are central to human health and illness, their interpretation, if any, is not usually done in the presence or with the help of a medical practitioner.

11 Personal communication, 28 April 1993.

12 All names of people interviewed are pseudonyms, as are names of neighbourhoods. In the Appendix I include a brief indication of the social identities of the people quoted in this chapter.

REFERENCES

Barone, Jeanne (1988) 'Can diet protect your immune system?' *Nutrition Action* 15(6): 3–7.

Bodanis, David (1986) *The Secret House*. New York: Simon & Schuster.

Burgess, Jeremy, Marten, Michael and Taylor, Rosemary (1987) *Microcosmos*. New York: Cambridge University Press.

Cambrosio, Albert and Keating, Peter (1992) 'A matter of FACS: constituting novel entities in immunology'. *Medical Anthropology Quarterly* 6(4): 362–84.

Cohn, Bernard S. (1987) *An Anthropologist among the Historians and Other Essays*. Delhi: Oxford University Press.

Corrigan, Philip (1988) '"Innocent stupidities": de-picturing (human) nature. On hopeful resistances and possible refusals; celebrating difference(s) – again'. In Gordon Fyfe and John Law (eds) *Picturing Power: Visual Depiction and Social Relations*, pp. 255–81. London: Routledge.

DeLillo, Don (1984) *White Noise*. New York: Penguin.

Elliott, Susan (1989) 'ABCs of immunology'. *Healthsharing* 10(2): 17–19.

Fox-Keller, Evelyn and Grontkowski, C. (1983) 'The mind's eye'. In Sandra Harding and Merrill Hintikka (eds) *Discovering Reality: Feminist Perspectives on Epistemology, Metaphysics, Methodology, and Philosophy of Science*. Dordrecht: Reidel.

Goldsmith, Maurice (1986) *The Science Critic: A Critical Analysis of the Popular Presentation of Science*. London: Routledge & Kegan Paul.

Hess, David J. (1992) 'Introduction: the new ethnography and the anthropology of science and technology'. In David J. Hess and Linda L. Layne (eds) *Knowledge and Society: The Anthropology of Science and Technology, Knowledge and Society*, 9. Greenwich, CT: JAI Press.

—— (1993). *Science in the New Age: The Paranormal, Its Defenders and Debunkers, and American Culture*. Madison, WI: University of Wisconsin Press.

LaFollette, Marcel C. (1990) *Making Science Our Own: Public Images of Science 1910–1955*. Chicago, Il: University of Chicago Press.

Latour, Bruno (1983) 'Give me a laboratory and I will raise the world'. In Karin D. Knorr-Cetina and Michael Mulkay (eds) *Science Observed: Perspectives on the Social Study of Science*. London, Beverly Hills, New Delhi: Sage.

—— (1986) 'Visualization and cognition: thinking with eyes and hands'. *Knowledge and Society: Studies in the Sociology of Culture Past and Present* 6: 1–40.

—— (1987) *Science in Action*. Cambridge, MA: Harvard University Press.

—— (1990) 'Postmodern? No, simply AMODERN! Steps towards an anthropology of science'. *Studies in the History and Philosophy of Science* 21(1): 145–71.

Lewontin, R. C. (1991) *Biology as Ideology: The Doctrine of DNA*. New York: HarperCollins.

Lynch, Michael (1985) 'Discipline and the material form of images: an analysis of scientific visibility'. *Social Studies of Science* 15: 37–66.

Markus, Gyorgy (1987) 'Why is there no hermeneutics of natural sciences? Some preliminary theses'. *Science in Context* 1(1): 5–51.

Martin, Emily (1994) *Flexible Bodies: Tracking Immunity in America from the Days of Polio to the Age of AIDS*. Boston: Beacon Press.

Nelkin, Dorothy (1987) *Selling Science: How the Press Covers Science and Technology*. New York: W. H. Freeman.

Preston, Richard (1992) 'Crisis in the hot zone'. *The New Yorker* 58–81.

Rasmussen, N. (1992) 'Saving the cell's power plant: the mitochondrion and biological electron microscopy in the 1950s'. Paper presented at the Princeton 'Visualization' Workshop.

Shapin, Steven and Schaffer, Simon (1985) *Leviathan and the Air-Pump: Hobbes, Boyle, and the Experimental Life.* Princeton, NJ: Princeton University Press.

Traweek, Sharon (1992) 'Border crossings: narrative strategies in science studies and among physicists in Tsukuba Science City, Japan. In *Science as Practice and Culture*, Andrew Pickering (ed.). Chicago: University of Chicago Press.

Chapter 3

Globalization and localization
New challenges to rural research

Norman Long

INTRODUCTION: A TURNING POINT IN HISTORY?

Many contemporary commentators and researchers have stressed that we are now living in an era of significant change: a moment in history, a turning point, a time of transition and radical social change; an end of industrial society and the end of the promise of the Enlightenment (Touraine 1984, 1989), the 'end of history' as 'the West' has conceived it (Fukuyama 1989). Important dimensions of change involve the rapid dissemination of scientific knowledge and technology, culture and communications, the restructuring of work, industry and economic life, and the fragmentation and reorganization of power domains leading to the emergence of new social and political identities.

Such change-processes – whether seen as the latest manifestation of some 'modernist' conception of history and 'progress' or as the beginnings of a 'post-modernist' era – not only affect the so-called 'advanced' or 'developed' societies but also the poorer nations of the world. Indeed much of what we now witness is essentially 'global' in scope, entailing the accelerated flows of various commodities, people, capital, technologies, communications, images and knowledge across national frontiers.

On the other hand, we should not be seduced into believing that globalization has a uniform impact everywhere. To do so would be to fall into the same trap as previous attempts at theorization, namely that of formulating a general (or universal) theory that seeks to identify certain 'driving forces' (e.g. the 'laws' of capitalist development or the imperatives of modern bureaucratic organization), 'prime movers' (e.g. technological or economic factors), or 'cultural facilitators' (e.g. religious asceticism or entrepreneurial rationalities) of change.

Discerning and interpreting these complex and interrelated processes is, of course, an enormous task (in fact this constitutes a major part of the research agenda for sociology) that goes well beyond what is possible in this chapter. My task here is much more modest: I aim to outline certain critical dimensions of social change in the late twentieth century and to identify key theoretical issues central to developing a new agenda for rural research on 'globalization' and 'localization'.

THREE INTERWOVEN FIELDS OF CHANGE

As I briefly indicated above, we can distinguish three fields wherein significant restructuring is taking place. The first concerns changes in production, work and economic life more generally. Here we encounter the following critical dimensions: (1) changes in the patterns of commoditization consequent upon the rise of new, and the 'reinvention' of old, modes of value, as consumer markets and interests become more diversified in the types and qualities of goods required; (2) an uneven transition from 'Fordism' and the vertical integration of firms towards a more flexible and global pattern of production and accumulation marked by the growing importance of more loosely structured horizontal linkages covering subcontracting, industrial or artisan homework, and a multiplicity of linked service and consumption-based activities; (3) changing notions of 'work' and 'occupational status' resulting principally from increased unemployment and part-time work and a reorganized gender division of labour, and (4) a move towards greater 'informalization' and fragmentation of economic life within the family/household, small-scale enterprise and local community, in some cases leading to the demise of local systems of care and social support.

The second field of change concerns the changing nature of the state, changing power domains, and the appearance of new social movements and socio-political identities. Central dimensions here include: (1) the decline of corporativist modes of regulation and organization, and the 'hollowing out' of the state as it relinquishes more of its functions to non-state bodies; (2) the emergence of new forms of coalition at local and regional levels as the politics, policies and organization of nation-states are transformed under the impact of more global interests, and as centralized political authority and control become increasingly delegitimized; (3) shifts in the relations and meanings of the 'public' versus the 'private' domain, bolstered by neo-liberal 'free enterprise' and 'back-to-the-market' discourse, and (4) the development of new social and political identities and movements based on diverse social commitments, class being only one among many other forms of association and social difference (such as gender, ethnicity, locality, religion, membership of environmentalist or human rights groups, or a commitment to 'transnational' or 'cosmopolitan' notions of 'citizenship').

The third field relates to issues of knowledge, science and technology. It focuses upon debates about the nature and impact of the rapidly growing 'information society', wherein sophisticated information, communication and media systems, production technologies and computerized modes of reasoning shape the social relations and the value orientations of contemporary societies. This field also encompasses issues concerning knowledge generation, dissemination, utilization and transformation; the encounter between so-called 'expert' and 'local' modes of knowledge; the clashes and accommodations that take place between contrasting cultural and epistemological frameworks; the affirmation of the 'power of science' to transform social life and steer change; and the transformation of knowledge and technology at the interface between intervening 'development' institutions and their so-called 'recipient' groups. In addition, it raises questions about the time–space compression of contemporary social life hastened by information technologies, as well as the central role that information processing plays in the development of 'institutional reflexivity' (Giddens 1991) which, it is alleged, facilitates the quick response of modern organizations to changed circumstances.

GLOBALIZATION: DIVERSITY NOT UNIFORMITY

So far we have concentrated primarily on delineating broad trends and identifying what seem to be critical dimensions. At this juncture, however, it becomes important to give more attention to certain contradictions and struggles that are generated within and between these different fields of change. This is imperative if we are to stand back from essentialist and reified interpretations of globalization that assume rather than demonstrate the force and uniformity of such change. It is also necessary to make a case against centrist and hegemonic modes of analysis.

As a first step, let us reassert the significance of social heterogeneity. We are in fact living in an increasingly diversified world which only has the trappings of homogeneity. The revolution in information and communication technologies has made the world look more uniform and interconnected. Yet even the most sophisticated modern communication and media systems and the development of integrated international commodity markets have not destroyed cultural, ethnic, economic and political diversity. Indeed globalization has generated a whole new diversified pattern of responses at national, regional and local levels.

Awareness of such heterogeneity is reflected in the questioning, in certain policy circles, of standardized solutions to problems of economic development, employment and welfare, in favour of what are described as more flexible, localized and 'sustainable' strategies. This shift implies, at least in public rhetoric, a greater recognition of the strategic contribution that local knowledge, organization and participation can make to development. Concomitant with this is an apparent decline of hierarchical and corporativist forms of organization and the emergence of new groupings and coalitions that delegitimize centralized political control and authority, thus reshaping power relations; although, at the same time, we must remember that so-called 'decentralized' patterns of government may often mask 'top-down' measures aimed at reducing the administrative and financial burdens of central government.

Alongside these trends is the swing back to market-led development where the language of free enterprise, competition and deregulation prevails, with the consequent pulling back or withdrawal of state institutions. Once again, though, we should not assume that liberalizing and privatizing strategies, spearheaded by international bodies such as the World Bank and IMF, imply the end of interventionist measures undertaken by the state. Indeed, the very implementation of liberalization policies requires a framework of state regulation, resources and legitimacy, and the use of a persuasive political rhetoric aimed at mobilizing people and enrolling them into this new type of strategic thinking. Moreover, policy measures that address themselves to the 'solution' of pressing economic problems often fall short precisely because they fail to come to grips with the everyday practicalities and diverse modes of making and defending a living. Thus strategic planning by government is always difficult to realize successfully when faced by a myriad local and regional adaptations, but especially so when the political conditions militate against the state being able to govern effectively and steer change. Many domains of state activity in fact increasingly require international backing to function at all.

GLOBAL DOMAINS AND 'NEW' SOCIAL MOVEMENTS

This problem of state 'governability' arises in part from the increased global character of the relationships affecting various domains of human practice. Recent geopolitical transformations (such as the breakup of the Eastern Bloc countries and the establishment of new regions of cooperation like the European Union and NAFTA, as well as the new agreements or 'conditionalities' concerning third world development aid and trade) question the sovereignty of nation-states, since their rights and obligations, their powers and autonomy, are clearly challenged and redefined. Yet, the immense flows of capital, goods, services, people, information, technologies, policies, ideas, images and regulations that these changes imply are not organized from a few centres or blocs of power, as world systems theory might suggest (see Sklair 1991: 33-4). Transnational enterprises may have localized sites of operation (e.g. London, New York, Tokyo and Hollywood) but they do not dominate their spheres of influence and investment. Rather they must contest them with their competitors.

It is equally difficult then to think of the nation-state or the transnational corporation as the appropriate power-container of important economic and social relationships in the global political economy. Instead we must replace such a model with that of global *orders* whose building blocks are groups and associations set within multiple and overlapping networks of power. These various networks are constantly reordering themselves in the face of changing global conditions. In doing so they draw upon diverse local and extra-local resources and values, frequently appealing to images of some new kind of 'global' scenario and 'cosmopolitan' civil society.

Such groups and associations include not only international trade organizations, financial corporations and newly emerging interstate political alliances, but also social movements where people group around pressing problems of a global nature. The latter manifest themselves in the growing commitment to new 'causes' which bring people together across the world – people of different nation-states and cultures. For example, there are 'green' movements that address themselves to the issues of world-wide pollution, degradation of the environment, depletion of natural resources and the loss of genetic diversity among animal and plant populations; movements that have sprung up around issues of health threats affecting the world population at large (and especially vulnerable groups), such as the HIV/AIDS associations and pressure groups; and 'alternative development' associations and groups that have launched campaigns against transnational companies that have introduced to the poorer nations what are considered to be nutritionally 'inappropriate' products such as baby bottle-feed formulas and Coca-Cola, as well as 'inappropriate' technologies promoting non-sustainable production methods and systems of labour control that are oppressive.

Other examples include consumers' associations (mostly based in the richer countries) that try to protect consumer interests by pressing for better quality or more organically grown produce and more favourable prices; and farmers' organizations that seek to advance their own particular interests – sometimes at loggerheads with each other (such as the French and British producers who have for a number of years been locked into a pitched battle over European Union agricultural export quotas which led in one instance to the slaughtering of imported British sheep in France), and occasionally mobilizing across national boundaries in order to pursue more global issues. Here the problem of the modern food chain is a critical factor, with transnationals and increasingly supermarkets making direct deals with producer groups in third world production zones in order to avoid state control and standards (see Marsden and Arce 1993).

Other cases highlight certain shifts in the character of peasant movements. Latin America in particular has a long history of struggles by small producers and agricultural labourers against landlords and local political bosses who monopolize access to the most productive land and to crucial marketing and servicing channels. But now we witness massive mobilizations of indigenous peoples. For example, around the Amazonian rim we find several different groups fighting aggressively not just for rights to land (i.e. plots for cultivation or livestock rearing) but for habitat rights (i.e. the right not to be disturbed by transnationals or ravaged by land speculators, and the right to determine how natural resources should be utilized and by whom). This struggle, of course, has a strong ethnic and human rights dimension to it which prompted the International Labour Organization to become involved in providing logistical support for the coordination of these Amazonian groups. It also sparked off protest marches directed towards the national governments of Bolivia and Ecuador by indigenous peoples who walked from the eastern tropical lowlands to La Paz and Quito to present their cases. The recent outburst in Chiapas, which focused upon resistance to the Mexican state and its free trade policies and which took place on the day NAFTA was inaugurated presents a similar mix of issues embracing land, ethnicity, political repression and human rights. This case is also notable for the rapidity with which the leaders of the uprising were able to disseminate their manifesto detailing their complaints and demands: almost as soon as they had taken their first offensive a statement from them appeared in e-mail inboxes throughout the global electronic network!

Another interesting global initiative concerns the expansion of women's and feminist associations to include women of diverse cultural and socio-political backgrounds, leading in recent years to the holding of World Summits to share experiences and to identity problems and areas for future strategic debate and action. Finally, of course, we should not forget the example of the long-standing Esperanto Association which has been promoting Esperanto as a world language, though somewhat unsuccessfully in the face of the accelerating spread of English.

As we stressed above, at the same time as these movements have been evolving and flexing their muscles, so we have witnessed a reordering of power relations due to a decline of hierarchical and corporativist modes of control. The interplay of these two processes has generated a variety of dynamic and contingent situations which contain both the organizational potentials for the creation of new globally-oriented coalitions of interest, as well as the possibilities of a fragmentation of existing power domains. While the latter may lead to the opening up of new political spaces, at least for some social groups, it may also heighten cultural and political confrontation, resulting (in the worst of scenarios such as the Balkans) in ethnic strife and civil war.

Clearly, then, globalization processes generate a whole new range of conditions and socio-political responses at national, regional and local levels. These changes, however, are not dictated by some supranational hegemonic power or simply driven by international capitalist interests. Changing global conditions – whether economic, political, cultural or environmental – are, as it were, 'relocalized' within national, regional or local frameworks of knowledge and organization which, in turn, are constantly being reworked in interaction with the wider context. It is for this reason that we need to study in detail the processes of 'internalization' and 'relocalization' of global conditions and trends (van der Ploeg 1992). These processes entail the emergence of new identities, alliances and struggles for space and power within specific populations.

People develop their own strategies to solve the problems they face through the use of interpersonal networks, community or neighbourhood ties, church or similar institutions, and through an appeal to certain widely accepted value positions, and they may do this either individually or in groups. They do not merely respond to programmes or services provided by 'outside' public or private interests; nor do they simply react to distant market conditions. On the basis of 'local' knowledge, organization and values, they actively attempt to come to grips cognitively and organizationally with 'external' circumstances, and in so doing the latter are mediated or transformed in some way (Long 1984, 1989; Long and Long 1992). In this manner, states, transnationals, markets, technologies and global images themselves become endowed with highly diverse and 'localized' sets of meanings and practices.

GLOBALSCAPES: CULTURAL FLOWS, 'IMAGINED WORLDS' AND CHANGING SOCIO-POLITICAL IDENTITIES

Global relations and cultures, as Appadurai (1990) and Featherstone (1990) convincingly argue, are sustained and transformed by global networks of communication and information. This has a number of implications.

The symbolic forms transmitted by communication media become central to contemporary cultural repertoires. The technology involved enables messages, images and symbols to be transmitted rapidly to audiences widely dispersed in time and space, thus creating and reinforcing new types of technically 'mediated' social relations which link individuals to various 'imagined communities' throughout the world (Anderson 1989; Thompson 1990). These 'imagined worlds' (as Appadurai renames them) are made up of 'historically situated imaginations of persons and groups spread across the globe . . . [and] are fluid and irregularly shaped'(Lash and Urry 1994: 307).

To be a member of an imagined world is not of course to be spatially contiguous or involved in direct interaction. In fact imagined worlds are always inhabited by non-existent people, in the sense that there is no one who exactly matches the qualities or profiles of those who are conceived of as being members. Yet individual and group identities (e.g. ethnic or gender belongingness or stereotypes, or simply the idea of what it means to be a train-spotter or a member of Manchester Football Supporters

Club) get constructed around these imagined peoples and places precisely when individuals compare and contrast themselves and their situations with those 'others'. This points to the potential ideological impact of media-transmitted images and symbols, although at the same time one must recognize that widespread and rapid communication entails the continuous transformation of meanings and 'reinvention' of old images and traditions.

But perhaps most important of all is the fact that these media networks project many diverse and often conflicting images which are then reworked by specific audiences in very different ways. For example, in rural Zambia, peasant Jehovah's Witnesses watching an American-made video about the coming of the 'New World' assumed that the paradise would offer them modern bungalows set within a beautiful country estate where they would dress European-style, all have handsome wrist-watches, splendid limousines and enjoy endless family picnics on the well-kept lawns. In short, they expected to receive all the material benefits now mostly monopolized by the whites. Their reading of the video then seized upon the materialist setting chosen to represent the paradise rather than upon what the makers would deem to be the 'spiritual' message. And no doubt numerous other interpretations of the same video film would arise among other audiences.

Thus, rather than generating an increasingly uniform cultural pattern, modern media technology helps to expand the cultural universe in many varied and unexpected ways. Some images, for example, are appropriated by oppositional movements to champion their own campaigns, as frequently happens with environmentalists or Friends of the Earth lobbyists. In this way images become highly localized and may be deployed to challenge established views; or, on the other hand, they may communicate certain supposedly negative attitudes and 'falsehoods' concerning particular cultures. The latter is powerfully demonstrated by Said (1978) in his exposure and critique of 'orientalist' views of Islamic society, which gained added saliency and legitimacy for the West through the media reporting of the Gulf War.

It is essential therefore to acknowledge what Appadurai calls the 'non-isomorphic' nature of global cultural flows: that is to say, the many movements of people, things and ideas do not neatly coincide or accumulate to produce a single overall pattern. Nor does culture merely flow from 'global centres' to subordinate 'peripheries'. Indeed in many cases it is the so-called 'periphery' that brings cultural innovation to the 'centre': see, for example, the constant reverberations of Caribbean, African and Latin American musical and artistic styles that shape the pop scenes of London and Paris.

A further tantalizing but complex aspect of global culture and identity concerns how the notion of citizenship, normally linked to the idea that a person's political identity and rights are defined and guaranteed by the nation-state, has become more elastic and unsure. Nowadays, many groups feel themselves less part of a nation-state, especially when the state is divided along sharp class, ethnic or language lines, and more in tune with the idea of belonging to a nation, such as 'the Scottish nation' to which many Scots claim allegiance, even if this is 'an aspiration rather than an historical fact' (see McCrone 1992 where it is argued that Scottish nationhood is actually built upon the *invention* of ancient Scottish kings and queens whose portraits now hang in Holyrood House in Edinburgh!).

Others claim to be part of an ethnic grouping with its own distinctive culture and language or dialect that cross-cuts nation-state boundaries. This often involves the creation of 'new' ethnicities as networks of people from specific homelands, seeking work, education or political asylum, build ties that span rural and urban locations and national frontiers. These networks constitute specific responses to changes in economic circumstances such as shifts in the international demand for labour (e.g. Mexican labour migration to the USA) or to the convulsions associated with the restructuring or breakup of nation-states (e.g. the Sudanese and Ethiopian refugees in Kenya escaping from war and famine).

As cross-border ties stabilize around regular flows back and forth, so migrants gradually develop a sense of self that is genuinely transnational. They also tend to form associations to further their own specific cross-border interests. This encourages the crystallization of a new kind of socio-political identity built upon ethnic bonds but cutting across national frontiers. Hence, for example, we find a growing propensity among migrant groups from Oaxaca, Mexico, in the USA, to articulate and defend their social rights as tomato workers *vis-à-vis* their Californian employers and the US government. Yet they do this not only as agricultural workers but also on the basis of a rejuvenated Mixtec identity, linking them to their villages of origin in Mexico, which they skilfully deploy in arguing their case against unfair treatment and inadequate housing. According to Kearney (1988), this militancy has spread to incorporate Mixtecs in the border cities of Tijuana, Mexicali, etc. in North-western Mexico, where Mixtec residents' associations have successfully fought cases involving, for instance, police harassment of Mixtec women street traders. Over time, these experiences have contributed to the emergence of a new conception of self which is essentially pan-Mixteca and which therefore goes beyond the normal criteria of citizenship.

This is a common characteristic among international migrant communities; as Hannerz (1990) suggests, even among those who make up the brigades of international migrant professionals who travel around the world working for the UN, development aid agencies and transnationals. These professionals quickly develop a cosmopolitanness that in many ways transcends national styles and identities, although at the same time their global networks remain relatively closed to outsiders. They are more interested in pursuing lifestyles that are largely unencumbered by the civic rights and duties of national citizenship, and of course they often receive tax-free salaries.

This, in turn, raises the thorny political and moral issue of redefining citizenship in terms of consumption so that we may argue that 'people in different societies should have similar rights of access to a wide diversity of consumer goods, services and cultural products', as well as the right to international tourism, that is, to '*consume* other cultures and places throughout the world' (Held 1991; Lash and Urry 1994: 309-10).

ANALYSING THE INTER-DYNAMICS OF 'GLOBALIZING' AND 'LOCALIZING' PROCESSES IN AGRICULTURAL AND RURAL DEVELOPMENT

The foregoing condensed account of key aspects of social change in the late twentieth century provides a baseline for a discussion of rural transformations. In it, I tried to highlight the complex inter-dynamics of globalizing and localizing processes that generate new modes of economic organization and livelihood, new identities, alliances and struggles for space and power, and new cultural and knowledge repertoires.

In the rural context we witness the increasing globalization of agriculture and the food chain, leading to changes in farm technology and the division of labour, with women assuming an increasing role in part-time agricultural work and in the food processing industries. Also, in some areas, we see the growth of new consumption and service activities linked to the tourist industry and recreational pursuits, or the consolidation of small-scale workshops that produce or assemble manufactured goods for transnational enterprises. Once again, these changes have tended disproportionately to recruit women into new and often poorly paid jobs.

Many such changes have exacerbated existing conflicts over land and natural resources, as well as over access to crucial socio-political or economic support. Also, depending on the situation, they have implied changes in legal frameworks, land use, environmental management, technology utilization, the network of technical and administrative institutions serving the farm, status and gender relations, and the internal organization of the household and farm enterprise. None of these transformations has been simply imposed from outside, since the different actors involved (e.g. peasant smallholders, commercial farmers, transnational companies, agricultural bureaucrats, credit banks and various agrarian organizations) have struggled to advance their own particular interests and outcomes have, as far as possible, been negotiated.

As I have argued in previous publications (see, for example, Long 1984, 1988; Long and Long 1992), farming populations are essentially heterogeneous in terms of the strategies that farmers adopt for solving the production and other problems they face. Although ecological, demographic, market, politico-economic and socio-cultural conditions differ and may shape the opportunities open to the farmer, it is the farmer (or more precisely the decision-makers of the farm enterprise) who must actively problematize situations, process information and bring together the elements necessary for the operation of the farming enterprise. Hence it is the enterprise managers who take a major role in constructing their own farming world, even to the extent of internalizing external rationalities (including the use of new technologies and computer software programs) and thus, as it were, appearing to carry out the commands of outside agents, whether they be government officers, representatives of transnational companies or research scientists.

Adopting such an actor-oriented perspective alerts us to the dangers of assuming the potency and driving force of external institutions and interests, when the latter represent only one set among a large array of actors who shape the outcomes. The organizational forms that result are complex and varied, since each 'solution' represents a specific configuration of interlocking actors' 'projects' which is generated by the encounters, negotiations and accommodations that take place between the actors, though not all of them meet face-to-face (Long and van der Ploeg 1994). The influence of actors who are remote from the action situation is of course especially pertinent in an age where information technology penetrates more and more into people's daily lives. Many commercial farmers in the third world, for example, now communicate through walkie-talkies with their farm overseers or foremen in the fields, and some possess computers that can directly access New York or other commodity markets for up-to-date information on prices and product turnover.

Patterns of agricultural development are therefore subject to the combined effects of globalization and localization: that is, 'local' situations are transformed by becoming part of wider 'global' arenas and processes, while 'global' dimensions are made meaningful in relation to specific 'local' conditions and through the understandings and strategies of 'local' actors. This produces a variegated pattern of responses, with some farms or production sectors orienting themselves towards producing for international markets, while others increase their commitment to locally specific production, consumption and distribution markets. Likewise, some farmers specialize their production, while others hedge their bets through crop diversification or by combining agricultural and non-agricultural activities. Nowadays, of course, such choices are complicated by the fact that technological developments are racing ahead of mechanization and chemical inputs to embrace biotechnological research and automation.

This throws up new choices and dilemmas as to the use of modern science and technology *vis-à-vis* local farmer knowledge and practice. However, even in this case, this does not entail a complete surrender to the 'imperatives' of advanced technology because, as Hawkins (1991) shows for British dairy farmers using embryo transplant methods of reproduction supplied by agribusiness, farmers still retain control of how they integrate this technology and its organizational implications into their farming activities and commercialization strategies.

The relationship between global and local dynamics is especially important for understanding the management of agro-ecological resources. Problems may be identified as global in nature when they have widespread consequences (e.g. destruction of the tropical rain forests) or ramifications that interlock a series of actors ranging from the local to the international arenas (e.g. intervention by transnational companies in particular production zones). But their solution requires 'localization'; that is, the localized management of available resources in accordance with existing local and regional knowledge, skills, potentialities and restrictions, although politically it may also be essential to lobby internationally. Frequently too, there are several possible socio-technical solutions to the same basic problems, with consequent differences in farm management styles, cropping patterns, levels of production and the differential use and transformation of knowledge.

Farm knowledge varies and is accorded different social meanings depending on how it is applied in the running of farms. This can readily be seen in the use of different technologies (e.g. tractor, plough, hoe or axe) but is also revealed in the meaning that a particular instrument or factor of production acquires as it is coordinated with other production and reproduction factors (van der Ploeg 1986). Adopted technology is forever being reworked to fit the production strategies, resource availabilities and social desires of the farm household. Included in this process is not only the process by which 'new' technologies or packages are adopted, appropriated or transformed, but also the ongoing processes by which particular farmers combine different social domains based, for example, on family, community, market or state institutions, as well as the struggles they pursue in order to retain or create space for manoeuvre.

Over recent decades non-agricultural dimensions have increasingly emerged as critical to the future of rural areas. One such factor is the massive increase in international migration flows from poorer to richer countries. The motivations for these movements have varied, many individuals and families leaving home in search of work and a better standard of living, and others joining the ranks of the already swollen number of persons displaced by natural disasters or civil war. A large proportion of these migrants originate from rural areas and, as we described for the Mixteca labour migrants, some are destined to return one day to their homelands, although a growing number remain in their host country working in poorly paid jobs in agriculture, the services and small manufacturing workshops.

Nevertheless, a majority retain important ties with their places of origin – even those who are refugees with no immediate prospect of returning. Over time these homeland ties consolidate into wide-ranging, cross-border networks that play a crucial role in the livelihood strategies of households at both ends of the migration flow, with the homeland households looking to their migrant kin and friends for help in finding jobs and raising cash, especially during periods when rural household incomes fall short of requirements, and the migrants expecting their compatriots to look after their homeland assets (e.g. land, housing and livestock) and to defend their interests whenever necessary. These migration networks also function as important conduits of information and opinions about the 'world outside' and disseminate the latest fashions in dress, music and films. In addition, they operate to promote and sustain attachment to homeland ways of life *vis-à-vis* the multiplicity of cultures that migrants encounter. This process facilitates the retention of migrant social identities.

Clearly the existence of such networks shapes the nature of rural social life and may be decisive in determining how rural producers respond to changing agricultural and economic circumstances. In this way, migrant networks, and especially those involving international migration, become central to understanding the restructuring of the countryside consequent upon the introduction of neo-liberal policies which have withdrawn or reduced subsidies and privatized many of the service-providing agencies previously responsible for credit, technical assistance and commercialization. Hence the ability of many farm households to adapt to these measures in order to survive or reap some benefit rests upon the effectiveness of their migrant networks.

'GLOBALIZATION', 'LOCALIZATION' AND 'RE-LOCALIZATION'

In developing further these observations on rural change, we must clarify a bit more what is implied in the notions of 'globalization' and 'localization', and why it is sometimes useful to speak of '*re*-localization'.

In the first place we use 'globalization' instead of 'internationalization' since the latter conjures up the idea of 'inter nation-state' relations, thereby suggesting that the constituent parts are composed of nation-states. Such a view is clearly too restrictive, especially given the present world situation where we are confronted with a complex and changing multiplicity of inter-connections based on financial commitments, commodity flows, producer and consumer associations, technology and knowledge disseminations, and political negotiations and struggles that are transnational in character in that they depend upon types of authority and regulatory practices other than those promoted by the state.

Second, as I indicated earlier, we wish to stand back from the 1960s idea of globalization which pictures an emerging world order in terms of 'centre-periphery', or 'metropolis-satellite' relations, thus implying simple asymmetries in economic, political and cultural terms. Instead we should view global ordering in terms of a complex changing pattern of homogenization and diversity. Moreover, the autonomy and boundedness of social and cultural units is better conceptualized as a matter of degree rather than as a set of sharply delineated forms. What we need then, as I suggested earlier, is a model that concentrates upon global flows involving movements of people (e.g. migrant workers, refugees, investors, traders and transnational employees), technology and information, money through financial operations, products through commodity markets, images and symbolic representations through various media (e.g. addressing notions of 'modernization', 'entrepreneurship', 'citizenship') and institutional designs (e.g. the role of 'modern' business organizations, cooperatives and 'partnership' arrangements) as promoted by the international development agencies. We should then attempt to identify the interest groups, organizations and stakeholders involved in stimulating, manipulating, steering or blocking these flows, and analyse the types and sources of power relations generated.

On the other hand, we use the concept of 'localization' to emphasize the *local embeddedness* of agrarian development. That is, we aim to examine the complex ways in which local forms of knowledge and organization are constantly being reworked in interaction with changing external conditions. We also find it useful to reflect upon issues of '*re*-localization' rather than simply 'localization', since this addresses questions concerning the resurgence of local commitments and the 'reinvention' or creation of new local social forms that emerge as part of the process of globalization. In fact globalization itself can only be meaningful to actors if the new experiences it simultaneously engenders are made meaningful by reference to existing experiences and cultural understandings, but in the process new social meanings and organizing practices are generated. To argue for the reassertion of local organizational and cultural patterns, the reinvention of tradition and the creation of new types of local attachment, is therefore not the same as arguing for a *persisting* set of local traditions. Rather, these 'reinvented' patterns are generated through the ongoing encounter between different frames of meaning and action. In this way, 're-localization' opens up new theoretical insights into processes of social transformation.

TOWARDS A NEW AGENDA FOR RURAL RESEARCH

The foregoing theoretical reflections on change in the late twentieth century underline the need for a new agenda for rural research. The present situation throws up a number of important theoretical and methodological challenges, some new and others a continuation of previous lines of enquiry. A central concern running throughout such a new agenda is, of course, how to analyse the complex sets of relationships that develop between policy discourse and intervention and the ideas and strategic actions of various social actors. It is the latter who, in the end, have to grapple with all the exigencies, dilemmas, vulnerabilities and contradictions of the new emphasis placed upon market-led development, ecological modernization and sustainability, and the accelerating impact of agricultural science and technology.

Yet, while stressing the significance of an actor perspective, we must also acknowledge that attempting to comprehend these processes requires a major rethinking of certain critical concepts and processes such as agrarian development, state intervention, commoditization and agricultural knowledge. This, of course, would necessitate a much fuller discussion than can be achieved in a chapter of this length. My aim then in this last section is to offer a sketch of some of the more interesting analytical problems we encounter.

An actor-oriented approach to issues of intervention

In previous research at Wageningen we have examined critically several of these key notions, stressing for instance the importance of treating state intervention and agrarian development as socially constructed and continuously renegotiated processes (see Long 1988; Long 1989; Long and van der Ploeg 1989; de Vries 1992; Arce 1993). We have also used this constructivist approach for studying the differentiated nature of styles of farming, agrarian enterprise and agricultural work (van der Ploeg 1990; Gonzalez 1994; Torres 1994), as well as for an analysis of the role of knowledge and power in the transformation of small-scale development projects (Villarreal 1994).

The time is now ripe, we believe, to build upon these insights to explore further the interrelations between market processes, government and other forms of planned intervention, and the organization of civil society. As one proceeds, it is important to counterpose theoretical forms of discourse with the actual ways in which different social actors – including here not only male and female producers, agricultural labourers and small-scale entrepreneurs, but also bureaucrats, politicians and planners –

conceptualize, deal with and become agents in the creation and reproduction of these dynamic and often volatile market, state and community relations.

Crucial to understanding the processes of intervention is the need to identify and come to grips with the strategies that local actors devise for dealing with interventionists so that they might appropriate, manipulate or subvert particular interventions. Similarly, the question of how far people make use of formal state or market frameworks and resources necessarily entails the consideration of how local knowledge, organization and values reshape these 'external' structures. In other words, to what extent do the state and the market become endowed with diverse and localized sets of meanings and practices? The latter include not only the well-trodden routines of 'local' culture, but also apparently trivial, contingent and experimental actions that can in no way be seen as simply determined either by planned intervention or by the exigencies of culture. Such a viewpoint we think can offer new insights into the interpretation and analysis of neo-liberal policies, theories and practices that go beyond the common tendency to explore them solely from a macro-economic or macro-political angle.

Differentiated nature of agrarian structures and interface actor networks

In order to accomplish this, we need to reconsider the concept of 'agrarian structure'. This has most frequently been used heuristically to identify the set of technical, natural resource and production factors involved in a particular farming system and to depict how wider legal, political, economic and spatial relationships fashion its reproduction. Rather less attention has been placed upon explaining the diversity of farming styles and enterprise types that are contained within such a system. Nor is there much detailed research on precisely how local producers and other actors are tied into more global actor networks.

These networks form part of complex food chains that link producers to traders, state agencies, transnationals, supermarket businesses, agricultural input suppliers, research enterprises, and eventually the consumers of the products. Each producer or group of producers is in effect part of an *interface* network which integrates the producer to his or her immediate farming environment composed of a series of actors involved in input and output service activities. Such interface networks take many different forms: some are built upon personal networks and commitments, while others entail membership of officially recognized organizations such as cooperatives, farmers' associations or water-users' organizations (see Long 1989; Hawkins 1991). Hence the ways in which the producer and his or her counterpart actors construct these social arrangements will vary significantly, thus shaping the organizing practices of the farmer and his or her farm enterprise. Systematic study of interface networks within particular farming populations affords a better understanding of the differentiated nature of particular agrarian structures. This will provide additional insights into the heterogeneity of farming styles and economic practice.

Food chains contain within them many other arenas within which commodity and non-commodity values are contested, negotiated and realized. Although often remote from the site of production, these arenas are also important for understanding farming styles, interface networks and agrarian structure. Shifts in consumer tastes, technology development and transnational or supermarket strategies set off a whole series of repercussions that can significantly affect farm decision-making. They may also have a disequilibrating effect on existing agrarian social relations, even to the extent of contributing to the downfall of key political groups and alliances within a region.

It is crucial, therefore, that the analysis of agrarian structures includes not only those forms of organization that emerge from the struggles which take place between different interest groups within the regional setting, but also those ordering and organizing processes that arise from the ways in which different farmers and other actors are bound into more global actor networks. The concept of agrarian structure is essentially a simplifying device for coming to grips with these multiple practices of agrarian life. Agrarian change evolves in the context of particular types of regional settings and identities and it is important to develop an analytical framework for understanding the patterns that emerge. But in so doing, one must avoid accepting uncritically the regional definitions and assumptions of administrators, planners and politicians. The life-worlds of farmers and other actors are not confined to the spatial and strategic options promoted by policy-makers even when these conceptions acquire a 'reality' as powerful instruments for allocating resources and for defining the discourse of policy and analysis.

Technologies and organizing practices of government

We also need some concept of government which concentrates upon the multifarious ways in which the state, through its various development programmes and organizational structures, attempts to control territory and people, and how this relates to non-state modes of control and regulation at both local and supranational levels. Although there is a burgeoning theoretical literature on social regulation in market, quasi-market, state and other institutional domains, there remains a dearth of detailed empirical studies exploring issues of 'governability'. One recent contribution draws upon Foucault's notion of 'technologies of government' to emphasize that we need to give more attention to the indirect mechanisms which link the conduct of individuals and organizations to political projects of others through 'action at a distance' (Miller and Rose 1990). The authors illustrate this by reference to the kinds of control exercised by so-called 'experts' concerned with economic planning or accounting practices that render certain things and people amenable to inscription and calculation. These new technologies (along with various other management, marketing, advertising and communicational methods) make up a concerted programme for promoting state policies geared to 'educating citizens in techniques for governing themselves'. Hence political authorities no longer seek to govern directly by putting as many of their own people on the ground as possible – everywhere state bureaucracies are being cut back – but rather to reinforce self-regulating processes among their subjects. Self-regulation, of course, constitutes a key objective of neoliberal policies, not so much 'deregulation' as is often argued.

The role played by these 'technologies of government' could be fruitfully extended to cover non-state bodies such as the World Bank which draws upon a large pool of experts to assist in the promotion of programmes of structural adjustment and 'good governance', as well as to various private enterprise initiatives aimed at encouraging competitiveness and entrepreneurship. We might also apply these insights in the field of rural development to the study of agricultural extension, and research and technology development programmes.

One shortcoming of this approach, however, is its emphasis on the part played by language and the discourse of experts. This view needs complementing by examining how discourses are deployed in particular social arenas, and by giving more attention to issues of strategy and social practice. Clearly the meaning and impact of particular arguments or images depend heavily on who is communicating to whom and on how the message is conveyed and received or transformed.

These dimensions can only be adequately explored by developing appropriate ethnographic methods for doing so. We need, that is, to document carefully how particular government officials, experts and professionals draw upon different conceptions of the functions of the state to legitimize their activities and task definitions, creating, for instance, images of the state as 'protector', 'arbitrator', 'facilitator', 'investor', 'judge' or 'cajoler'. Attention must also be directed towards understanding how government policy concretely affects the lives and life-chances of agrarian populations and how, in turn, the character of the government and its policies are affected, and sometimes transformed, by the actions of rural peoples. We must at all costs avoid a reification of state institutions and actions, in the sense of attributing to them an 'internal logic' or a fixed rationality. However, having said this, we must also recognize that images and ideologies of the state clearly shape the attitudes and guide the actions of all those individuals involved in or affected by the activities of state organizations.

Understanding issues of intervention and regulatory practice entails developing a methodology for studying administrative processes and the work and strategies of bureaucrats, especially in respect to the bottom end of the agricultural bureaucracy. Such an analysis should look at problems of access to and rationing of services, as well as at the types of labelling (e.g. of target groups, or of state 'functions', etc.) practised by administrative, planning and technical personnel. We also need to refine our understanding of organizational styles and the transformation of policy that occurs during implementation.

These dimensions can be integrated into a framework of studies dealing with rural development 'interface' (Long 1989). Interface studies are essentially concerned with the analysis of *discontinuities* in social life. Such discontinuities imply discrepancies in values, interests, knowledge and power, and typically occur at points where different and often conflicting life-worlds or social domains intersect. More concretely, they depict social contexts wherein social relations become orientated towards the problem of devising ways of 'bridging', accommodating to or struggling against other people's social and cognitive worlds. One such critical point of inter-section is, of course, where government officers or representatives of transnationals encounter various local actors and institutions (for further discussion of the concept of interface and how to place it theoretically, see de Vries 1992: Chapter 5).

Social differentiation, social identities and commoditization processes

A new agenda for rural research would also necessitate developing new insights into social differentiation among rural populations, but, unlike much previous work on this topic which concentrates largely on class dimensions, greater attention (as already evident from the literature) should be accorded to issues of age, gender and ethnicity. Research should focus particularly on questions concerning the formation and transforma-tion of social identities that arise in part from the above social differences. This implies addressing issues concerning the negotiation and struggle over self-images, and analysing the interplay of discursive practices whereby the behaviour and perceptions of particular actors are shaped by how others ascribe social meanings to them, and by whether or not they themselves embrace or disown these. These processes generate certain types of power relations and establish the relevance or otherwise of specific normative frameworks. They are also likely to reveal the frailty of authority and the ambiguity of status ascriptions.

Far from being remote from issues of agrarian development, these dimensions become central to the changes taking place. For example, it has become commonplace to assume that with increased commoditization the social identities of people and groups are fundamentally transformed, although in fact relatively little detailed ethnographic research has been conducted on this topic (Taussig 1980 is somewhat of an exception but adopts a political economy position). Given the kinds of globalizing processes that we now face, which draw people into different social worlds – many of which are 'imagined' rather than directly experienced – it seems highly relevant once again to tackle such dimensions.

Types and levels of commoditization and 'externalization' (i.e. the delegation of production and reproduction functions to external bodies) affect the scale and specialization of production, the degrees of capitalization and styles of enterprise management. In the contemporary scene, as agribusiness and food industries compete for increased shares of the market, so they become more sensitive to the differential and localized organization of agricultural production, while at the same time often attempting to commoditize peasant labour through new forms of temporary labour and contract farming. These changes generate the opening up of different 'action spaces' for farmers and peasants and can lead to the growing 'opting out' of some farmers from certain styles of farming.

Linked to this issue is the interrelation of 'commoditized' and 'non-commoditized' relationships in agriculture. Many theories of agrarian development simply assume that the autonomy and functioning of the peasant farm is undermined by the extension of commodity relations, but the empirical evidence shows the matter to be much more complex. This issue merits special attention, since commoditization and externalization only become real in their consequences when introduced and translated by specific actors (including here not only farmers but also others such as traders, bureaucrats and politicians). It is necessary therefore to analyse closely how farmers and householders deal with these problematic situations and develop their own 'livelihood projects'. Moreover, since farmer- or householder-initiated strategies draw upon and may reshape socio-cultural resources and identities, it becomes important to introduce into this type of research an appreciation of how particular cultural repertoires and social organizational resources can create or constrain choice.

The social construction of local and scientific knowledge

One way in which the new agenda should take up these cultural dimensions is through the study of agricultural knowledge. This type of work can draw upon the sociology of knowledge and on cognitive anthropology to analyse how farmers or other relevant actors generate, reproduce, transmit and transform knowledge relating to agricultural practice. Such studies focus, in part, on the schemes of classification used by farmers for coordinating production and reproduction tasks and for guiding their farm decisions on technology, investment and on labour mobilization. They also bring out differences based on the type and scale of enterprise, as well as differences by age and gender. In the same way, we should be interested in identifying the conceptual schemata of agricultural scientists or extensionists when dealing with farming matters. Exposing the underlying assumptions and rationales of these various bodies of knowledge and their bases for reproduction (e.g. the institutions and interactional networks that function to maintain them) reveals the points at which the conceptual models and expectations of the different actors coincide or collide. Through this, one can learn a lot about the ideational impact of new technologies or the incorporative power of existing local cultural models.

More recently, the sociology of knowledge has embraced a more robust social constructivist perspective which provides fresh insights into how 'expert' and everyday forms of knowledge relate to development processes. Such a perspective takes full cognizance of social actors, their values and understandings in the construction of knowledge, and in the scientific design for alternative or competing 'projects of society'. It also takes a stand against treating science and everyday knowledge as being ontologically different.

Hence the demystification of science through the ethnographic study of scientific practice and everyday knowledge (in this case, we are interested in agricultural types) brings into focus a whole new set of images and representations of how the social/scientific world is constructed and organized. The creation and transformation of knowledge, we argue, can only effectively be studied and analysed through an appreciation of how knowledgeable and capable actors – whether peasants, bureaucrats or scientists – build bridges and manage critical knowledge interfaces between their diverse life-worlds (Arce and Long 1987; Long and Villarreal 1993). This requires giving close attention to the practices of everyday social life, involving actor strategies, manoeuvres, discourses, speech games and struggles over social identity, since only in this way can one tease out the intricacies of how knowledge is internalized, used and reconstructed. Such an actor-oriented perspective helps us to go beyond earlier dichotomized representations that overstress the differences between the nature and application of modern science and forms of local knowledge.

Understanding the encounters between various types of knowledge and ideology is central to the analysis of rural development. The interactions between government or outside agencies involved in implementing particular development programmes and the so-called recipients or farming population cannot be adequately understood through the use of generalized conceptions such as 'state-peasant relations' or by resorting to normative concepts such as 'local participation'. These interactions must be analysed as part of the ongoing processes of negotiation, adaptation and transfer of meaning that take place between the specific actors concerned. Interface analysis provides a methodology for doing this. This is a difficult research topic, but one which is central to understanding the intended and unintended results of planned intervention carried out from above by public authorities or development agencies or initiated from below by local interests.

REFERENCES

Anderson, P. (1989) *Imagined Communities*. London: Verso.
Appadurai, A. (1990) 'Disjuncture and difference in global cultural economy', *Theory, Culture and Society* 7(2 and 3).
Arce, A. (1993) *Negotiating Agricultural Development: Entanglements of Bureaucrats and Rural Producers*. Sociologische Studies no. 43. Wageningen: Agricultural University.
Arce, A. and Long, N. (1987) 'The dynamics of knowledge interfaces between Mexican agricultural bureaucrats and peasants: a case study from Jalisco', *Boletin de Estudios Latinoamericanos y del Caribe*, no.43.
Featherstone, M. (1990) 'Global culture: an introduction', *Theory, Culture and Society*, 7(2 and 3).
Fukuyama, F. (1989) 'The end of history', *The National Interest* no. 16 (Summer).
Giddens, A. (1991) *Modernity and Self-Identity*. Cambridge: Polity Press.
Gonzalez Chavez, H. (1994) *El Empresario Agricola: En El Jugoso Negocio de las Frutas y Hortalizas de Mexico*, Ph.D. thesis. Wageningen: Agricultural University.
Hannerz, U. (1990) 'Cosmopolitans and locals in world culture', *Theory, Culture and Society* 7(2 and 3).
Hawkins, E. (1991) 'Changing technologies: negotiating autonomy on Cheshire farms', Ph.D. thesis. London: South Bank Polytechnic.
Held, D. (1991) 'Democracy, the nation-state and the global system'. In D. Held (ed.) *Political Theory Today*. Cambridge: Polity.
Kearney, M. (1988) 'Mixtec political consciousness: from passive to active resistance'. In D. Nugent (ed.) *Rural Revolt in Mexico and U.S. Intervention*. San Diego: Centre for USA-Mexican Studies.
Lash, S. and Urry, J. (1994) *Economies of Signs and Space*. London: Sage.
Long, N. (1984) 'Creating space for change: a perspective on the sociology of development'. Inaugural lecture, Wageningen Agricultural University. A shortened version appears in *Sociologia Ruralis* XXIV (3/4).
—— (1988) 'Sociological perspectives on agrarian development and state intervention'. In A. Hall and J. Midgley (eds) *Development Policies: Sociological Perspectives*. Manchester: Manchester University Press.
—— (ed.) (1989) *Encounters at the Interface: A Perspective on Social Discontinuities in Rural Development*. Wageningen Studies in Sociology, no. 27. Wageningen: Agricultural University.
Long, N. and Long, A. (eds) (1992) *Battlefields of Knowledge: The Interlocking of Theory and Practice in Social Research and Development*. London: Routledge.
Long, N. and van der Ploeg, J. (1989) 'Demythologizing planned intervention: an actor perspective', *Sociologia Ruralis* XXIX (3/4).

— (1994) 'Heterogeneity, actor and structure: towards a reconstitution of the concept of structure'. In D. Booth (ed.), *Rethinking Social Development: Research, Theory and Practice*. London: Longman.

Long, N. and Villarreal, M. (1993) 'Exploring development interfaces: from the transfer of knowledge to the transformation of meaning'. In F. J. Schuurman (ed.), *Beyond the Impasse: New Directions in Development Theory*. London: Zed Press.

McCrone, D. (1992) *Understanding Scotland: The Sociology of a Stateless Nation*. London: Routledge.

Marsden, T. K. and Arce, A. (1993) 'Constructing quality: globalization, the state and food circuits'. In *Globalization of Agriculture and Food*, Working Paper no. 1, The University of Hull and Wageningen Agricultural University.

Miller, P. and Rose, N. (1990) 'Governing economic life'. *Economy and Society* 19(1).

Ploeg, J. van der (1986) 'The agricultural labour process and commoditization'. In N. Long *et al.*, *The Commoditization Debate: Labour Process, Strategy and Social Network*. Wageningen: The Agricultural University.

— (1990) *Labour, Markets and Agricultural Production*. Boulder: Westview Press.

— (1992) 'The reconstitution of locality: technology and labour in modern agriculture'. In T. K. Marsden *et al.*, *Labour and Locality: Critical Perspectives on Rural Change*, Vol. 4. London: Fulton.

Said, E. W. (1978) *Orientalism*. New York: Random House.

Sklair, L. (1991) *Sociology of the Global System*. New York/London: Harvester Wheatsheaf.

Taussig, M. (1980) *The Devil and Commodity Fetishism in South America*. Chapel Hill: University of North Carolina Press.

Thompson, J. (1990) *Ideology and Modern Culture*. Cambridge: Polity Press.

Torres, G. (1994) *The Force of Irony: Studying the Everyday Life of Tomato Workers in Western Mexico*. Ph.D. thesis, Wageningen: Agricultural University.

Touraine, A. (1984) 'Is sociology still the study of society?' *Thesis Eleven*, no. 23.

— (1989) 'The waning sociological image of social life'. *International Journal of Comparative Sociology* 25 (1 and 2).

Villarreal, M. (1994) *Wielding and Yielding: Power, Subordination and Gender Identity in the Context of a Mexican Development Project*. Ph.D. thesis, Wageningen: Agricultural University.

Vries, P. de (1992) *Unruly Clients: A Study of How Bureaucrats Try and Fail to Transform Gatekeepers, Communists and Preachers into Ideal Beneficiaries*. Ph.D. thesis, Wageningen: Agricultural University.

Chapter 4

Anthropology, China and modernities
The geopolitics of cultural knowledge

Aihwa Ong

INTRODUCTION: ANTHROPOLOGY, AUTHORITY AND THE NEW WORLD DISORDER

When I was a child growing up in a predominantly Chinese city in Malaysia, it seemed as though we were always trying to catch up with the West, represented first by Great Britain and later by the United States. Although Malaya gained independence from the British in 1957 (and became Malaysia in 1962), British-type education and the mass media constructed our worlds as failed replicas of the modern West. This colonial effect of trying to learn from and imitate the global centre has been a preoccupation of post-colonial elites seeking to articulate a destiny that is a mixed set of western and Asian interests. Now a resident in the United States, my annual visits to South-east Asia intensify my awareness that an alternative vision of the future is being articulated, an increasingly autonomous definition of modernity that is differentiated from that in the West.

The first half of this century saw the collapse of western colonial empires; in the second half we are witnessing the emergence of a multipolar world. What do these global circumstances mean for anthropology as a western theory of knowledge about culture? In *Culture and Imperialism* (1993), Edward Said notes that a western 'structure of attitude and referencing' uses the third world (cultures, places and peoples) as sources of materials to produce knowledge, and as 'cases' to explicate western theory without recognizing non-western roles as equal partners in cultural production.[1] In today's world, such a structure of attitude actually reflects a defensive western cultural nationalism more than the supreme cultural confidence at the height of western imperialism, the era dealt with by Said in his book. This chapter considers how anthropology can make itself more responsive to the current shifting boundaries of cultural power, and to the changing dimensions of global politics, so as to be a more truly cosmopolitan and politically relevant discipline.

WESTERN SELF-EXAMINATION AND
RECAPTURING OF ANTHROPOLOGY

In recent years, the shrinking of western hegemonic influence abroad and the growth of restive minorities at home have led American anthropologists to suggest a reformulation of our ethnographic goals. There is a disturbing trend of turning inward, a process which converts anthropological knowledge to a defensive form of western self-examination.[2] Whereas in the past, male anthropologists could be said to be engaged in soul-searching through a study of the colonized other,[3] the more recent inward-turning gaze is directed at the cultural self and body at home.

Recently, younger anthropologists have again problematized our representation of cultural others in political terms.[4] A popular work in this discussion is *Writing Culture* (Clifford and Marcus 1986), which analyses the ways male anthropologists have constructed anthropological texts to establish 'ethnographic authority'. However, by reducing the politics of representation to a question of literary techniques, the book offers few suggestions as to how anthropological knowledge may be reformulated in a transnational, post-colonial world. In a companion volume entitled *Anthropology as Cultural Critique* (1989), George Marcus and Michael Fischer invoke Margaret Mead to suggest an appropriate response to the 'crisis of representation'. The book prescribes the location of cultural others in the integrated world system: 'If cultural others are to be contrasted with us, to make a critical point, they must be portrayed realistically and in the round, *sharing modern conditions* that we experience also' (p.162, emphasis added). The implication is that the West invented modernity and other modernities are derivative and second-hand. Even more disturbing, the message of the book is that western interest in cultural others acts only as a foil to the West, as a strategy of defamiliarization and (western) cultural critique of western societies (pp. 158–62). Thus anthropology as cultural critique reveals itself as a neo-liberal defence of the asymmetries of modernity. What is at stake is our modernity (and view of the world), not theirs. As Mayfair Yang notes (see Chapter 5, this volume), the book 'supposes that only the West is in need of, and can provide, critique' (p. 000). We remain comfortably lodged in a Eurocentric notion of modernity, regardless of the rest of the world's views and plans for the future. This is a dangerous anachronism considering the new claims of other modernities, while European modernity is itself under attack at home.

A third form of inward-turning is represented by studies of colonialism which tend to focus on white male power, and the forms of control over white female colonists (see e.g. Callaway 1987), or ideological domination of the lower orders 'back home' (Comaroff and Comaroff 1991). Such approaches to colonial societies seem to reflect two current concerns: a concern with the rise of European modernity/white hegemony on the one hand, and the feminist struggles against male ideologies on the other. The inescapable impression is that the third world, colonized or decolonized, is primarily of interest when viewed as acted upon by the West, or places where western hegemony can be deconstructed. Such current interests in colonialism of course intersect with the struggle over multiculturalism in western democracies, and are part of a renegotiation of western national identities at home and abroad. Anthropological studies of colonialism and the third world are deeply embroiled with western interests in the age of economic restructuring, but rarely with the concerns of non-western nations redefining their own realities.

How should we treat non-western cultural production of difference that attempt to disengage from western cultural hegemonies? In what ways can anthropology as a form of western knowledge enact a political decentring by attending to other narratives of modernity that are neither wholly derivative of the West nor based entirely on the interests of western democracies? Under current shifting geopolitical conditions, 'the periphery [forces] itself upon the attention of West' (Kipnis 1988: 165) in an entirely new way. How can we make anthropological writings of cultural knowledge address the current concerns and criticisms of cultural others?

For inspiration, I turned to a new collection dedicated to 'recapturing' anthropological authority (Fox 1991).[5] An 'anthropology of the present', in the words of Paul Rabinow (1991), should be 'resolutely late modern'; but he focuses on the micro-politics of departments and the discipline and gives little hint as to how our collective attitude might be changed in relation to the late modern non-western world. Towards this end, Joan Vincent (1991) appeals to anthropologists to historicize their work in a 'cosmopolitical system', while Arjun Appadurai (1991) suggests the configurations of a 'cosmopolitan ethnography' by delineating 'ethnoscapes' of exchange and contestation emerging from the global circulation of people, cultures, media images and goods. These are necessary steps to deepen, broaden and recontextualize the scope of anthropological investigations, but can anthropological authority be recaptured through reified western notions of historicism and transnationalism, without seeing itself as speaking from a vantage point limited by its own historical, cultural and geopolitical situation?[6] Indeed, the current focus on the transnationalized world made by late capitalism may actually represent an anthropological recodification of western knowledge 'about' those others. Our authoritative gaze still emanates from a fixed western vantage point, and our structure of attitude and referencing is deeply invested in these tropes. We rarely ask how other societies view transnational exchanges in relation to their specific economic, cultural and nationalist interests.

DISORDERING GEOPOLITICS, DESTABILIZING CATEGORIES

To be relevant to the changing world, anthropology must enact a decentring from its western vantage point and engage with other forms of cultural knowledge arising out of other historical situations and concerns. By discussing two different strands of Chinese modernity, I hope to suggest possibilities for a shifting anthropological subjectivity that would treat non-western cultures as effective producers of knowledge that can interact with anthropological knowledge about our collective late twentieth-century condition.

In the USA the multiculturalism debate has sparked a remarkable response: how much diversity can (or should) modernity take? An ironic question. Throughout the first sixty years of this century, western modernity claimed to be internationalist in its scope and ambition, supremely confident that it could incorporate all kinds of diversity and make the world over in its image. In our changed global circumstances, modernity, as based on Eurocentric experiences, is forced to acknowledge its limits (confusion), or its refusal to absorb the cultural diversities of the world. A recent article in a major American newspaper is unusually critical of the foreign policy establishment's view of the USA as bound to lead the multipolar new world order. Christopher Layne notes that

> While Washington may believe its aspirations for world order reflect universal values, they reflect American preferences that may not comport with others' interests. . . . We [can't] indefinitely prevent new powers . . . from rising, or old ones . . . from staging comebacks.[7]

There is also a changing political economy of knowledge that we have been reluctant to confront. What is social knowledge for: to buttress outmoded hegemonic views of the world, or to increase our understanding of its complexities through exchange and mutual understanding? Recent interest in cultural hybridity and transnational flows of culture have radically overturned notions of culture as a seamless whole. We are told that in the late twentieth century, anthropology is to be dominated by the study of cultural hybridity and alternative cosmopolitanism, whether in terms of self-fashioning from 'bits and pieces' of cultures (Clifford 1988; Hannerz 1989) or in understanding how social lives are partially fabricated from global media-generated fantasies (Appadurai 1991) as local forms of resistance. However, little attention has been paid to geopolitical or political economic conditions that condition and produce these hybrid cultural forms. Another approach to the study of transnationalism focuses on the political economy of accumulation and nation-building, while the cultural differences among mobile third world petit-bourgeoisie tend to be erased.[8] At this point we might ask whether the study of cultural hybridity and transnationalism merely represents a reassertion of the western vantage point in multicultural global capitalism, since our key assumptions about history, capitalism and modernity have remained largely unchanged by the ways social knowledge elsewhere remakes other worlds.

A promising approach is suggested by post-colonial scholars, especially of the Subaltern Group, who have participated in critiques of western modernity as outsiders from within the West. Partha Chatterjee, for instance, has criticized the Indian national project as based on western models of modernity, while bypassing 'many possibilities of authentic, creative, and plural development of social identities' from the marginalized communities in India (1993: 156). He suggests that an alternative imagination, drawing upon the 'narrative of community', would be a formidable challenge to narratives of capital.

Unfortunately, this brilliant work unproblematically accepts the notion that both modernity and capitalism are universal forms against which non-western societies like India can only mobilize 'pre-existing cultural solidarities such as locality, caste, tribe, religious community, or ethnic identity' (Chatterjee 1993: 217–218). Even among scholars who are beginning to acknowledge that the definition of modernity is relative, there is little attention to how non-western centres 'rework modernity' except through cultural responses (Pred and Watts 1993; see also Lash and Friedman 1991). There has been no attempt to consider how non-western societies themselves make modernities after their own fashion, in the remaking of the rationality, capitalism and the nation in ways that borrow from but also transform western universalizing forms. Indeed, as another post-colonial scholar notes, 'The narrative of capitalism is no longer a narrative of the history of Europe; non-European capitalist societies now make their own claims on the history of capitalism' (Dirlik 1994: 350). As we shall see, post-1970s China has begun the latest phase of its modernization project, but this time she claims an increasing degree of independence from western categories, and insists upon the distinctive racial, cultural and economic roots of Chinese modernity.

CHINA'S OFFICIAL CONSTRUCTION OF MODERNITY

It is claimed that the next largest economy in the world is emerging in China. With the end of the cold war, the Chinese state has embarked upon a narration of modernity and cultural difference that is centred in Asia. How is China's conversion to a market economy imagined, and what does it tell us of its alternative modernity? I suggest that modernity is an evolving project in different parts of the world, and in this chapter will focus on two types of modernist imaginaries: a post-Maoist official state project that is tied to the fixed territory of China, on the one hand, and a coastal phenomenon that envisions Chinese modernity in transnational terms. These two views overlap to some degree, but important tensions exist over the divided loyalties to territorial and political affiliations.

In China, knowledge is clearly understood as power, and the state plays a major role in the construction of proper knowledge. There is a pervasive ideological distinction between what is considered 'official' (*guanfang*) and 'unofficial' (*feiguanfang*) discourses about society (Link *et al.* 1990: 2). Mayfair Yang argues that 'state power in China today is both the product of the western Enlightenment optimism in reason, social engineering . . . and "modernization", as well as the eruption of an older, native rationality of the state' (1994: 174). In everyday life, official discourse, as disseminated in the official press and electronic media, exhorts 'both the people and officials to aspire to a higher loyalty' (p. 175). The official narratives of a national imagined community (Anderson 1991)[9] inextricably links modernization and modernist aspirations to the strengthening of the motherland, and the territorial space of the nation-state.

During the Mao era, the state was influenced by the Soviet Union in its view of modernity. Socialist modernization stressed the development of science (*kexue*) and technology (*jishu*) to strengthen the economy on the one hand, and the overcoming of feudalism (*fengjianzhuyi*) in order to liberate social forces for development on the other. These principles were later encapsulated in the 'Four Modernizations' (*sige xiandaihua*) that identified development in industry, agriculture, science and technology, and national defence. Thus progress in both the fields of production and political thought were mainly dependent upon borrowings from the West, by way of the Soviet Union. The Great Cultural Revolution (*wenhua dageming*) clearly indicated that at least from the official perspective, Chinese culture was viewed mainly in terms of 'feudal' features obstructing Chinese socialist modernity.

With Deng Xiaoping coming to power in the late 1970s, market reforms (*shichang gaige*) have replaced continual class struggle as the language of modernization. Official discourses now, building on the four modernizations, have begun to valorize Chinese traditional culture (*chuantong wenhua*), but purged of its 'feudal superstitions'. With the rejection of the Soviet Union as a model of modernization, socialism (as western political philosophy) became sinicized as 'socialism with Chinese characteristics' (*you zhongguo tese de shehuizuyi*), just as market reforms would also be detached from the West and made Chinese. Such official and elite rethinking about modernity is reflected in Premier Deng Xiaoping's historical visit to South China in 1992.

A new state vision of modernity was proclaimed in Shenzhen, the foremost 'special economic zone' driving China's economic take-off. Deng called for one hundred years of market reform (*sichang gaige*) or modernization (*xiandaihua*) by pointing to the newly industrializing Asian countries as models of China's development.[10] The growth of 'a capitalism with Chinese characteristics', he declared, depended upon setting up 'a number of Hong Kongs' (*jige Xianggang*) along China's coast. Deng was referring to the entrepreneurial dynamism of Hong Kong, while blithely ignoring its waning British rule. Today, a gigantic poster of Deng, emerging like a Judaeo-Christian God from sun-streaked clouds, raises a finger in seeming admonishment at the chaotic traffic below in downtown Shenzhen. This image of Chinese modernity is a reminder that the state modernization project has not abandoned socialism, and that market forces have been released for the strengthening of the nation. Market reform is ultimately intended for developing the 'productive forces', increasing 'comprehensive national strength' and 'the living standards of the people'. Modernity, and capitalism, are bounded to national interests and the political integrity of the state.

Some have argued that Deng's model of 'authoritarian modernization' shares features in common with the economic plans of his non-Communist predecessors on the one hand, and with overseas Chinese modernist projects on the other (Cohen 1988: 535). Like the current regimes of Taiwan and Singapore, capitalism is controlled by the state for the overall good of society and country, while democratic rights are firmly curtailed. 'Capitalism with Chinese characteristics' is an Asian reconstruction of capitalism that puts the state in the driver's seat, and emphasizes productivity (of the labour forces), security (jobs and a rising standard of living) and seduction (expanded consumer choice) for the population. Wealth accumulation and modernist reforms are ultimately for the strengthening of the state. Thus by learning from the ways capitalism has coexisted with strong state controls in Asian countries, Chinese modernist narratives stress collective values while eschewing democracy often associated with capitalism in the West.

Furthermore, I argue that in official discourse, Chinese modernity is being recast in terms of a blending of capitalism with Chinese race and cultural tradition. State power implements modernity not only in discourses of market reforms, but also in the regulation of the population, in the interests of improving China's labour productivity, household income generation and consumer power, all in competition with other Asian capitalist economies. In the process, the uniqueness of the Chinese race is continually invoked, together with the economic success of overseas Chinese communities as a way to exhort Chinese citizens to constantly improve their economic performance and thus strengthen the Chinese economy.

In the twentieth century, indigenous notions of the Han race-nation have been strengthened through drawing selectively from western theories of eugenics and progress. By the turn of the century, the long-held Chinese notion that race (*zhongzhu*) and culture (*wenhua*) were inseparably linked had been reinforced by Han resistance to the Manchus, who despite or because of their long rule in China, were still viewed as a separate and degenerate race (Crossley 1990). The coming of other western 'barbarians' like the English and French seeking imperialist concessions was experienced first and foremost as racial domination. For instance, in the Shanghai western concessions, the notice 'Chinese and dogs not allowed' was posted in parks. Furthermore, the language of western modernity assumed the fundamental superiority of the West over China's inferior cultural traditions (Chow 1960). The profound influence of social Darwinism and Henry Morgan's savagery-to-civilization scheme recast within a Marxist model of historical determination convinced many Chinese intellectuals that they were an inferior race and culture. Both the westerners and the Chinese saw themselves as biologically separated in terms of race. A 1920 textbook for primary schools claimed that 'Among the contemporary races that could be called superior, there are only the yellow and the white races.... Only the yellow race competes with the white race' (Dikotter 1992: 162–3). Thus for Chinese thinkers, whether partial to liberal democracy or to communism, modernization was seen as totally inseparable from westernization (*zifangjuyi*) and from the white race. Those Chinese who desired social change but feared cultural deracination came to view themselves only as 'occasional modernists' (Shih n.d.).

By the 1930s, the influence of eugenics produced many discussions on race improvement in order to save the 'nation' (*minzu*), a concept that means a biologically distinct group (Dikotter 1992: 178–80, 192). Thus race–culture–nation was an intertwined whole in the struggle to strengthen China. Chinese leaders were haunted by one question: since imperialists were the standard-bearers of modernization and the colonizers of Asia, how can the Other (as race/culture/nation) itself become modern?[11] Again and again, Chinese officials returned to the theme of 'Chinese learning for the fundamental principles, western learning for practical application' (*Zhongxue weiti, Xixue weiyong*), or in other words, a mixture of Chinese cultural–racial difference with western science/technology appeared the only path to modernization.

After the communist victory in 1949, racialist discourse was banned as discriminatory to Chinese minorities, but the basic assumptions about racial exclusiveness and the continuum between nation, race and culture remained (Dikotter 1992: 191–2). Today, a resurgent Chinese nation-state crafting a new course of modernization focuses strongly on race/nation/culture as the means to achieve developed country status within Pacific Rim affluence. At home, complex strategies in redefining Chinese modernity includes the othering China's minorities in the interior as representing the backward and the historical past (Schein 1993; White 1993). More dominant is the discourse of Han exceptionalism not only at home but also overseas. Newly industrializing countries like Hong Kong, Taiwan and Singapore are often held up as models to emulate, not least because of the Chinese populations and Confucian heritage. Official Chinese discourses emphasize the need to raise China's labour productivity to those transnational Asian-Pacific standards.

The new socialist-modernist imaginary, stimulated by comparisons with overseas Chinese communities, fundamentally depends upon state attempts to ensure the 'improvement of the quality of the population' (*gaijin renminde suzhi*). This discourse on population quality has displaced earlier images of the population as a political force in history. About 40 per cent of China's population of over one billion is aged 19 or younger.[12] Concerned that the population is 'the source of China's backwardness' (Anagnost 1989: 5–6), the government has launched campaigns to improve conditions in the fields of public health, education, family planning, law and technology. China is well known for its one-child family policy which in many cases relied on compelled abortion or sterilization. Recently, the Public Health Ministry announced that these measures have been extended to 'prevent or reduce the number of births of seriously sick and disabled children [in order to] improve the quality of the Chinese population.' The statement goes on to defend the 'essence' of the policy as 'totally different' from Nazi eugenics policy.[13] Such attempts to control and correct the composition of the population arrived on the heels of a shake-up in welfare supports.

Discourse on the quality of the population also includes promoting the household as a model of class solidarity but as an adaptable form of capitalism. Ann Anagnost (1989) notes that the 'moral discourse of wealth' now honours the wealth-accumulating household. Labels such as the '10,000 yuan household' (*wanyuan hu*), 'nouveau riche household' (*baofu hu*) and 'civilized household' (*wenhua hu*), though often the target of resentment and envy by neighbours, have become the new measures of Chinese living standards. In many cases, households have been able to improve their living standards because of daughters and sons working in factories.[14] The household responsibility system has revived Confucian discourses on family values and solidarity that will contribute to a kind of competitive productivity that will only strengthen the motherland.

Market reform also entails a dramatic change in the relation between state and workers. Socialist forms of security have been suddenly removed from selected industries, plunging workers into labour market competition. In the 'break the three irons' campaign, the state rescinded the iron rice bowl or guaranteed employment, iron chair or guaranteed posts for managers, and the iron salary or the guarantee that wages will not be cut. Workers looking to be improved by market competition have complained bitterly about trading their iron bowl for a porcelain one (the latter is elegant but fragile). By thus exposing Chinese workers to the uncertainties of international capitalism, the state puts its economy in direct competition with the flexible labour regimes of the Pacific Rim countries. When Chinese newspapers now talk about Chinese workers as literate and healthy, *and* willing to work for £50 or less a month, they are identifying young women in South China's special economic zones, which attract labour migrants from all over China. Increasingly, manufacturing firms perceive Chinese women as better workers than their counterparts in South-east Asia, and many overseas Chinese capitalists are relocating their factories from Indonesia and the Philippines to South China.

Improving the quality of young workers by making them available and flexible to exploitation also involves remaking them as consumers. For instance, a visitor to Shenzhen, China's pace-setting industrial zone, observed in surprise: 'A model woman worker dressed in gold and jade? Suddenly I understood. Model workers of the 1980s are good at creating wealth, and they also understand how to enjoy it. This is probably the charm of our times' (Honig and Hershatter 1988: 39). Thousands of young single women have flocked to the Guangdong and Fujian provinces where much of the new industrialization has been spawned by overseas Chinese capital, and a consumer culture inspired by Hong Kong. Whether employed in timber mills, electronics factories or hotels, many rush to spend their earnings on consumer items like beauty aids. In Guangzhou, there is a virtual 'empire of Avon ladies' who serve a market of sixty million. These sales representatives earn much more than most young women. Their faces and finger-nails, displaying the colour spectrum of Avon products, promise Chinese working women the 'beautiful world' to be gained through working hard and making over as a marketable product of Asian capitalism.[15] Currently, thousands of professionals from Hong Kong, Singapore and Taiwan are teaching mainlanders how to organize modern selves, offices and industries in all fields. The strategy of raising the quality of the population not only integrates China into the Pacific Rim world, but also promotes a transnational modern Chinese market sensibility. Official narratives of Chinese modernity thus promise productivity (competition and greater income), security (rising standard of living) and seduction (expanded consumer choice). We see here the reworking of Confucian tradition – of loyalty, solidarity and diligence – as a rational instrumentality for advancing Chinese modernity.

Official discourse on Confucianism (*rujia sixiang*) has also been employed as a brake on the more rampant versions of 'money worship' that threatens to wreck national solidarity. Recently, the official press printed front page articles calling for a renewal of Confucianism as a moral force 'that can serve as a single source for building a new culture'. It continues:

The Confucian school does not oppose profiting through merchandise and money but advocates fairness in buying and selling, and neither is it opposed to making money and wealth but it advocates that such practices be guided by morality.[16]

Thus official constructions of Chinese modernity, working with the premise of race–culture–nation as an inseparable entity, employs Confucianism (often by invoking its '2,000-year-old history') both as an instrumental rationality of futurist modernism and as a moral force to domesticate capitalism. Such ritual invocations of disciplinary practices define the ideological contours of Chinese modernity as a distinctive entity that is bounded to the nation-state.

Thus, when Asian entrepreneurs coined the concept 'Greater China', many Chinese academics, whose public pronouncements reveal the effects of official power, are careful to point out the territorial boundedness of the Chinese nation-state (*guajia*). I am told by scholars from China that the concept has generated much heat in public forums, with Chinese academics differentiating between the concept of 'China's Economic Zone' (*Zhonghua jinji quan*), which includes the mainland, Hong Kong, Macao and Taiwan, and the idea of 'Greater China' (*da Zhonghua*), which in addition may include Chinese communities in South-east Asia. The argument goes that the China Economic Zone reflects a new Chinese modernity, since Hong Kong, Macao, and Taiwan are technically part of (or will soon be incorporated within) the motherland; together with the mainland, they represent a single territorial, economic and political entity. Greater China, on the other hand, implies the mixing of nation-states – China, Singapore, Malaysia – that do not add up (*buhe*) into a single entity. The discussions thus attempt to deflect the challenges of transnational capitalist formations to the territorial power of the state, the official reiteration of the fixed state position in opposition to the capitalist discourse of deterritorialization.

BRIDGING OVER NATIONS, PLUNGING INTO THE OCEAN

This second construction of Chinese modernity is thus one associated with the coastal cities of South China, and the world of the capitalists, professionalists and overseas Chinese (*huaqiao/huayi*). In cities like Shanghai, Guangzhou, Xiamen and Shenzhen, the modernist imaginary is directed outwards, towards Hong Kong, Singapore and other overseas Chinese communities that are the centres of new affluence.

In 1988, the Chinese Central TV showed a series called *He Shang* ('Yellow River Elegy'). Written by intellectuals, the television epic portrayed the Yellow River through its entire journey. Symbolizing China's life-force, history and traditions, the river is depicted as turbulent, tyrannical and destructive. Only as it enters the ocean does it gain an openness and richness as it mingles with the waters of the Pacific. This highly acclaimed film was widely read as an urgent call for Chinese society to change its ancient traditions by flowing into 'the blue ocean culture' (*lanhai wenhua*) of the Pacific. What is exactly meant by the blue ocean culture remains ambiguous. For many, it is an image of the West, especially its industrialization, science and democracy from which China must learn in order to be modern (Feld 1991: 6). Yet the blue oceanic societies can also stand for Asian Pacific Rim countries which are widely viewed as having achieved western material standards without losing their cultural heritage. The controversy surrounding *He Shang*'s ambiguous messages created such a storm that it was later banned, and blamed for inciting the student movement in 1989.

Some scholars have argued that the emergence of a new urban Chinese identity is based on international symbols of democracy so widely displayed during the Tiananmen demonstrations (Watson 1991). While this view has some appeal among urban professionals, it is the fever of making overseas connections that is fuelling much of the popular vision of a Chinese future, a modernity that is inextricably linked to overseas Chinese communities in the rest of Asia. Historically, a Beijing-centred northern China had always been an expression of the nation-state, whereas southern China, linked by diaspora to South-east Asia (the Southern Ocean or Nanyang), has always explored its identity, and future, in relation to the outside world (see Friedman 1994). It is not surprising then that a transnational construction of China's modernity should evolve in the coastal cities, where overseas Chinese investments have fuelled the world's greatest new industrial development. There is talk of a southern wind (*nanfeng*) blowing across China (Guldin 1992: 179), transnational forces that are symbolized by Chinese acumen and accumulation overseas.

Huaqiao as bridge-builders

The term *huaqiao* is used to denote Chinese nationals who live abroad, while the term *huaren* refers to Chinese citizens of foreign countries.[17] In practice, they are linked as *huaqiao/huaren* to refer to all Chinese living abroad, denoting the overriding importance of same race/culture as compared to different nationalities. For generations, overseas Chinese have been constructed as traitors of the motherland, but now, in the coastal regions, they are viewed as major investors and returning native sons, and they have come to symbolize the persistence of primordial/patriotic sentiments (over socialist ideals) and kinship mutual assistance (over economic inequality), i.e. the new old collective values for strengthening the links between individuals, families and the race-nation (*zhongzu*), even across oceans.

There are innumerable stories of returnee *huaqiao* who demonstrate their Confucian reverence for their home towns and clan associations by building factories and providing employment for relatives and compatriots. Overseas relatives, once they have revealed themselves, are reclaimed by mainlanders as people to whom one can rightly appeal for funds to pay anything from the funerals of distant cousins to rebuilding the local school. They are also sought as patrons to provide services and knowledge about access to resources in the outside world. These gifts and favours are possible because overseas Chinese continue to operate according to the Chinese norms of personal relationships (*guanxi*). Although many return to China for business, they establish relationships of trust and mutual obligation on the basis of personal relationships, which are indispensable for conducting business. Thus the business activities of overseas Chinese are constructed as inseparable from building *guanxi* which facilitate the channelling of funds, favours and people across national borders.

A recent news story used banner headlines to proclaim, 'Let the overseas Chinese build bridges, let them create prosperity!' (*Yi qiao daqiao, yi qiao shengchai!*)[18] Something is lost in the translation, but the pun on huaqiao and daqiao merges overseas citizenship with a bridge overseas. The article reports that in Shanghai almost half a million inhabitants have overseas connections forming 'a large invisible bridge' (*wuxin ta qiao*) that is developing the local economy and integrating it with Chinese abroad. Other articles refer to the huaqiao's capitalist skills and flexibility , as in a report entitled 'In an Overseas Chinese Hometown, the More Bridge is Played, the More Flexible it Gets' (*Qiaoxian Quanzhou, qiao pai yue ta yue huo*), which compares Taiwanese manipulation of capital to bridge-playing (*qiaopai*, puns with *huaqiao*).[19] Such accounts[20] represent overseas Chinese investments in their ancestral hometowns as acts of patriotism, inseparable from reinvestment in blood connections to kinsmen and to the ancestral race/culture. By investing in China, overseas Chinese are 'adding wings to the tiger' (i.e. China as the new economic Asian powerhouse).

More explicitly, another stream of articles lauds the patriotism of overseas Chinese by appealing to traditions of loyalty to the family and the motherland. One report opens by invoking a poetic couplet:

> Time will not age the migrant's heart,
> High mountain pass cannot break the longing for home.[21]

These Confucian sentiments are ritualistically invoked in meetings welcoming overseas investors. At a reunion conference in Fujian, an overseas Chinese claims:

> We Fujian Chinese from Japan have for a long time raised the flag of love of motherland (*zuguo*), love of hometown (*qiaoxian*). . . .

For the first generation of emigrants, this is our dream come true. For the second, third, and even fourth generations, these ties can deepen their understanding of the hometown and the motherland.[22]

The traditions of paternalism, filial piety and everlasting loyalty to the motherland have become the language of investments and flexible accumulation, while traditional objects are displayed at investment-scouting meetings. After the conference, the overseas visitors planted pine trees in the city garden called 'Love of Hometown' (*ai qiaoxian yuan*). The trees symbolize the claim (and hope) that the love for the hometown will be evergreen. These enduring symbols of Chinese roots stress the indestructible nature of ancestral home and kinship ties, thus reinforcing the timeless and unchanging quality of Chinese culture, even in the age of flexible accumulation.

A parallel narrative constructs the *huaqiao*'s capitalism as the expression of Chinese cultural difference from the West, because it is based on *guanxi*, on humanistic feelings considered the touchstone of Chinese culture. Stories about returning overseas Chinese deal with their sojourns in the West and renewed ability to appreciate their Chineseness, expressed as an inescapable kinship and racial particularity. The following story illustrates the theme that although western scientific knowledge can be applied to help China develop, the overseas Chinese's cultural/racial identity remains a key to guiding China's future. Mrs Yuan, who trained as a linguist in the United States, returns to her father's Shanxi hometown.[23] As a filial returning daughter, Mrs Yuan allows local officials to use her family name for a new retirement home she built for the hometown. In the opening ceremony, Mrs Yuan notes that in the United States, the elderly live in beautiful environments but in loneliness and neglect by their children: 'Let us use the profound humanity of the Chinese people to attract elderly overseas Chinese people back to China.' Western training has not destroyed her identification with her Confucian roots. Chinese humanist values are invoked to contrast the different ways modern sciences are used by the Chinese and western others.

In another story of filial piety, a Mrs Li, who trained as a scientist in America, returned to Hubei to set up a scholarship fund in her father's ancestral hometown.[24] She had been 'very moved at how the government had led the people in constructing modern China'. Besides giving lectures on advanced foreign management techniques in China's major cities, Mrs Li wanted to help young students 'understand one's motherland in relation to western societies'. Her lecture *March to Success* was selected as one of the ten most popular books in Beijing in 1988. Her message is China's fundamental difference from the West; Chinese race has its own originary development and only needed western scientific learning to help build its greatness.

The Chinese nation (*minzu*) is full of aspirations (*xiwang*). I was born in mainland China, grew up in Taiwan, and established my career in the US. (Nevertheless) I have a profound identification with my people (*minzu*).

She goes on to confide that she had sent her daughter to study in Beijing in order to 'remind her that she is one of the Chinese people, with their black eyes (*hei yanjing*) and yellow skin (*hwang pifu*)'. Filial piety, profound identification with Confucian traditions and the Chinese people are inseparable from being at one with the race.

What are the everyday opinions of ordinary Chinese about *huanqia/ huaren* and do they reflect these official views? In China's booming coastal cities, the reactions to overseas Chinese are probably more diverse than elite views, and the local reactions veer between open admiration and overt hostility. In the Fujian province, across the water from Taiwan, local knowledge of Taiwanese developed during the forty years of Communist rule was as smugglers and criminals. Now the influx of overseas Chinese money has transformed the major port Xiamen into a 'Little Taipei', with skyscrapers, department stores and karaoke bars. Anti-Taiwan feelings are freely expressed by a customs official: 'They may be rich, but they aren't very polite. Lots of the Taiwanese who come here are the dregs of society. They bring over the worst of their world, and when we see them smuggling or going out with hookers, naturally we are turned off.'[25]

On my recent visit, residents told me that Taiwanese businessmen had the local policemen in their pockets. They mention an incident in which four Taiwanese supervisors severely beat a female worker, and were taken into custody. The next day, after the intervention of their Taiwan boss, the men were released and no charges pressed. Although their investments and free-spending habits are welcome, people feel that Taiwanese managers tend to exploit local women, increase corruption and intensify relations of inequality.

In Quanzhou, also on the Fujian coast, locals complain about the sale of dozens of failing state enterprises at rock bottom rates to a wealthy Indonesian Chinese. He was also offered generous tax breaks to set up joint ventures with the city government. A worker made an anonymous call to the mayor's office asking him 'Why don't you sell your wife too?'[26] Economic development is linked to selling women in other ways too. Hong Kong truck drivers working inter-city circuits in Guangdong are well known for perpetrating the 'mistress phenomenon' through their 'railroad policy' of keeping women at different stops along their routes. Although there is the feeling that Hong Kong visitors have reduced the general morality, a female official commented, 'We no longer talk about these things'.

These stories indicate that in the coastal provinces, ordinary people view overseas Chinese as foreigners who consider mainland Chinese as pawns to be exploited, who import 'dirty things' like brothels, and who raise land prices; but they also promote the prosperity so much desired by everyone. They are viewed as crude businessmen who have learned their capitalist skills, management techniques, treatment of women and forms of entertainment from the Japanese occupation of Taiwan. *Huaqiao* are thus ambivalent figures, the sharp entrepreneurs and free-spenders who gamble with the fate of local people, but because they also set up hospitals, city parks and downtown businesses, they build *guanxi* with local people in a way that will eventually benefit everyone. Warts and all, the *huaqioa* are still symbolized as both the window and the bridge to a distinctive kind of Asian affluence and modernity.

'Leave the country fever'

The images of overseas Chinese as possessing clever western skills yet embodying the Chinese tradition of *guanxi* also become a beacon that attracts ambitious mainlanders to become entrepreneurs and cross the oceans themselves. A scholar explains that for ordinary Chinese, the country is viewed as a train on a fast track leaving an agrarian society and rushing towards a commercial and industrial one, symbolized by the 'blue ocean culture' (*lanhai wenhua*). In the booming cities of Shenzhen, Xiamen and Guangzhou, I met young Chinese workers and students whose main goal is to 'plunge into the ocean' (*xiahai*), a phrase that means plunging into business, the sea standing for a number of things. It connotes learning a new skill for peasants and landlubbers, and the constant struggle to survive in turbulent, often cruel conditions. It is a place of suffering and risks, but it also promises great wealth unobtainable in agriculture (and on the mainland?). The actual seas around China also stand for the western expansion into Asia, and the emergence of great maritime centres of capitalism like Hong Kong and Singapore. Thus 'plunging into the ocean' can mean making the transition from farming, writing or government employment to capitalism, or it can also mean actually leaving China as emigrants to plunge into the blue oceanic cultures of the world. Indeed, for the up-and-coming modern Chinese, becoming an entrepreneur is often inseparable from the desire/fever to leave the country (*chuguore*). A popular song in China called *My 1997*, the year Hong Kong returns to mainland rule, captures some of this desire to embrace overseas Chinese culture:

Let 1997 come sooner, so I can go to Hong Kong
Let 1997 come sooner, let me stand at the Hongshi stadium
Let 1997 come sooner, so I can go to the midnight shows with him!

Karaoke modernity

Writing about urban China in the 1980s, Orville Schell claimed that discos were 'the living symbols of modernity' for China's youths (1988: 355–6). Schell's notion of modernity is unproblematized as simply western forms of leisure and entertainment that the Chinese were mindlessly imitating. I maintain that, while some popular dances and songs have originated from the West, their forms and meanings have been mediated and transformed by overseas Chinese into expressions of a different Asian modernity. For instance, take the karaoke-ization of China's urban scene today. The explosion of desires associated with becoming rich and leaving the country is garishly expressed in the new urban 'cultural market' (*wenhua sichang*) in which karaoke clubs reign supreme as the icon of this imitative, mobile and borderless form of Chinese modernity. In Shenzhen, which is considered the dreamland of China's future, karaoke bars are found on every city block, sometimes in every building. Increasingly, villages have their own karaoke bars, becoming as common an institution as the village tea-shop. The video karaoke player, which includes sing-along equipment, is a mobile window to the 'opening' (*kaifang*) of China to the world of the future. The karaoke bar is a space and experience for Chinese eager to tap into the new culture of transnationalism associated with South-east Asian affluence. First, there are the images and music, produced mainly in Hong Kong and Taiwan, and although participants sing along in their own voices, lines are scripted for them, often in 'Cantopop' (Cantonese pop songs). Attending a karaoke bar is an opportunity to indulge in a spot of dreaming about one's glorious future in places like Hong Kong and Singapore, where preconfigured forms of Asian modernity are taken as China's own future. Imagine my surprise when in a major South China campus, after a day-long conference, young male and female professors filed into a karaoke lounge to relax for the evening. The bravest man picked up a microphone and sang along to a video film of Hong Kong, as the camera panned slowly over panoramic views of skyscrapers and city landscapes. He was soon joined by most of the people in the room, singing in harmony and with feeling. The next few videos cannot be called anything but 'soft pornography', with images of Hong Kong starlets, scantily dressed, displaying their bodies in languid and inviting positions. The faculty lip-synced sentimental love songs without any trace of embarrassment. When the video switched to a rousing, arm-waving song *We are Chinese People*! (*Women si Zhongguoren*!), I felt it was time to leave. If we can read anything from this incident, young people like to sing and dream together, and bathe in the sense of being borne along into the same Chinese future. It occurred to me that this may be a 1990s version of Red Guard group performances. In fact, thanks to the karaoke medium, by simulating the images and desires, young people are already participating in overseas Chinese modernity.

Karaoke lounges are places for local women to meet foreign men, preferably overseas Chinese. Marriage bureaus arranging for Chinese women to marry overseas men have opened up in major cities like Shanghai and Shenzhen.[27] For many working women, the karaoke bar is the first step into the transnational world of the overseas Chinese. Karaoke videos and Hong Kong television stations are primary sources of images of modern sexuality, fashions and gender relations. A young working woman confesses that she frequents karaoke bars, even though she has a perfectly respectable and devoted mainland boyfriend with a good government job. She is hoping to meet foreign men in order to 'develop a bridge to leave China'. Karaoke clubs are thus places for women to make a living as attendants (or sometimes as prostitutes), to learn about foreign culture, to meet boyfriends, and hopefully to make a passport marriage. Dropping into karaoke bars is a very expensive pastime, but for ambitious women, karaoke bars are an investment in a different future, an expression of their desire to marry out of the socialist market economy and into the transnational Chinese world.

Finally, video karaoke players and karaoke clubs operate, not surprisingly, as the new tokens of prestige in the *guanxi* networks, especially between locals and overseas Chinese. Luxury cars fitted with karaoke systems are an especially attractive gift to local officials. Karaoke bars are places to bring acquaintances one hopes to establish *guanxi* with. Thus in addition to providing the normal round of banquets, businessmen concluding deals may take their guests to private rooms fitted with karaoke systems for an evening of togetherness. It is an expensive but effective way to 'gain a lot of face'.[28] Since much of *guanxi* depends on facial management and verbal agreements, karaoke images and sing-along are the ideal medium to establish good feelings of fellowship and solidarity.

As a space of transnational connections, a *guanxi*-building medium and a window on China's modernity, karaoke uniquely expresses the combination of individualist quest for wealth and success through overseas connections on the one hand, and its dependence upon the cultivation of *guanxi* on the other. Mayfair Yang talks about the ambivalences of *guanxi* as 'born in a conflict between a state-espoused "public" (*gong*) collectivist ethic and a "private" (*si*) ethics of personal relationships' (1994: 71–2). As a medium and practice of *guanxi*, karaoke expresses the privatized, individualistic ethics of Chinese subjects eager to participate in a modernity that is not bound by the interests of the state, but that seeks to cross borders into overseas Chinese communities.

CONFUCIANISM, *GUANXI* AND A NEW NORMATIVE REGIME OF ASIAN MODERNITY

The tensions between the state project of modernity, as one fixed within China's territorial and political interests, and the popular vision of modernity as an individual, self-propelling quest for a future outside China is the latest expression of twentieth-century Chinese rule. In the early Republican period, scholars argued that in Confucian culture, Chinese familialism (*jiazuzhuyi*), as opposed to western individualism (*gerenzhuyi*), was a positive factor in preserving the race's vitality. Chinese nationalism depended upon kinship duties taking precedence over individual rights in order that 'the race' may succeed in its struggle for survival (Dikotter 1992: 175). In post-Mao China, Chinese familialism and its links to national strengthening have again become the ideological framework for articulating a distinctive Chinese modernity. At the same time, China's development as a superpower is dependent upon its relations with other countries. Thus state narratives of modernity increasingly seek to learn from the 'Asian Dragons' in South-east Asia without blurring the political and territorial entity of China as a nation-state. In this section, I will argue that while modernist imaginaries in China oscillate between the territorial boundedness of China and the transnational world of the overseas Chinese in the Asia-Pacific world, there are new expressions of a varied but co-extensive Asian modernity that have continuities with China's historical role in the region, and are in part embedded in Confucian regimes of rule and *guanxi* networks.

In recent years, historical revisionism in Japan firmly rejected the western view that Confucianism and patrimonial bureaucracies obstructed capitalism. Contrary to the popular view that Commodore Perry's visit was the catalyst for Japan's move towards industrialization, Japanese scholars are now tracing the roots of Asian modernity to the China-centred tributary and trade system in East and South-east Asia (Hamashita 1988: 193). Europeans arriving in South-east and East Asia were required to penetrate tributary networks in order to participate in regional trade. In the nineteenth century, intra-regional economic competition between mainland Chinese, overseas Chinese and Japanese merchant groups was the initial impetus for the Japanese shift towards industrialization. Such revisionist history views Asian modernity as rooted in regional economic and cultural exchanges, and stresses its autonomous development that although borrowing heavily from the West, constructs Asian forms, practices and meanings of modernity that is distinctively Asia. After centuries of 'a political economy of exclusion' (Sahlins 1988), a different modality of China's engagement in the world is emerging at the end of the twentieth century.

European colonialism in Asia however broke apart the traditional links between the Chinese commercial classes and the Chinese state, thereby redirecting the merchant families to the task of wealth accumulation without any concern for the wider polity (Ong 1993). In the post-colonial era, China refers to overseas Chinese communities as 'married-out daughter' communities that were no longer formally part of China, although kinship links of sentiments remained.[29] However, since the 1970s, South-east Asian states that are dominated by large Chinese populations have begun to assert a modernity that is in dialogue with the West but is increasingly drawing upon local traditions to construct a distinctively Asian future. The economically successful South-east Asian countries are characterized by the mix of free-wheeling capitalism, with few social and economic constraints on the one hand, and authoritarian governments with tight controls over political and social life on the other (Tai 1988; Appelbaum and Henderson 1992). The term 'flexible accumulation' (Harvey 1989) might have been invented for the forms of capitalism originally associated with overseas Chinese: trade and subcontracting industries based on family firms, and business networks that form commodity chains across national borders (Hamilton 1991). Indeed, generations of scholars of overseas Chinese have tried to demystify the ways overseas Chinese capitalism is embedded in *guanxi* networks (Omohondro 1981; Nonini 1983; Mackie 1992). In South-east Asia, a balance is struck between the free-flowing horizontal networks that crisscross national economies, and the harnessing of capitalism for strengthening state power (see Ong and Nonini 1996).

Inspired by these flexible accumulation/state authoritarian models, the Chinese state often looks to Singapore as a model of China's development, with its combination of western rationality and Confucian authoritarian rule. Although the offspring of an Anglo-Asian encounter, Singapore's modernization project is not to copy any European countries, but to supersede them through an alternative kind of modernity that combines an authoritarian state relationship to capitalism, the subordination of civil liberties to economic development and an overt valorization of Chinese tradition. Although there has been extensive borrowing from the West in science, technology and the economy, many Asian leaders consider western democracy and human rights as alien implants unsuited to Asia. Thus in the aftermath of the Tiananmen crackdown and western attempts to tie trade relations to human rights concerns, the former prime minister of Singapore, Lee Kuan Yew warned:

> It is a mistake to follow mindlessly the present politically correct and stridently advocated view that democracy is the precondition for economic development.[30]

Lee's opinions are shared by the neighbouring Malaysian government which insists that the concept of human rights is relative and specific to particular cultural formations. The increasing chorus of Asian voices over their different pattern of modern development had won over Francis Fukuyama (1992), who earlier claimed that with the end of the cold war, democracy has triumphed all over the world. Now he notes that the 'soft authoritarianism' of countries like Singapore 'is the one potential competitor to western liberal democracy, and its strength and legitimacy grows daily'.[31] Indeed, since it began an ambitious development plan in the 1960s, the Singapore regime had embarked upon a series of struggles over the creation of values – 'rugged society' (not individuals), 'hard' Confucian culture (versus 'soft' Malay ones), culminating, by the 1980s, in compulsory Confucian studies in high schools. 'State fatherhood', in a double sense, also included campaigns to encourage educated women to marry and produce children as a kind of patriotic motherhood (Heng and Devan 1992). Harvard historian Tu Wei-ming was invited to give expression to an overseas Chinese cosmopolitan which he claims is infused with Confucian humanistic values. In his writings, Tu maintains that overseas Chinese 'ethical-religious' values, in contrast to western 'anthropocentricity' will produce an alternative modernity that transcends the instrumental rationality of the West (1988: 27). Thus Singapore has most thoroughly institutionalized Confucian values and practices both within and outside the state, despite its formal status as a multiracial country. State-sponsored Confucian renewalism has also been implemented in Taiwan (Chun 1994). The links between Confucian discourse and disciplinary rule on the one hand, and double digit economic growth on the other have provided the ground of common sense, often cutting across class, gender and even ethnic lines in accepting such regimes of truth. In the most extreme pronouncements of Asian difference, there appears to be nothing to learn from western political philosophies; in contrast, Confucianism is celebrated for its humanistic values, while its instrumental rationality, both in authoritarian rule, in the market-place and in everyday relations is legitimized as an inevitable guarantee of that paternalistic humanism.

Such a model of an official Chinese modernity that is based on Confucian state paternalism, disciplinary regimes and *guanxi*-based capitalism resonates among political leaders on the mainland. In South China, where there is rampant celebration of the fruits of capitalism, local officials see no conflict with authoritarian rule. For instance, an official in Shenzhen explains it to me:

Democracy has limits, like traffic lights. We have not reached the stage of democracy in the West. The freedom will grow as development advances. We need to eat first, then have a good job, then only can we have freedom. Be rich first! Can't just let democracy be imposed on us. We have millions of peasants who don't understand these things. It will lead to chaos (*luan*). Democracy will only bring freedom (*zhiyu*) if people understand the rules of democracy.

This statement reveals an interesting combination of western linear thinking about modernization, and a Confucian assumption that only the elite should rule and construct regimes of truth. He ends by declaring 'Let them [the masses] have their desires. If they have money, they can do what they want. Just no more Tiananmens!' My conversations with other officials and intellectuals in southern Chinese cities reveal similar arguments based on a step-approach or priority model whereby democracy must always be the deferred goal in the journey to developing China as a superpower. They are the echoes of the 'new authoritarianism' (*xin quanweizhuyi*) formulated by Beijing academics and supported by top Party officials. Again, drawing on the examples of the Asian dragons – Taiwan, Hong Kong, Singapore and South Korea – and influenced by Samuel Huntington's writings, the theory maintains that for an underdeveloped country like China, 'transition to a full-fledged democracy is neither politically feasible nor economically advisable' (White 1994: 119–21).[32] Indeed, scholars and officials I spoke with were doubtful that Chinese people *as a whole* will ever be ready for full democracy. Instead, proponents of human rights and the right to oppose government policies are viewed as an assault on Chinese culture and its reverence for the stability, collective responsibility and state authority. Official Chinese discourse frequently uses the examples of Asian dragons to argue that only a Confucian-style rule will ensure greater productivity in the economy so that citizens can enjoy economic security and the pleasures of the market.

While official Chinese discourse state invokes affluent Asian regimes as examples to emulate, it avoids the idea of Greater China, since it smacks of hegemonic intentions in the region. At the same time, the concept of *Da Zhonghua* has become the reigning topic in innumerable scholarly and business meetings held both on the mainland and in South-east Asia, where speakers, after ritually denouncing the idea as an attack on the integrity of nation-states, move on to celebrate the enduring cultural continuities between the mainland and the married-out daughter communities. These forums are the sites for generating narratives that define a larger racial and cultural reality that has emerged at the core of a deterritorialized Asian imaginary that is underpinned by overseas Chinese business, social and cultural networks.

A key player has been the Singapore Chinese Chamber of Commerce which in 1991 arranged the first international meeting for overseas Chinese entrepreneurs from all over the world, including South America. Critical *guanxi* networks were set up to engage in trade between overseas Chinese communities and with mainland China. The second meeting, held in 1993 in Hong Kong, was attended by over 800 Chinese entrepreneurs and politicians from Asia and Australia. A Hong Kong tycoon hosting the meeting noted that the goal was not to discuss the Greater China economic zone, but for overseas Chinese to share their experiences. He casts their interests in terms of shared racial origin and cultural affinity:

> [T]he fact we inherit the same cultural heritage and that we belong ultimately to one big family means that the time has come for ethnic Chinese businessmen to work together and take full advantage of the many opportunities around us.[33]

The 'one big family' theme was echoed in Lee Kuan Yew's talk which notes the advantages of electronic innovations for the 'networking between people of the same race'. Furthermore, he argues, such *'guanxi* connections through the same language and culture can make up for a lack in the rule of law and transparency in rules and regulations'.[34] *Guanxi* has become the practice and the symbol of mobile and far-flung Chinese capitalism, one that appears so exclusively Chinese that it can bypass the laws of countries.

Although Lee warned against 'Chinese chauvinism', these themes of racial and cultural exclusivity were also raised and frequently reified at another meeting in Shantou University. Academics criticized the Greater China concept for inciting fears among China's neighbours, but discussions focused on the 'one big family' picture. One scholar noted that the big question is not Greater China, but that there are 'Chinese people inside and outside China' (in South-east Asia). They share 'the same language, same culture, and same stock' (*dong yuyan, dong wenhua, dong zhu*). This new favourable image of overseas Chinese is due to the perception that although overseas Chinese have become clever at being capitalists, they express their instrumental rationality in an inherently 'Chinese' manner, i.e. through reverence for Confucian discipline, paternalistic duties and observing *guanxi* obligations.

The theme of a culturally exclusive capitalism raised fears among westerners that they were no longer calling the shots when it came to questions of global trade. A British economist notes that

> The Chinese world may appear relatively westernized and modern to western eyes, but its inner spirit is quite different. The universalism and egalitarianism of the West is replaced by a sense of hierarchy and cultural affinity.[35]

But since Asian countries and capitalists do depend on trade with the rest of the world, attempts were made to construct *guanxi* as networks of 'open architecture'. Again, Lee provided the proper articulation of how the *huaqiao/huayi* are the modern intermediaries between China and the West. Their mastery of the English language and western skills has been part of their success in transnational economic activities. Thus overseas Chinese can teach the mainland 'the economic value of multiculturalism, derived from co-existing with and absorbing the good points of other cultures'.[36] The implication seems to be that although they have lived among other cultural groups, they have remained 'Chinese' in a basic, unchangeable way, and multicultural lessons were only significant for Chinese economic advancement. This construction of a profound Chineseness in opposition to non-Chinese[37] even muted former political suspicions of married-out daughter communities, which are now viewed as sending patriots to help strengthen the motherland while raising the prestige of the Chinese in the world. Thus some mainland scholars agreed with a Taiwan investor that overseas Chinese can transform Tibet, clearly viewed as a 'backward' Other to be 'civilized' by the Chinese, 'from a desert into a flourishing place'.

These interweaving, cross-border narratives about Chinese economics and race in Asia clearly set up the West as Other, a place from which one can learn the utilitarian tools of economics and science, but not political ideas that will be useful in shaping Asian modernity. In contrast, overseas Chinese communities in Asia have become the modern pace-setters in defining the larger contours of a organic unity of the Chinese people scattered throughout the world. They are presented as possessing and deploying western knowledge and skills without becoming in essence occidentals. Despite their cosmopolitanism and sojourns in the West, these overseas communities have not become inferior versions of westerners, but have remained in a sense 'internal outsiders' distributed in different sites, who are critical agents and models of a racial 'genius' in China's re-emerging role in the Asia-Pacific region.

What is being constructed is the cultural homogeneity of a Greater China that is rooted in the primordial sentiments of race, familial economism and Confucian values that are considered an irreducible and unchanging part of Chinese people everywhere. The married-out daughter communities of overseas Chinese have provided the forms and practices of a distinctive modernity that borrows from the West and transforms capitalism into a Chinese phenomenon. These events from China's periphery are part of an ongoing reintegration of mainland and deterritorialized Chinese populations, and the development of a new normative regime of state practice, restricted individualism and *guanxi*-based capitalism that cuts across political boundaries.

These developments thus contradict a post-colonial argument that third world nationalisms have remained a prisoner to western rationalist discourse and need always to assimilate to the West in order to be modern. It is perhaps not surprising that such a view is expressed by scholars from India, a country that was colonized by Great Britain, and many Indian intellectuals remain beholden to British education and sensibility. In contrast, Chinese modernist discourses reject the 'the legitimacy of the marriage of [western] Reason and capital' (Chatterjee 1986: 168) by constructing Confucian tradition as the source of the moral authority, instrumental rationality and networking associated with powerful nation-states and the dynamic, mobile capitalism reconfiguring the Asia-Pacific world.

Arising in different sites of South-east Asia, the new social imaginary privileging Chinese cultural practices and values push what Prasanjit Duara calls the 'soft boundaries' of a Chinese nationalism beyond the boundaries defined by the nation-state ideology (1993: 20).[38] The symbolic remapping of Chinese nationalism surges oceanward to incorporate overseas Chinese communities, which though adulterated by other cultural influences, are the key models of an Asian counter-discourse of modernity. Furthermore, the borders of the imagined Greater China powerfully recall the contours of the fifteenth-century Chinese tributary system that was held largely in place by Chinese traders. The narratives of a transnational Chinese modernity continue to evolve, in continuity and also in contradiction to other discourses of the future, but able for the time being to contain and marginalize them. The flowering of a Chinese modernity, shifting across a number of zones, overlapping and contradictory, claims a distinctive Confucian spirituality and instrumentality that is ultimately in dialogue with the West, and also operates as a check on its universalistic claims. We are witness to a transnational production of an emerging normative regime of modernity in the Pacific region.

CONCLUSIONS: CONTRAPUNTAL ANTHROPOLOGY AND THE HOMELESS ANTHROPOLOGIST

Western scholars have begun to talk about the 'multiple modernities' created by the 'multiplicities of capitalisms' operating worldwide (Watts 1993: xiv). It is no longer sufficient, I think, that we understand particular modernities by focusing on local cultural protests *against* western modernity, or the interdependence between 'bits and pieces' of culture found in the global supermarket. It is important and necessary to study Islamic revivalist critique of western culture, to explore the meaning of break-dancing in Mongolia, or the spread of karaoke bar culture in the West. However, as late twentieth-century analysts, we must also execute a political decentring away from seeing everything from the western vantage point. In our multipolar world, emerging powers are playing a major role in defining their own modernity in their own terms and reflecting their own concerns. Western categories of social change, and the concepts of rationality, nation-state and capitalism, while having roots in the Enlightenment, have been made over according to Asian historical traditions. A China historian, tired of our propensity to view the other through the prism of what we take to be our modernity, observes that the 'kinds of theories scholars deploy secure them in particular modernities' (Barlow 1993).

I have tried to deploy a decentred, even mobile theory of modernities that brings tensions to bear on anthropological production of knowledge about the present. By presenting different constructions of Chinese modernity and modern subjects,[39] I problematize anthropological knowledge as itself based on key western modernist assumptions that (1) science and knowledge will disenchant the world, destroy or gain the upper hand over culture; (2) the West will act as catalyst of modernization and the source of modern forms, and the rest of the world will eventually be assimilated to an international modernity determined by the West, and (3) that multiple modernities arise only through resistance to the West's universalizing trajectory. The different constructions of Chinese modernity – from the perspectives of the state, coastal cities and married-out daughter communities – all indicate that modernities are evolving in a series of sites, in dialogue and tensions with each other in the region, while seeking to define their overall distinctiveness from the West. There are of course other conversations, dialogues and dissensions from lower classes, women's groups and indigenous communities I do not have the space to go into here (but see Ong 1987, 1991, 1992, 1993; Dirlik 1994; Ong and Peletz 1995; Ong and Nonini 1996) that contest these perspectives, but their presence only serves to confirm the force of this emerging hegemony of Asian modernity to contain them, to provide the concepts and enunciative modality that symbolically remaps their future.

The decolonization of anthropology requires that we cease colonizing other parts of the world simply to validate western theories of modernization, Marxism, feminism, socialism or capitalism. If we continue to use pre-articulated categories of western knowledge we are merely redeploying our particular vision in transnational descriptive narratives. The third world and other 'interstitial places' will continue to be places where we gather field data to add to anthropological knowledge, but are not themselves considered producers of knowledge and critiques that can change anthropological understanding of the world. We may change our language and the places we are studying, but nothing is changed if anthropological knowledge refuses to consider non-western societies as producers of cultural knowledge about their own worlds. By exploring the production of alternative modernities in shifting geopolitical contexts, we are also debunking the static, geographical division of the world into discrete 'cultures'.

As anthropologists of the late twentieth century, we would want to be secured not in a singular modernity, but to explore the exchanges between different kinds of modernity. Our ethnography can address not only the meanings and uses of alternative modernities, but also explore how they are produced in relation with each other, in the shifting currents of geopolitics. Although focused on recent Chinese narratives, this chapter has tried to suggest its borrowings, reactions and oppositions to western modernist thought. Such a 'contrapuntal analysis' (Said 1993) encourages anthropologists to write not from within the homogenous, stable representations of national regimes, global hegemonies and nativist doctrines, but from the interstitial places between them. Indeed, as a post-colonial, Malaysian/Chinese/American woman, triply displaced and exiled from a home culture, there is no possibility of subscribing to a singular authority. One's very uprootedness requires the refusal of the totalizing claims of gender, race, discipline, culture or nation (Ong 1995). Indeed, belonging nowhere and everywhere has been the necessary condition for understanding twentieth-century human experience.[40] This displacement can be converted into a critical practice whereby anthropology critiques not only western hegemonic knowledge, but also the kind of nativistic modernist ideologies developing out of Asian capitalism. Writing this essay is both a warning to western academic blind-spots and complacency as well as an expression of alarm over the cultural constructions of Chinese modernity.

Some may misread this call for a mobile anthropological subjectivity[41] as falling back upon cultural relativism, and its implied stance of apolitical detachment. My point is that we can no longer afford cultural relativism, but must acknowledge the making of other worlds in their own terms, outside of western political domination. At the same time, emergent world powers like China can enact other forms of cultural hegemony that inspire both fear and resistance. This does not mean that there are no longer universalistic values one would want to defend, only that one is forced to recognize that western modernist values (including fully-fledged democracy) can have limited application to non-western countries emerging as capitalist powers in their own right. This recognition introduces a severe radical doubt in anthropology which, at least in its early twentieth-century American rebirth, is based on democratic liberalism. A mobile anthropological sensibility, I suggest, should retain this radical doubt, while remaining committed to the values of minimal modern human rights (freedom from hunger and torture, and the right to survive as a people) as a 'weak' human universal that we must nurture throughout the late twentieth-century world.

ACKNOWLEDGMENTS

A Hewlett grant from the International Studies Institute, University of California, Berkeley, provided funds for my field trip to South Chinese cities. I thank Ching Kwan Lee and Connie Clark for introducing me to the human side of Shenzhen, and Jiemin Bao for help in researching Chinese newspaper articles. I also benefited from helpful comments by Henrietta Moore, Mayfair Yang, Vincanne Adams and Lisa Hoffman.

NOTES

1 For a similar perspective on academic feminism, see Ong 1989.
2 Although I am talking mainly about American anthropology, I also include British and Eurocentric views formed in the context of western global hegemony.
3 Sontag 1990.
4 Earlier criticisms of the politics of representation were led by Talal Asad's edited volume, *Anthropology and the Colonial Encounter* (1973). However, in recent decades, the perception that most of the third world is now free of colonial control by western powers has perhaps contributed to the tendency to view the political economy of anthropological knowledge as merely a matter of textual representation.
5 The collection (especially papers by Joan Vincent, Dick Fox, Lila Abu-Lughod and Jose Limon) is to be commended for protesting the silencing of some anthropologists in the micropolitics of defining academic anthropology.
6 For instance, the Marxist-based historical narratives represented by Wallerstein (1974) and Wolf (1982) ignore alternative historical discourses emanating from different starting points in non-western places. For instance, Asian historical narratives cannot fit into western historicism (with its sequential history) although in the twentieth century they have been influenced by social Darwinism and Marxist schemes of development and agenda of universalism. For a similar criticism, see Sahlins 1988. In any case, since the 1960s, many of the categories and stages of modernization have become scrambled and over-turned by actual historical events like the collapse of communism worldwide, the revival of ethnic nationalisms and the rise of Asian capitalism.

   Rather than the historicism of Marxist and western concepts of modernity, we can begin with non-western cultural narrativization of identity which may very well use a different sense of temporality that is non-linear but circular and discontinuous. For instance, see Bhabha 1991 for his discussion of the complex strategies of narrativization and liminal displacement, of crisis and continuity in nationalist discourses.
7 *New York Times*, 13 March 1993, op-ed page.
8 See e.g. Basch *et al.* 1994.
9 Anderson linked the emergence of the nation-state to 'print capitalism' but he seems to have overlooked the capacity of socialist regimes to use modern media outside the market context for political ends.
10 *New York Times*, 13 March 1992, A6; *The Economist*, 29 February 1992, 35.
11 Barlow 1993; see Teng and Fairbank 1965 for extracts of Chinese texts on this issue.
12 *Wall Street Journal*, 2 March 1992.
13 *San Francisco Chronicle*, 30 December 1993, A20.
14 See e.g. Chan *et al.* 1992.
15 *Wall Street Journal*, 3 April 1992, B1.
16 *Renmin Ribao* (national edn), 19 September 1994.
17 Relations between the Chinese state and emigrant Chinese (considered subjects of China) have gone through many cycles of rejection and embrace by the motherland. For instance, the Manchu invasion of Northern China brought about the gradual collapse of the Ming Dynasty in the seventeenth century, spawning an outflow of loyalist subjects like Koxinga who fought off the invaders in Taiwan, and are still celebrated as true patriots. During the Ching dynasty, Chinese who ventured abroad were considered traitors who would be beheaded upon returning to China (See Chen 1939). Following the

overthrow of the Ching dynasty in 1916, overseas Chinese played a major role as patriots who supported Sun Yat Sen's Republication efforts and who provided the needed funds in resisting the Japanese invasion of China. When the Communist victory was achieved in 1949, overseas Chinese were once again considered traitors of the motherland, and thousands of emigrant Chinese were forced to either return to China or to give up claims on its citizenship.

Although overseas Chinese citizens (*huayi* or *huaren*) continued to play a major role in providing financial support to their relatives in the PRC, it was not until the late 1970s that the Chinese government once again considered overseas Chinese as an important social as well as economic force in the transformation of the country. Both Fitzgerald (1972) and Willmott (1956) discuss in some detail changing Beijing policy towards overseas Chinese in South-east Asia both before and after the Second World War.

18 *Renmin Ribao* (international edn; henceforth *RMRB*), 7 January 1993.
19 *RMRB*, 15 October 1991, 5.
20 See also *RMRB*, 2 October 1991; 21 November 1991.
21 *Shui ye bu lao you zixin,*
    guan shan nan duan gu xiang qing
    These lines are probably by the poet Liu Po (*RMRB*, 22 October 1991).
22 *RMRB*, 22 October 1991.
23 *RMRB*, 11 January 1992, 5.
24 *RMRB*, 11 November 1991.
25 *New York Times*, 3 February 1992, A9.
26 *South China Morning Post*, 29 November 1992.
27 *South China Morning Post*, 15 January 1993.
28 *Wall Street Journal*, 10 October 1993, A1.
29 The term was coined by the late Chinese premier Zhou Enlai to describe the changing citizenship status of overseas Chinese communities and their attenuated political claims on China, just like married-out Chinese daughters in relation to their patrilineal natal homes.
30 *International Herald Tribune*, 23 November 1993, 6.
31 *Time Magazine*, 18 January 1993, 36.
32 White goes on to discuss the feasibility of fully-fledged democracy in China's future, given its demographic, political, cultural and economic realities.
33 *International Herald Tribune*, 23 November 1993, 4.
34 Ibid.
35 Ibid.
36 Ibid.
37 Wang Gungwu, a leading scholar of overseas Chinese and the president of a new international organization of overseas Chinese, entitled a recent paper *Among Non-Chinese* (1992).
38 Duara (1993) makes the useful distinction between nationality with the soft boundaries permeable to other cultural influences, and the nationality with hard boundaries that seeks to fix the cultural difference of the community in relation to those around it. Thus nationalism 'is never fully submerged by the nation-state' and should be understood as the interaction and contestation between different narratives defining fluid and shifting boundaries of identifications (pp. 2, 9).
39 When overseas Chinese operate in western contexts, they occasionally participate in orientalist discourses as a means to inscribe themselves into various political economies and societies. Their self-narratives are never simply complicitous in hegemonic discourse, but are a complex strategy of self-positioning in relation to local hierarchized spaces and moral economies (Ong

1992, 1993). My view thus challenges Said's (1978) presentation of orientalism as a one-sided discourse, and claims that its objects are invariably rendered silent by its construction.
40 For a more explicit feminist restatement of this point, see Ong 1995. See also Said 1993, 335–6.
41 I borrow the phrase 'mobile subjectivity' from Ferguson (1993).

REFERENCES

Anagnost, A. (1989) 'Prosperity and counter-prosperity: the moral discourse on wealth in post-Mao China'. In Arif Dirlik and Maurice Meisner (eds) *Marxism and the Chinese Experience*. Armonk, NY: M. E. Sharpe, Inc.
Anderson, Benedict (1991) *Imagined Communities*. London: Verso
Appadurai, Arjun (1991) 'Global ethnoscapes: notes and queries for a transnational anthropology', pp. 191–210. In R.G. Fox (ed.) *Recapturing Anthropology*.
Appelbaum, Richard P. and Henderson, Jeffrey (eds) (1992) *States and Development in the Asian Pacific Rim*. Newbury Park, CA: Sage Press.
Asad, Talal (1973) *Anthropology and the Colonial Encounter*. London: Ithaca Press.
Barlow, Tani (1993) 'Colonial modernity and gendered agency'. Presented at the East Asian Institute, University of California, Berkeley, 3 May.
Basch, Linda, Schiller, Nina G. and Blanc, Cristina S. (1994) *Nations Unbound: Transnational Projects, Postcolonial Predicaments, and Deterritorialized Nation-States*. New York: Gordon & Breach.
Bhabha, Homi (1991) 'DissemiNation: time, narrative, and the margins of the modern nation'. In *Nation and Narration*. New York: Routledge.
Callaway, Helen (1987) *Gender, Culture, and Empire: European Women in Colonial Nigeria*. London: Macmillan.
Chan, Anita, Madsen, Richard and Unger, Jonathan (1992) *Chen Village Under Mao and Deng* (expanded and updated version). Berkeley: University of California Press.
Chatterjee, Partha (1986) *Nationalist Thought and the Colonial World: A Derivative Discourse?* London: Zed Books.
—— (1993) *The Nation and Its Fragments: Colonial and Post-colonial Histories*. Princeton: Princeton University Press.
Chen, Ta (1939) *Emigrant Communities in South China: A Study of Overseas Migration and its Influence on Standards of Living and Social Change*. Shanghai.
Chow, Tse-tsung (1960) *The May Fourth Movement: Intellectual Revolution in Modern China*. Stanford: Stanford University Press.
Chun, Allen (1994) 'From nationalism to nationalizing: cultural imagination and state formation in postwar Taiwan', *The Australian Journal of Chinese Affairs* 31: 49–69.
Clifford, James (1988) *The Predicament of Culture: Twentieth Century Ethnography, Literature, and Arts*. Cambridge, MA: Harvard University Press.
Clifford, James and Marcus, George (eds) (1986) *Writing Culture*. Berkeley: University of California Press.
Cohen, Paul A. (1988) 'The post-Mao reforms in historical perspective', *Journal of Asian Studies* 47(3): 517–41.
Comaroff, Jean and Comaroff, John (1991) *Of Revelation and Revolution: Christianity, Colonialism, and Consciousness in South Africa*. Chicago: University of Chicago Press.
Crossley, Pamela (1990) *Orphan Warriors: Three Manchu Generations and the End of the Qing*. Princeton: Princeton University Press.

Dikotter, Frank (1992) *The Discourse of Race in Modern China*. Stanford: Stanford University Press.

Dirlik, Arif (1994) 'The post-colonial aura: third world criticism in the age of global capitalism', *Critical Inquiry* 20: 328–56.

—— (ed.) (1993) *What is in a Rim?* Boulder: Westview Press.

Duara, Prasenjit (1993) 'De-constructing the Chinese nation', *The Australian Journal of Chinese Affairs* 30: 1–28.

Feld, Stephen. (1991) 'He shang and the plateau of ultrastability', *Bulletin of Concerned Asian Scholars* 23 (3): 4–13.

Ferguson, Kathy E. (1993) *The Man Question: Visions of Subjectivity in Feminist Theory*. Berkeley: University of California Press.

Fitzgerald, Stephen (1972) *China and the Overseas Chinese: A Study of Peking's Changing Policy, 1949–1970*. Cambridge: Cambridge University Press.

Fox, Richard G. (ed.) (1991) *Recapturing Anthropology*. Santa Fe: School of American Research Press.

Friedman, Edward (1994) 'Reconstructing China's national identity: a southern alternative to Mao-era anti-imperialist nationalism', *Journal of Asian Studies* 53(1): 67–91.

Fukuyama, Francis (1992) *The End of History and the Last Man*. New York: Avon.

Guldin, Gregory E. (ed.) (1992) *Urbanizing China*. New York: Greenwood Press.

Hamashita, Takeshi (1988) 'The tribute trade system and modern Asia'. Tokyo: *Memoirs of the Research Department of The Toyo Bunko*, No. 46.

Hamilton, Gary (ed.) (1991) *Business Networks and Economic Development in East and South-east Asia*. Hong Kong: Hong Kong University.

Hannerz, Ulf (1989) 'Notes on the global ecumene', *Public Culture* 1(2): 66–75.

Harvey, David (1989) *The Condition of Postmodernity*. Oxford: Basil Blackwell.

Heng, Geraldine and Devan, Janadas (1992) 'State fatherhood: the politics of nationalism, sexuality and race in Singapore'. In A. Parker *et al.* (eds) *Nationalisms and Sexualities*. New York: Routledge.

Honig, Emily and Hershatter, Gail (1988) *Personal Voices: Chinese Women in the 1980s*. Stanford: Stanford University Press.

Kipnis, Laura (1988) 'Feminism: the political conscience of postmodernism?'. In Andrew Ross (ed.) *Universal Abandon?*. Minneapolis: University of Minneapolis Press.

Lash, Scott and Friedman, Jonathan (eds) (1991) *Modernity and Identity*. Oxford: Blackwell.

Layne, Christopher (1993) 'Pox Americana, not pax Americana', *New York Times* 13 March 1993, op-ed page.

Link, Perry, Madsen, R. and Pickowicz, P. G. (1990) 'Introduction'. In P. Link, R. Madsen and P. G. Pickowicz (eds) *Unofficial China*. Boulder: Westview.

Mackie, James (1992) 'Overseas Chinese entrepreneurship', *Asian-Pacific Economic Literature* 6(1): 41–64.

Marcus, George and Fischer, Michael (eds) (1989) *Anthropology as Cultural Critique*. Chicago: University of Chicago Press.

Nonini, Donald (1983) *The Chinese Community of a West Malaysian Market Town: A Study in Political Economy*. Ph.D. Stanford: Stanford University Press.

Omohondro, John T. (1981) *Chinese Merchant Families in Iloilo: Commerce and Kin in a Central Philippine City*. Athens: Ohio University Press.

Ong, Aihwa (1987) *Spirits of Resistance and Capitalist Discipline: Factory Women in Malaysia*. Albany: SUNY Press.

—— (1989) 'Colonialism and modernity: feminist re-presentations of women in non-western societies', *Inscriptions* Nos. 3/4: 79–93.

—— (1991) 'The gender and labor politics of postmodernity', *Annual Review of Anthropology* 20: 279–309.

—— (1992) 'Limits to cultural accumulation; Chinese capitalists on the American Pacific Rim', *Annals, New York Academy of Sciences* 645: 125–44.

—— (1993) 'On the edge of empires: flexible citizenship among Chinese in Diaspora', *Positions* 1(3): 745–78.

—— (1995) 'Women out of China: traveling tales and traveling theories in post-colonial feminism'. In Ruth Behar and Deborah Gordon (eds), *Women Writing Culture*, Berkeley: University of California Press.

Ong, Aihwa and Nonini, Donald (eds) (1996) *On the Edge of Empires: Capitalism and Identity in Modern Chinese Transnationalism*. New York: Routledge.

Ong, Aihwa and Peletz, Michael G. (eds) (1995) *Bewitching Women, Pious Men: Gender and Body Politics in Southeast Asia*. Berkeley: University of California Press.

Pred, Allan and Watts, Michael (1993) *Reworking Modernity: Capitalism and Symbolic Discontent*. New Brunswick: Rutgers University Press.

Rabinow, Paul (1991) 'For hire: resolutely late modern'. In R.G. Fox (ed.) *Recapturing Anthropology*, pp. 59–71. Santa Fe: School of American Research.

Sahlins, Marshall (1988) 'Cosmologies of capitalism: the trans-Pacific sector of "The World System"', *Proceedings of the British Academy* LXXIV: 1–51.

Said, Edward (1978) *Orientalism*. New York: Random House.

—— (1993) *Culture and Imperialism*. New York: Alfred A. Knopf.

Schein, Louisa (1993) *Popular Culture and the Production of Difference: The Miao and China*. Ph.D. in anthropology, UC Berkeley.

Schell, Orville (1988) *Discos and Democracy: China in the Throes of Reform*. New York: Anchor Books.

Shih Shu-mei (n.d.) 'Subjects and non-subjects in the discourse of occidentalist modernism in early modern China', *Positions* (forthcoming).

Sontag, Susan (1990) 'The anthropologist as hero'. In *Against Interpretation and Other Essays*. New York: Doubleday.

Tai, Hungchao (ed.) (1988) *Confucianism and Economic Development: An East Asian Alternative?* Washington: Washington Institute Press.

Teng, Ssu-Yu and Fairbank, John K. (1965) *China's Response to the West: A Documentary Survey 1939–1923*. New York: Atheneum.

Tu, Wei-ming (1988) 'A Confucian perspective on the rise of industrial East Asia', *Bulletin of the American Academy of Arts and Sciences* XLII(1): 32–50.

Vincent, Joan (1991) 'Engaging historicism'. In *Recapturing Anthropology* (ed.) R.G. Fox, pp. 44–58. Santa Fe: School of American Research.

Wallerstein, Immanuel (1974) *The World-System*. New York: Academic Press.

Wang, Gungwu (1991) 'Among non-Chinese', *Daedalus* 120(2): 135–58.

Watson, James L. (1991) 'The renegotiation of Chinese cultural identity in the post-Mao era', Social Science Research Center, University of Hong Kong, Occasional Paper 4.

Watts, Michael (1993) 'Introduction'. In A. Pred and M. Watts *Reworking Modernity*. New Brunswick, NJ: Rutgers University Press.

White, Gordon (1994) 'Democratization and economic reform in China', *The Australian Journal of Chinese Affairs* 31: 73–94.

White, Sydney (1993) *Medical Discourse, Naxi Identity, and the State: Transformation in Socialist China*. Ph.D. in anthropology, University of California, Berkeley.

Willmott, Donald F. (1956) *The National Status of the Chinese in Indonesia, 1900–1958*. Ithaca: Cornell University South East Asia Program.

Wolf, Eric (1982) *Europe and the People Without History*. Berkeley: University of California Press.

Yang, Mayfair M. H. (1994) *Gifts, Favors, and Banquets: The Art of Social Relationships in China*. Ithaca: Cornell University Press.

Chapter 5

Tradition, travelling anthropology and the discourse of modernity in China

Mayfair Yang

What fascinated me about fieldwork in rural Wenzhou in coastal South-eastern China was the local revival and reinvention of a rich corpus of traditional organizations, popular religion, traditional customs, rituals and festivals by entrepreneurial and prosperous peasants and townspeople engaged in privatizing and industrializing the rural economy. However, in the course of the fieldwork, I also encountered restrictions on this research from local officialdom and surveillance by the Public Security Bureau or police. They wanted me to focus on the economic development, but not on the accompanying revival of traditional peasant forms of culture. These fieldwork experiences in 1991, 1992 and 1993 serve as a point of departure for the following ruminations on the fate of something called 'tradition', and the roles that anthropological knowledge and a state discourse of modernity have played in tradition's demise. An enquiry into the complex set of historical reasons for state officials to restrict my research leads me to some reflections on the use and abuse of modernist discourse in twentieth-century China. I found that, in order to frame my study of this revival of local traditions, I needed to ponder the genealogy of knowledge and power that had produced this official attitude towards tradition, and towards its study by an outsider like myself.

In the outline of my research interests which I submitted to local authorities in Wenzhou, I wrote that I wished to look at the variety of temples (*simiao*) and lineage ancestor halls and the social activities which surrounded them. This was because on my first visit I had marvelled at how economic prosperity and the privatization of production into family- and joint-stock enterprises had brought with them two paradoxical social phenomena. First, as one Chinese economic researcher in the area remarked to me, 'What's curious about Wenzhou is that in most places where you get economic development, traditional customs and the person-alistic quality of human relations (*renqingwei*) disappear. But in Wenzhou, what you have is the *strengthening* of tradition'. Indeed, since the economic reforms of the 1980s, this area has witnessed the revitalization of Daoist and Buddhist temples, the return of temples devoted to various gods and goddesses, the renewal of lineage organizations, the re-enactment of traditional rituals and the jubilant celebration of festivals in the lunar or agricultural calendar. This is quite amazing in a country where much of the countryside still remains stripped of all cultural and religious elaborations[1] except the bare essentials necessary for a state-organized society whose dominant discourse is the utilitarianism of nationalism, production and modernization.

Second, it seemed to me that economic privatism had paradoxically produced, not so much individualism, as a great deal of community partici-pation in the rebuilding of local infrastructure and traditional culture. That is, frequent donation drives among the people, called *minjian jizi huodong*, were led by organized groups of old people who collected money from the community for the building and repair of roads and bridges, temples and ancestor halls, and community-sponsored festival celebrations.

I had anticipated official restrictions to the research for the reason that the current unstated official policy was to loosen and open up in the economic arena (*fangsong jingji*), but to quietly tighten up on the political front. After the Tiananmen disaster in 1989, the state moved swiftly to ban and dissolve all spontaneous grass-roots organizations and associa-tional life across the country. Indeed, state law forbids the establishment of independent and 'illegal cliques' (*feifa jituan*), since all organizations and associations must belong to an arm of state bureaucracy. However, besides these ostensible political reasons, I also detected another deeper rationale for the local official attitudes to tradition which I had not noticed before. This other reason, which I call the state discourse of modernity, is what I would like to discuss here.

Unlike the West and most of its third world colonies, in modern China, capitalism and industrialization's assault on tradition were halted in mid-twentieth-century China by the Communist Revolution which threw out the West and put an end to the capitalist process. However, the process of detraditionalization not only continued in China but was intensified, in a quite different way through the other modernizing force, the state. The state emerged as an agent of revolution which called for liberation of the people from the oppressive and cruel forces of tradition. Yet, why is it that as soon as the state relaxes its war against tradition in order to pay more attention to economic production, some of those whom it had liberated proceed to revive some of the very customs from which they had been saved?

Anthony Giddens has recently shown that modernity has been respon-sible for the dismantling and destruction of two forces that have shaped much of pre-modern human history: the non-human force of nature, and the human one of cultural tradition (1994). Despite their differences over the distribution of material wealth, both capitalist and socialist discourses have subscribed to the modernist and humanist elevation of human will, rationality and labour in conquering nature and overcoming tradition. They share a common underlying rationality of 'productivism', an 'ethos where work is autonomous and where mechanisms of economic development substitute for personal growth, for the goal of living a happy life in harmony with others' (Giddens 1994: 247). So successful and enticing have modernity and its discourses been that we are just starting to realize that we are now living in a 'post-traditional' and 'post-natural' world. We are no longer battling with the oppression of tradition and nature, but are everywhere faced with their ruins and vestiges. In this world of rapidly disappearing and extinct species and traditions, new post-modern discourses of 'conservativism' (i.e. conservationism and preservationism) can challenge the hegemonic modernist narratives of liberation, development and progress. As we will see, such counter-discourses are also emerging in China.

When I arrived in the Wenzhou area, two officials visited me and informed me that they had read my research outline. I was welcome to enquire into the astounding developments in local economy, but as for temples (*simiao*), I could look at 'Buddhist temples' (*si*) because they were a religion protected by the Chinese constitution, but not at 'deity temples' (*shenmiao*) which were not 'religion' (*zongjiao*), but 'feudal superstition' (*fengjian mixin*). Said one official, 'We want to get rid of them, but it is hard. This shows that "our people" (*women de laobaixing*) are slow to change and still very "backward" (*luohou*).'

My interest in lineage revivals also met with official displeasure. After Liberation, Communist Party policy was to ban all lineage organizations and confiscate lineage land and property. In this rural town, the ancestor halls of a certain lineage I shall call the Lins were turned into a primary school and factories. Since the economic reforms of the 1980s, the Lin lineage has been allowed to repair their ancestor hall and engage in some group activities. Originally I had permission to film a Spring ritual of ancestor sacrifice which the Lins had started to perform for the first time in forty years. The lineage organizers had painstakingly reconstructed the ritual from old people's memories and old lineage records from the Ming and Qing dynasties. These records had survived the almost blanket destruction of antiquities during the Cultural Revolution (1966-76) because they were kept in the Wenzhou City library. The lineage's old paintings of illustrious ancestors, and the most important lineage artefact, the genealogy of its membership, were all burned. The officials explained to me why they were not letting me see or film the ritual, and why they had ordered the Lin lineage to thoroughly scale down or even cancel their ritual festivity, saying, 'This matter is very "sensitive" to us because the lineage is very "feudal" (*fengjian*) and "backward". In fact, they are even more ancient than feudalism, so they are *really* backward'.

What was even more disconcerting was that this classification of religious and cultural practices along a linear progression of historical stages was not limited to officialdom, but could also be found among the peasants. Asked to explain why there were so many lighted candles placed beneath several large banyan trees in the area, a peasant hastened to tell me not to videotape the scene because, he said, 'the worship of tree spirits is even more backward than Buddhist temples, it's the most backward of all. Most of us don't believe in this sort of thing anymore, you know'.[2]

Edward Said has drawn attention to what he calls 'travelling theory' in an increasingly interconnected and global world. He points out that 'by virtue of having moved from one place and time to another an idea or a theory gains or loses in strength, and . . . a theory in one historical period and national culture becomes altogether different for another period or situation' (1983: 226). Such has been the case with the movement of Henry Lewis Morgan's nineteenth-century anthropological knowledge, via Marxism and Stalinism, to twentieth-century China. Morgan's three-stage theory of social evolution (the state of savagery, barbarism and civilization) as laid out in his *Ancient Society* (1967), was expanded to five stages of 'relations of production' by Stalin: primitive communism, slave society, feudalism, capitalism and socialism (1940). This latter formulation became the official as well as the intellectual and popular view of universal human history in the 1950s in China. It served as the basis for the reinterpretation of Chinese history according to 'historical materialism' (*lishi weiwu zhuyi*) by such prominent historians as Guo Moruo and Hu Sheng (Chao 1986: 155–6).

This stage theory remains the official view of Chinese historical development in high school and university textbooks today. China's minority peoples underwent a classification process whereby they were pegged into the first three stages of this universal evolution (Chao 1986). As Chinese anthropology became a project of affirming and proving Morgan's theory, ethnic minorities in China became 'living fossils' (*huo huashi*) of earlier stages of evolution, while the Han were presented as more evolved (Gladney 1991: 72). So entrenched and politically invested are the Morgan and Stalinist models of social evolution that a recent critique of Morgan by a Chinese scholar, in the light of twentieth-century Western anthropological findings about primitive societies, had to be couched in delicate language:

So although this article points out some mistakes in Morgan's theoretical framework, it does not mean that the writer already has a well-developed new theory to replace it. . . . Under the correct guidance of Marxism . . . [I] merely wish to point out that as persons who laid the foundations, Morgan and Marx have not completed their understanding of truth, but the whole of what they have asserted can still be discussed further.

(Tong 1989: 352)[3]

Han Chinese history was also subjected to a project of periodization according to the five stage schema, so that the pre-Qin dynasties of Xia, Shang and Zhou became 'slave societies' and the two thousand years after Qin unification in the third century BCE became 'feudalism' (*fengjian zhuyi*).[4] Given that feudalism usually suggests some sort of dispersed rule and local autonomy, there is a tremendous historical irony in calling the Qin state centralization in 221 BCE the launching of 'feudalism' in China. European Marxism, which emerged out of an analysis of western feudalism and capitalism, did not sufficiently theorize the state, perhaps because both these modes of production already had/have counter-state and decentralizing tendencies. However, this was the doctrine applied to China, which desperately needed to bring the state into discursive consciousness. Marxism did address the serious impoverishment of the Chinese population and the severe class situation in the first half of the twentieth century. However, in a culture where there is an ancient and historically continous centralized state tradition, this also meant that state power, a key aspect of China's situation, could not be addressed. The modern Chinese state first showed its ferocity in the form of the Guomingdang. Later, in another guise, it mounted state projects of modernity which led to the death of 30–40 million people after the Great Leap Forward, and the death of 15–25 million in the Cultural Revolution.

Marxist evolutionist discourse served very different ends in the West and in China. Marx and Engels were inspired by Morgan's stage theory of social evolution in *Ancient Society* because they wanted to show that the institutions of capitalism in the modern West were not 'natural' and had not always existed in human society, and therefore could be dismantled (Bloch 1983: 8–9, 11). In China, Marxist evolutionism served the purpose not only of eliminating capitalism which had come from the West, but also traditional and native Chinese institutions which were considered even more backward. Whereas Marx and Engels were interested in the 'gens' or 'clans' of primitive societies because they displayed a communalism opposed to private property and exploitation (Bloch 1983: 15), in China, lineages were cast as a privatistic and backward institution to be eliminated and replaced by public state-run units of production and social reproduction, such as brigades, communes and Party organizations.

I ventured to ask one Wenzhou local official why the Confucian ancestral ceremonies in Qufu, his hometown in Shandong Province, could be broadcast on national television, but I could not witness the local lineage ritual.[5] In that confident paternalistic manner of officials, he replied that the Confucian ceremonies are now separated from any living lineage organization. 'It is a historical activity by now. It's all right to "appreciate" (*xinshang*) and study lineage as a historical phenomenon of the past, but not as a living thing in the present.' They would permit me to enquire about the architectural history of ancestral halls built in the area, which date back to the sixteenth-century Ming Dynasty, but I was not to understand current lineage activities. Thus they assigned me to talk with the Office for the Preservation of Cultural Relics (*wenwu baohuju*), the state office which provides some money for the maintenance of the Wang ancestral hall, as an historical site, not as a place for Wang lineage members to commemorate their ancestors. In other words, lineages are only to be understood as cultural relics shut away safely in museums, not as viable social organizations in the present[6] because they are an embarrassing reminder, as well as an ongoing threat, of a reversion to backwardness.[7]

This paradoxical attitude of wanting to ban and preserve tradition at the same time does not seem so strange when we compare it with the attitudes of Euro-American authorities towards the North-west Coast Indians in the USA and Canada in the late nineteenth and first half of the twentieth century. Native American customs were regarded as 'barbaric' and 'superstitious'. In 1884 the Canadian government passed a law to prohibit the holding of 'potlatches', the traditional ritual and competitive feasting of the Indians (Jonaitis 1988: 53). When a Kwakiutl Indian chief violated that law in 1921 with an extravagant six-day long potlatch, the state cracked down hard on the Indians, demanding that they either go to gaol or relinquish forever their precious potlatch masks and ceremonial heirlooms. When the Kwakiutls chose to do the latter, the state sold and transferred the treasures to museums, with very little compensation to them (Jonaitis 1988: 229). Thus a native state in China and a colonial state in the New World share a similar discourse of modernity and their repressive means of building a post-traditional order in which tradition is still visible, not as a living field of action, but as a neutralized and inert object of contemplation.

I asked a 68-year-old male peasant in rural Wenzhou, 'You're from a poor peasant family, why do you want to revive the lineage, when it was controlled by wealthy landlords in the old days?' He replied, 'Our ancestors did great things. They used their blood and sweat to build the ancestral hall and the town wall. And they fought the invading Japanese pirates. So our generation should honour and remember them. If we did nothing to commemorate them, then we will not have the face to stand before our descendants *houdai*. Our descendants will say, "Look at you, you did not live up to your responsibilities".' It would seem that for many Chinese, honouring the ancestors creates chains of interconnectedness and indebtedness across the generations. When these chains are suddenly broken, then other means may be sought to restore a sense of connectedness and integration into the wheel of life.

As various writers on western modernity have pointed out, Enlightenment thought 'embraced the idea of progress, a break with history and tradition ... [it was] a secular movement that sought the demystification and desacralization of knowledge and social organization in order to liberate human beings from their chains' (Berman 1982; Harvey 1989: 12–13). This modernist break or rupture with tradition, of a rejection of the cultural past, has been realized much more radically and suddenly, and therefore more traumatically in modern China than in the West. Traditional Western social institutions underwent a gradual evolution over hundreds of years, rather than a sudden transformation by revolution and social engineering, as was the case in modern China. The modernizing West never totally rejected its Greek, Roman and Christian heritages. Churches and temples of Christianity and Judaism continue to thrive in the late twentieth century, and classics departments survive in western universities. Already in the 1930s some Chinese intellectuals were alarmed that people could no longer understand 60 per cent of the Chinese Classics, and in the 1980s another added that the percentage is sure to be higher today (Zhang 1987: 53).

Indeed, in rural Wenzhou, I met a young female high school graduate from a peasant background in the mountains who did not know what a lineage was. This cultural amnesia is the product of a paroxysm of anti-traditionalism in modern China, beginning as a May Fourth intellectual movement, and reaching its logical extreme in the state-sponsored 'Destroy the Four Olds' (po sijiu) campaign of the Cultural Revolution against 'old thoughts, old culture, old customs, and old habits'. In rural Wenzhou, the Lin lineage performed their last ancestor sacrifice in 1950. The last collective ritual singing of the saga of the mother-goddess Chen Shisi, which was performed to heal the community of social strife, also took place in the 1950s. Her temple was converted into an elementary school. During the Cultural Revolution, schoolchildren fired up with revolutionary zeal ransacked the ancestral halls, destroyed buddhas, bodhisattvas and gods in their temples, and desecrated the ancient tombs of the ancestors. The ritual gift-giving among kin and neighbours and between villages, which accompanied weddings, births and funerals, and traditional festivals such as Chinese New Year and the Dragon Boat Festival, became forbidden 'feudal' practices, continued only in secrecy until recently. For the Lin lineage and others, the ancestors received no offerings from the living for a while.

One local official told me that, on orders 'from above' (shangmian), cadres would go in periodic campaigns throughout the area on appointed days and smash the buddhas and gods that the peasants erected illegally, and sometimes tear down their temples. He himself had participated several times in such campaigns. It was only around 1986 that they started to let the temple-building alone, and adopted a policy of 'open one eye, close the other' (zheng yigeyan biyigeyan) towards such activities. A few peasants and townspeople I spoke with confirmed such practices, although they said temple-smashing lasted until 1988. They gleefully told me that once someone from inside the ranks of officialdom tipped off the old people in charge of the temple to the local god Yang that it was about to be demolished. This tip gave them time that night to remove the heads of the temple gods and conceal them for safe-keeping. Generally, after a few months, the peasants quietly re-erect their gods in their temples.

As Prasenjit Duara has shown, campaigns against popular religion did not start with the Communists, but can be traced back to the first decades of the twentieth century when local governments confiscated temple property, converting them into modern-style schools (1988: 149–55), or making them generate revenues for an expanding modern state at the village as well as higher levels (Duara 1991: 75–76). In the Communist period, Ann Anagnost has analysed the ways in which the state has persistently assumed the voice of scientific reason against magical belief in shamans and diviners and their money-making (1987). In the process, the state seeks to replace not only the shaman's authority with its own, but also the shaman's personal relationship with local communities. Thus the twentieth century has seen the unprecedented state penetration of local communities and the displacement of popular religion by modern state values.

One Wenzhou peasant in his fifties told me that the cadres generally went after the small deity temples, not the temples of institutitionalized religions like Buddhism and Daoism. Indeed, many small deity temples seek protection by labelling themselves Daoist. Both Buddhism, and to a lesser extent Daoism, are integrated into state bureaucracy, and are part of a religious administrative system stretching upwards to Beijing. In many ways the monks are like civil servants collecting state wages. Since the 1980s, Christian churches who agree to join the state Patriotic Committee (*aiguo weiyuanhui*) which overseas Christianity in China are now also supported by the state. In rural Wenzhou, I found that the same distinction between 'superstition' and 'religion' that was made in the 1920s state campaigns against popular religion (Duara 1991: 79) continues today, so that organized textual religion, which is more susceptible to state control, is favoured, while popular 'superstition' is attacked.

In a 1986 statement on religious policy, a state document declared that such things as reciting Buddhist scriptures, burning joss-sticks and going to church were 'normal religious activities' (*Guangming Ribao*; quoted in Dean 1993: 174). However,

> building clan temples, drawing genealogical charts . . . and performing rites in honour of ancestors are feudal, patriarchal activities, impermissible under our Socialist System. . . . All activities which seriously infringe on the interests of the State and jeopardize the lives and property of the people must be resolutely suppressed.

There is a strange irony in the fact that a western religion like Christianity should be approved, but a native and very ancient culture of ancestor worship and lineages should be banned.

Stepping back and viewing modern Chinese history, we can see the gathering strength of the discourse of modernity from the introduction of social evolutionism with the translation by Yan Fu of Huxley's *Evolution and Ethics* (1898) to the anti-traditionalism of the May Fourth Movement (1919–20s) by urban youth and intellectuals. The May Fourth Movement relied upon 'new literature' (*xin wenxue*) in an effort to transform a Chinese thought to be mired in traditional religion and oppressive Confucian family systems to a westernized culture of scientific rationality, democracy and individualism (Chow 1960: 300–26). In the process, argues the writer A Cheng, traditional novels, which had expressed and celebrated 'customs' (*shisu*) were transformed into romantic and ambitious efforts to redirect customs and reshape national character (1994: 103).

The early twentieth century was a period of frenetic translation of 'travelling theories' from the West, often via Japan, when new terminologies and discourses were introduced into the native language (Liu 1993). Indeed, the very word 'tradition' (*chuantong*) came into usage at this time, as did 'religion' (*zongjiao*), 'evolution' (*jinhua*) and 'modern' (*xiandai*) (A Cheng 1994: 71–2). As Nick Dirks has written, 'The modern not only invented tradition, it depends upon it' (1990: 27). Modernity sets itself apart from an Other which it labels 'tradition'. Its emancipatory discourse paves the way for the introduction of a new regime of power.

Fired up with this new discourse of modernist liberation, May Fourth intellectuals also participated in the dismantling of traditional temples (A Cheng, personal communication, LA). Running through such movements as the May Fourth, the Guomingdang's 'New Life Movement' (1930s), and the Communist Party's 'Destroy the Four Olds and Erect the Four News' campaign (1960s), there is a common thread in modern China of the conscious and systematic effort to change customs, abolish tradition and erect a new morality (Yang 1988; A Cheng 1994: 25). However, the true successor of the May Fourth movement is the Communist Party because it was the most determined and systematic in employing evolutionist knowledge to set up a new schema of Chinese historical development and in rooting out old customs of everyday life.

If one of the main features of modernity is that reflexivity is built in as an intrinsic part of its mode of operation, as Anthony Giddens has argued, then in one sense, modernity went much farther in China than in the West, and in another sense, modernity was incomplete and halted. 'Reflexivity' refers to the fact that in modern life, social practices are constantly altered by new information and reflections upon those practices, so that 'reflexive' knowledge is a constitutive component of social change (Giddens 1990: 38). In this sense, Foucault's insight into the interconnections between knowledge and power also thematizes a unique aspect of modernity. One of the most important forms of 'reflexivity' in twentieth-century China has been the 'use of history to make history' (Giddens

1990: 50). Evolutionism, notions of scientific and industrial progress and historical materialism have been employed to break with the past. In these histories we can see that modernist discourse in China has been intricately tied in with the history of anthropology.

The Chinese break with the past has been more radical than in the West because first, the opposition traditional versus modern was intensified by its conflation with the opposition China versus the West. Whereas western modernity only rejected certain aspects of western culture, modernity in China has meant the repudiation not only of the past, but of all that made for Chinese identity. Second, through two revolutions and countless modernizing movements, reflexivity in knowledge has been translated into deliberate and systematic projects of social engineering. However, modernity in China has also been an arrested process, denied full and continuous reflexivity by the social institution which not only survived modernity but was renewed and expanded by it, that is, the state.

When a 'travelling theory' becomes transformed into a state doctrine, it means that certain troubling issues cannot be opened up for public discussion; thus the reflexive process is brought to a close. It becomes difficult to point out that having 'feudalism' follow 'slave society' (which Marx modelled after ancient Greece and Rome) does not fit a Chinese history where already in 221 BCE, a centralized bureaucratic state had not *preceded*, but instead *replaced* a system of dispersed aristocratic segmentary kinship states (see Yang 1994a). Historical materialism was developed in the age of industrialism, when it seemed natural that the prime mover of history was the development in the forces of production. The archaeologist K-C. Chang, however, has shown that in the origins of the Chinese state, the invention of bronze was not tied to agriculture, subsistence or economic needs, but to the realm of ritual and politics (1983: 104; 108–9). Bronze was not used for farming implements but in the making of two trappings of the state: ritual vessels and weapons of war. He hypothesized that states in the Three Dynasties period (2200–300 BCE) moved their capitals in order to follow new sources of copper and tin, and to be close to the mines. So important were ritual vessels as symbols and embodiments of states that a state could overcome a rival by capturing its precious set of vessels and art treasures.

Similarly, although the theory of landownership was irrelevant in many local areas, it was still applied in a blanket fashion, as in Ding County, North China, where in 1936 only 0.7 per cent of households were landlords who hired labour (Friedman et al. 1991: 81–4), and tenants farmed less than 2 per cent of the private arable land. Where landlords did not exist they had to be invented, in order to carry out the state policy of class struggle. A Cheng recounts that when he was living in the mountains of Yunnan during the Cultural Revolution, there was a minority group who 'were slash-and-burn types who tied knots on ropes for their memory' and who moved on to open up new clearings after they harvested from one area (A Cheng 1994: 28). A work team from higher levels of government was sent down to divide these people up into the standard class categories of 'landlord', 'rich peasant', 'poor peasant', etc. that applied all over China. Not only did this work team have great trouble chasing the people from one clearing to another in the forest, most difficult of all was assigning them to these class categories when they did not even have private ownership of land. When the work team departed, A Cheng writes satirically, 'they left behind a very confused bunch of "landlords" and "poor peasants" to continue on with their slash-and-burn.'

Three features of Chinese discursive modernity and its effects can be discerned. First, a cyclical or spiralling dynastic history and moral discourse of virtuous and sage emperors was replaced by an evolutionary meta-narrative of progressive linear history and a tale of competition and survival. A culture that had looked to the ancients for inspiration and cultivated the memories of ancestors was suddenly confronted with a world which rejected the past and valorized the future, a teleological future which already existed as an external threatening force in the form of western powers.

Second, the Chinese discourse of modernity was also carried out in terms of the West as the standard-bearer and forerunner of what was considered modern, advanced and superior.[8] 'China found itself narrated into [the West's] meta-narrative as a weakling in danger of extinction' (Wu 1992: 103). In Morgan's schema, the vast array of human cultures were so many different stages that advanced Western civilization had itself already passed through and transcended.[9] Eventually, the Chinese also participated in narrating themselves into this story. The Chinese adoption of the modernist discourse of evolutionism was therefore in a way acceding to the colonial binary construction of eastern backwardness versus western progress. For the Chinese, this sort of imposition and self-positioning with regards to an Other created a cultural and psychic crisis that the modern West has not had to deal with. As one Chinese scholar has observed, in the development of the West, it has not had to 'take an external culture as its reference point in re-evaluating and examining itself and its traditional culture ... in order to renovate and remake its own culture' (Zhang 1987: 48).

Much of modern Chinese history, in all its trauma and tragedy, can be understood as the psychic crisis which follows upon the sudden adoption of the western meta-narrative of modernity and evolution. Borrowing the language of psychoanalysis, Wu Xiaoming points out that when the love object of one's culture and identity, tradition itself, must be forcibly given up in order to substitute a new and alien culture in its place, the sense of longing for that which has been lost can lead to such cultural disorders as 'melancholia' and 'paranoia' (1992: 103). Giving up the love of one's own culture which has been for so long a satisfying love object is very difficult. The forbidden love that lingers on for tradition can be culturally denied or repressed through projecting the love object, a traditional way of life, as a persecuting and destructive force. Lu Xun's famous story 'Madman's Diary', in which a madman thinks the people around him want to eat him, and he sees in an old book nothing but the words 'eating people', exemplifies modern China's paranoia and loathing of its tradition. China's history was seen as thousands of years of oppression and cannibalism. Thus, '"going mad" is perhaps the high psychic cost that the Chinese cultural self in the early twentieth century has had to pay for relinquishing and turning away from [tradition]' (1992: 104).

Beginning with the May Fourth Movement of the 1920s, the whole of the traditional Chinese order was called into question and blamed for failing to provide resources for survival in the present. However, it was after 1949 that anti-traditionalist activities were carried out on a wide social scale. And this brings us to the third feature of the discourse of modernity in China, that is, from an intellectual movement it was progressively taken over by a modernizing state. Whereas in the West, different institutions and groups participated in defining the vision of the modern and corroding the traditional (such as scientific knowledge, capitalist economic forces, and critical artists), by the mid-twentieth century in China, the state had monopolized and coordinated all modernizing efforts and attacks on tradition. In China, state modernism was unrelieved by critical aesthetic modernism (Lee 1990), which in other contexts served as a perpetual challenge to modernism as an ideology.

In recent years, there has been much theorizing about colonialism in the third world, especially India and Africa. While it has been pointed out that there is a diversity of modernities in the world (Rofel 1992), when it comes to discussing colonialism, seldom has it been pointed out that there is also a diversity of colonial experiences. Unlike India, Africa or the Americas, China was never fully colonized by the West. It retained its sovereignty, even though it was that of the Manchus. Furthermore, the reaction to colonialism, in the form of the establishment of state socialism, is quite different from the various third world post-colonial capitalisms. I would have to agree with Wang Jing that the Chinese experience of modernity cannot be readily appropriated into the discourse of post-colonialism which stems from the Indian and Middle Eastern experience (1994). First, since post-colonial theory implicitly gives priority to the critique of capitalism, it cannot address the Chinese situation where modern state power has been much stronger than capitalism. Neither can it appreciate the role of market economies, especially at the local and rural level, in maintaining a modicum of independence for society and social processes from the state.[10] Although what is now emerging in 1990s China is a new version of state capitalism the world has not yet seen (Anagnost

1992; Ong 1994a, 1994b), state power will most likely remain a force to contend with, albeit in new forms.

Second, it seems to me that post-colonial theory often draws too sharp a line between the colonizer and the colonized. Writes Nick Dirks, 'Under colonialism tradition was consigned not just to a past but to a place. If modernization has not fully done its job, it is because it was an imposed rather than an intrinsic process' (1990: 27–8). I would like to take issue with Dirks's claim that modernity is an imposed or extrinsic process rather than an intrinsic process. The discourse of modernity and evolutionism of the imperialist West was soon taken over by Chinese reformers and revolutionists who saw themselves not only as national liberators of China from the West, but also as liberators of China from its oppressive tradition. We therefore need to examine a situation where, in the process of resisting colonialism, the colonized comes to internalize aspects of the very colonialism they wanted to resist in China. Wu Xiaoming has pointed out that Marxism served both the need to reassert Chinese self-identity as well as to critique the West (1992: 106–7). Both these tasks were defined and expressed in terms of a western discourse of modernity, a discourse which was also applied to address internal social disintegration and impoverishment. At the same time, this new discourse of modernity was linked up and integrated with innumerable practices traceable to a native despotic state tradition. Therefore, modernity in China became very much an intrinsic process.

Mao once said, 'A sheet of blank and white paper bears no burden, so it's easy to write the newest and most beautiful words on it, and it's easy to draw the newest and most beautiful pictures on it' (1971: 194). The Revolution saw to the stripping of culture to make a blank and white slate for a new picture. The two major State-initiated campaigns to root out tradition were the 'Destroy the Four Olds' and the 'Criticize Lin Biao, Criticize Confucius' campaigns where the intensity of the people's hatred of tradition was matched by the fervour with which they embraced the all-encompassing state as its substitute. There is an eerie quality about this destructiveness and the desperate attempt to speed up the social revolution which would allow China to make a 'Great Leap Forward' over and ahead of the West and its capitalism to a more advanced historical stage.

An internal logic can be detected where loss and advancement are mutually dependent. The more China wiped itself clean of its old culture, the more it embraced a teleological state vision of evolutionary advancement. This is especially evident in the Cultural Revolution where anger and hatred of tradition can be found alongside an intense love for the icon of the unified nation, the person of Mao the Leader (Yang 1994b). It is as if, having destroyed tradition, the social body had to turn to a new love object to fill the empty void which the modernist project of cultural self-alienation had created.

Francois Lyotard makes an important point in his post-modern critique of modernism in aesthetics when he portrays it as a stance which, when confronted with the unpresentable, becomes melancholy, opts for a form which is reassuringly familiar, and seeks an illusion of totality and unity to assuage the shock of the shattering of a recognizable world. 'The nineteenth and twentieth centuries have given us as much terror as we can take. We have paid a high enough price for the nostalgia of the whole and the one' (1984: 81). Here I think he is referring to the totalitarianism of fascism and Stalinism which were modernity's nostalgic and desperate grasping for unity, wholeness and certainty in the form of the nation-state. This was also a Chinese experience, but in China, modernity as the collapse of a total social formation and way of life did not even have the luxury of choosing to be nostalgic. With the breakdown of traditional cultural mechanisms of social order in China, the longing for unity and certainty was less a choice than a life and death matter. For now only the unity of a powerful and repressive state could hold the shattered pieces of culture and the disconnected and warring social groupings together and keep them from falling apart. And certainly modern China has paid a high price for unity and life at the hands of the state.

Elsewhere I have written about how the inability to properly mourn the loss of tradition leads to a burying of the grief that cannot be expressed (Yang 1994b). The inability to mourn derives from a reluctance to admit a feeling of loss and longing. This is due to the discourse of modernity which instils a cultural shame at still being attached to a tradition that is now regarded as bankrupt and 'backward'. In rural Wenzhou, a local official said something memorable to me: 'You're also a Chinese, you know there are still a lot of backward things in our country. Foreigners [i.e. the West] have two kinds of attitudes towards our backward aspects. One, they are curious, they have never seen these things before. The other is they look down upon us (*kan bu qi women*), they think it is backward. So in your research, please exercise some judgement (*yaoyou fencun*), don't show the backward things.' I hope I have exercised judgement in my presentation, but perhaps not the kind that he was requesting, for it is this very modernist discourse of backwardness and progress which I wish to interrogate.

This shame felt at traditional culture has been responsible not only for its systematic destruction, but also for the lack of cultural resources to deal with the impact of its sudden loss. The failure to mourn the passing of tradition means that it lingers on, causing disquiet to the living. Like the resentful 'hungry ghost' of someone who was killed violently and unjustly, it threatens to haunt the living at every turn. That is why there is so much vigilance to guard against a tradition whose ghost lives on. That is perhaps why the officials did not want the lineage ritual to be re-enacted, nor me to report on its persistence or revival.

This example of what happened in China due to an anthropology which travelled, brings us back to a consideration of anthropological knowledge. In Morgan's day, the Others of the West provided raw material with which the modernizing West could ponder its uniqueness in human history. Knowledge was thought to be a painstaking approximation of the truth, and the quality of the true was independent of moral and aesthetic criteria. Nowadays, after Foucault and Habermas, we know that knowledge has 'power-effects' and is embroiled with 'human interests'. There is no external fulcrum or privileged and objective vantage point from which to conduct the study of human societies. There are only relative vantage points limited by their cultural location and historical situation.

Much effort in recent western anthropology has gone into the discovery and dissemination of this insight about the constructedness of knowledge. Less time has been spent considering the translation and reception of knowledge, and the destinations of 'travelling theories'. As Lydia Liu has noted, 'When concepts pass from the source language into the target language, [they are] (re)invented within the local environment of the latter' (1993: 165). In crossing cultural, historical and national borders, the character of knowledge is affected as much by the conditions of its introduction into an existing discursive formation and historical situation, as by the conditions of its original production.

The de-legitimation of anthropology as an objective science has opened up a salutary space for a rich variety of discussions. Interpretive and reflexive anthropology have explored how the production of knowledge and representation can involve the native in a dialogical or multivocal process (Clifford and Marcus 1986; Clifford 1988). However, the specific destination and form of reception of that representation is usually not addressed, or is assumed to be the same as that of the anthropologist. *Anthropology as Cultural Critique* (Marcus and Fischer 1986) has also not considered its own possibilities as a 'travelling theory', for it assumes that only the West is in need of, and can provide, critique. In an increasingly interconnected global community, not just anthropologists but also their knowledge cross borders, often long before the anthropologist arrives. This knowledge is often put to new and different uses from those of its point of origin. Given the unforeseen cultural violence wrought by Morgan's anthropology in China, it would seem that we must start to build an awareness of the local conditions and context for knowledge and critique into anthropological understanding. In other words, anthropological knowledge must not only reflect upon its point of origin, but also its non-western destinations.

It is not sufficient to acknowledge that anthropology has often been a western discourse whose western bias must be criticized. Anthropology is also a rich body of discourse which can be made available for non-western native self-critique and diagnosis of illness. With its concern for cultural difference, its interest in pre-industrial and pre-colonial cultural formations,[11] anthropology can help define a different modernity which develops not by a wholesale extermination of the past, but by working with and adapting existing cultural elements. It can also provide resources for non-western subjects seeking alternatives to modernist discourse in grappling with native traumas and adjustments to modernity. To do so, anthropologists must engage with third world intellectuals and become more aware of voices of native critique. This means that anthropologists must also become more proficient in the written language of those modernizing cultures with a strong textual tradition of its own.

In the case of China, modernist discourse is so entrenched that not only the state speaks its language, but even most dissident intellectuals adopt it in their rhetoric, accusing the state of being mired in 'tradition' and 'feudal thought'. A good example of dissident modernist discourse is the now banned television series *He Shang*, which portrayed traditional Chinese culture and rural China as hopelessly backward, like the strange and exotic customs of primitive minority peoples. Unlike the state, which wants 'socialism with Chinese characteristics', *He Shang* wanted 'total westernization' (*quanpan xifanghua*) in order to modernize.[12] One intellectual who applauded the show saw the Cultural Revolution, not as a modern form of mass madness, but blamed it on tradition, and he went so far as to call it 'barbaric feudalism' (*fengjian mengmei zhuyi*) (Liu 1989: 101). Thus in China it is often difficult to see that part of the awesome power of the state lies in its very modernity.

However, in the mid-1980s a cluster of literature called 'Seeking Roots' (*xungen*) emerged with an outlook markedly different from the discourse of modernity. These works sought meaning in the lives and customs of rural folk, in the land and in nature, and in traditional culture and philosophy, rather than in heroic sagas of modernization or revolution (Han 1984; Li 1987; Cao 1988; Shi 1989; Wang 1994). They questioned the destructive and 'nihilistic attitude' (*xuwu zhuyi taidu*) of the May Fourth Movement and the Cultural Revolution towards the cultural heritage (A Cheng 1985). Writing allegorically, A Cheng ponders:

> When I was in Yunnan, each day I shouldered an axe and gazed at the tropical jungle. After gazing for ten years, I understood that the high and low growths before my eyes had developed naturally (*ziwei*) over hundreds of millions of years. Whether fragrant flowers or poisonous weeds, nothing can be removed, for if you move a blade of grass or tree, you will alter the whole forest, not to mention what would happen with a Revolution's frenzy of chopping down. ... Once a primeval forest or grasslands are despoiled, they will never return, and herein lies the key point.
>
> (A Cheng 1994: 104)

He is referring to the wholesale depredation of a body of traditional but flexible and adaptive customs and culture which his generation participated in dismantling during the Cultural Revolution and before. Like the tropical jungle, traditional culture is the cumulative growth and development of millennia, but its deracination can be accomplished overnight, leaving a scarred and barren land. Indeed, A Cheng employs some strong language in describing China after the Cultural Revolution as culturally 'emaciated':

> The Mainland is a 'vast expanse of empty whiteness' (*bai mangmang da di*). ... It's as if the earth's forests have disappeared, its water becomes contaminated, its air is polluted, its food chain is broken, there is a spread of pestilence, and its people do not have the ability to emigrate to another planet, so they wait for death.
>
> (A Cheng 1994: 191–2)

In these passages, both tradition and nature are put into the same categories as the casualties of modernity and its radical destructiveness. At the same time the author mourns the loss of nature and tradition, and suggests the need to preserve what is left of them.

Wang Jing has pointed out that 'Seeking Roots' literature is not simply a nostalgia for tradition and the primitive, but a reflection on an 'aborted utopia and ... betrayal by the Revolution' (1994: 128). The return to Nature by this group of writers is a 'laborious self-reflection and a poignant testimony of historical guilt' (1994: 128) for the massive damage done to customs, traditions and artefacts of history under the influence of the discourse of modernity. There is also a recognition that the space vacated by custom and culture has come to be occupied by the state: 'My experiences tell me that to sweep away a self-constituting space of customs (*ziwei de shisu kongjian*) and to establish a modern state in its place, is like a tasteless and insipid watery soup, not a life for even fish to live' (A Cheng 1994: 26). It is to these native cultural critics for whom modernism is not a taken-for-granted good, but a social force requiring reflection and critical examination, that anthropological knowledge can address itself.

A question that anthropologists could help tackle is one posed by Giddens: 'How shall we live after the end of nature and the end of tradition?' Except that anthropologists would not pose this question so generally, but would be specific as to cultural and historical context. Different cultures will come to their own particular solutions to this question. What in Chinese tradition is worth preserving? The old society was horrible in many ways: class oppression; the low position of women; arranged marriages for the youth; the servant system, and the market in humans, so well described by Rubie Watson (1991). And yet, in Wenzhou I also felt the reviving and energizing force of tradition. The revitalization of tradition knitted together local community relationships, created a sense of community identity and commitment, and enhanced local cultural, economic and political autonomy from the state.

Traditional China had many features which could benefit modernity. Many aspects of traditional lineages have the exact qualities which Giddens says are worth saving about tradition. 'Succouring traditions means preserving a continuity with the past which would otherwise be lost and doing so as a way of achieving a continuity with the future as well' (1994: 48). Although Chinese patrilineal lineages had an effect of devaluing women and depriving the female line from honouring their ancestral identity and depriving women of the chance to hand down property and teachings, they also had other features and social effects. Lineages also linked the living with the dead in the past, and imparted a sense of responsibility and concern for their future descendants.

Both state socialism and capitalism are modernizing forces which have brought about the radical 'eradication' or 'uprooting' of tradition and nature. In both social formations there have emerged sentiments of counter- or post-modernism which see the need to protect tradition and nature from further pillaging. Rather than obliterate lineages and replace them with the state, post-modernist alternatives would be to deploy lineage logic and its reservoir of kinship ethics as oppositional moments against the state, or to work within lineage logic to promote bilineal descent, especially descent in the female line, a task made easier now by lineages facing the state birth control policy. In a world forever and permanently altered by human intervention, to ponder the various ways to deal with the disorder and traumas of modernity, by preserving links with the past and adapting selected elements of tradition, that is what anthropological knowledge is for.

ACKNOWLEDGEMENTS

I am grateful to Wang Jing, Anthony Giddens, Abdellah Hammoudi and Aihwa Ong for helpful comments on this chapter and to Li Weimin for library and reference assistance. All Chinese names are pseudonyms, except those of famous people.

NOTES

1 Another area which has seen an astounding revival of traditional popular religion and rituals in the last decade is the Zhang-Quan region of coastal Fujian Province. The strength of popular religion in Wenzhou and Fujian is perhaps due to their relative geographic isolation from the rest of China and the political centre in Beijing by mountains on one side, and the sea on the other. For a detailed study of the history and contemporary practice of popular deity cults and Daoist liturgical traditions, see Kenneth Dean's work (1993).

Dean vividly describes a tense stand-off he witnessed between local participants of a Daoist deity cult ritual procession in 1987 and the Public Security
force which tried to stop them. A tractor driver who dumped a pile of stones
across the path of the police was arrested, and a shot was fired (1993: 113).

2 An American ethnologist travelling through rural Sichuan Province in the
1920s also documents the worship of old cypress and banyan tree divinities in
areas of the province (Graham 1928: 77–8) (my thanks go to Greg Ruf for
this reference). In rural Wenzhou I also saw many dead cats hanging in trees
to flush out their internal poisons, which would seep into the ground if they
were buried.

3 Tong (1989) critiques both Morgan and the rigid and doctrinaire use of Morgan
in Chinese anthropology. He challenges Morgan's belief in technology as the
single force of social change, the easy assumption that contemporary primitive
societies represent past stages of human evolution, that similar technologies
necessarily mean the same social organizations or stages, that kinship termino-
logy is a transparent indicator of social structure, that there was an original
matrilineal society, and that all societies go through the necessary sequence of
'matrilineal society', 'patrilineal society', 'tribal federation', 'patriarchal slave
system', etc. However, he does not directly challenge the applicability of either
Morgan's or Stalin's stage theory to Chinese history.

4 For a fascinating account of the discursive struggle around the notion
of 'feudalism' in modern China, see Prasenjit Duara 1993. From the sense of
decentralized government and federalism, the term later came to mean 'backwardness' in a schema of historical evolution and progress.

5 The state support for the revival of Confucian ritual represents a new post-
Cultural Revolution state approach and attitude towards tradition in the 1990s.
This is one of collaboration with cultural conservatives in promoting state
traditionalism, which is more in keeping with the modern Taiwan (Chun 1994)
and Singapore (Heng and Devan 1992) state's appropriation of Confucian
tradition. This new development of state and tradition is beyond the scope of
the present discussion.

6 Helen Siu has also shown that the revival of traditional rituals has an important
and new role to play in the transactions of ongoing social life in the present
(1990).

7 Other reasons for official restrictions on lineage activities include the inequality
of men and women because lineages only focus on male descent, and the
tendency for interlineage conflicts which disturb the peace of the community.
These will be discussed in a separate work on lineage revival in rural Wenzhou.

8 Since the Tiananmen crackdown of 1989, both the state and intellectuals in
China have begun to explore an alternative Chinese modernity not based on
the western model. The offshore discourse of the so-called 'Four Asian
Dragons' which points to the Confucian cultural role in economic development
has fuelled a new confidence in seeking an independent path from the West
(Wang Jing, Li Fan, personal communication; see also Aihwa Ong, Chapter
4, this volume).

9 Morgan writes, 'The history and experience of the American Indian tribes
represent ... the history and experience of our own remote ancestors when
in corresponding conditions' (1967: Preface).

10 Jonathan Friedman, Mark Selden and Paul Pickowicz have shown how rural
markets before the Revolution were crucial to maintaining not only peasant
livelihood, but also a flourishing peasant culture of festivals, life-cycle rituals
and popular religion (1991). The state socialist destruction of rural markets
was disastrous for rural culture.

11 Of course, as Abdellah Hammoudi has pointed out (personal communication), even anthropology can never be able to fully understand the pre-modern, pre-colonial and pre-industrial, because anthropology itself as a form of knowledge only emerged in the late nineteenth century after modernity had already affected diverse cultures.

12 In Shanghai in 1993, I talked with some Chinese intellectuals and learned that most now find fault with *He Shang*'s blanket rejection of Chinese tradition, but no one wants to start a general debate on the issue because the state has condemned the show for failing to acknowledge socialist achievements. For an intellectual to criticize the show might be misinterpreted by others as being opportunist and siding with the government.

REFERENCES

A Cheng 阿城 (1985) *Wenhua zhiyue zhe ren* 文化制约着人 ('Culture delimits humanity') in *Wenyi bao* 文艺报 (*Literature and Art*), 6 July, p. 2.

—— (1994) *Xianhua xianshuo: Zhongguo shisu yu zhongguo xiaoshuo* 闲话闲说:中国世俗与中国小说 (*Leisurely Chats: Chinese Customs and the Chinese Novel*). Taipei: Shibao wenhua chubanshe.

Anagnost, Ann (1987) 'Politics and magic in contemporary China', *Modern China* 13(1), pp. 40–61.

—— (1992) 'Constructions of civility in the age of flexible accumulation'. Unpublished paper given at the American Anthropological Association meetings, San Francisco.

Berman, Marshall (1982) *All That is Solid Melts into Air: The Experience of Modernity*. New York: Penguin.

Bloch, Maurice (1983) *Marxism and Anthropology: The History of a Relationship*. Oxford: Clarendon Press.

Cao, Wenxuan 曹文轩 (1988) *Xun 'geng' re* 寻"根"热 ('The seeking 'roots' fever') pp. 234–50 in *Zhongguo bashi niandai wenxue xianxiang yanjiu* 中国八十年代文学现象研究 (*The Study of Chinese Literary Phenomenon in the 1980s*). Beijing: Beijing daxue chubanshe.

Chang, Kwang-Chih (1983) *Art, Myth, and Ritual: the Path to Political Authority in Ancient China*. Cambridge: Harvard University Press.

Chao, Weiyang (1986) *Evolutionary Theory and Cultural Diversity: A Study of the Ethnology of China's National Minorities*. Ph.D. dissertation, U.C. Berkeley. Ann Arbor: University Microfilms International.

Chow, Tse-tsung (1960) *The May Fourth Movement: Intellectual Revolution in Modern China*. Cambridge: Harvard University Press.

Chun, Allen (1994) 'From nationalism to nationalizing: cultural imagination and state formation in postwar Taiwan', *Australian Journal of Chinese Affairs* 31, January.

Clifford, James (1988) *The Predicament of Culture: Twentieth Century Ethnography, Literature, and Art*. Cambridge: Harvard University Press.

Clifford, James and Marcus, George (eds) (1986) *Writing Culture: The Poetics and Politics of Ethnography*. Berkeley: University of California Press.

Dean, Kenneth (1993) *Taoist Ritual and Popular Cults of Southeast China*. Princeton: Princeton University Press.

Dirks, Nicholas (1990) 'History as a sign of the modern', *Public Culture* 2(2), Spring.

Duara, Prasenjit (1988) *Culture, Power, and the State: Rural North China, 1900-1942*. Stanford: Stanford University Press.

—— (1991) 'Knowledge and power in the discourse of modernity: the campaigns against popular religion in early twentieth-century China', *Journal of Asian Studies* 50(1), pp. 67–83.

—— (1993) 'Provincial narratives of the nation: centralism and federalism in Republican China'. In Harumi Befu (ed.) *Cultural Nationalism in East Asia*. Berkeley: Institute of East Asian Studies, University of California, Berkeley.

Friedman, Jonathan, Pickowicz, Paul and Selden, Mark (1991) *Chinese Village, Socialist State*. New Haven: Yale University Press.

Giddens, Anthony (1990) *The Consequences of Modernity*. Stanford: Stanford University Press.

—— (1994) *Beyond Left and Right: The Future of Radical Politics*. Cambridge: Polity Press.

Gladney, Dru (1991) *Muslim Chinese: Ethnic Nationalism in the People's Republic*. Cambridge: Harvard University Press.

Graham, David Crockett (1928) *Religion in Sichuan Province*. Washington, DC: Smithsonian Institution.

Guangming Ribao (newspaper) 光明日报 (1986) 1 March.

Han, Shaogong 韩少工 (1984) *Wenxue de 'geng'* 文学的根 ('The 'roots' of literature'), *Zuojia* 作家 (*The Writer*) no. 4, April.

Harvey, David (1989) *The Condition of Post-Modernity*. London: Basil Blackwell.

Heng, Geraldine and Janadas, Devan (1992) 'State fatherhood: the politics of nationalism, sexuality and race in Singapore'. In Andrew Parker *et al.* (eds) *Nationalisms and Sexualities*. New York: Routledge.

Jonaitis, Aldona (1988) *From the Land of the Totem Poles: the Northwest Coast Indian Art Collection at the American Museum of Natural History*. New York: American Museum of Natural History.

Lee, Leo Ou-fan (1990) 'In search of modernity: some reflections on a new mode of consciousness in twentieth-century Chinese history and literature'. In *Ideas Across Cultures: Essays on Chinese Thought in Honour of Benjamin Schwartz*. Cambridge: Harvard University Press.

Li, Hangyu 李杭育 (1987) *'Wenhua' de ganga* "文化"的尴尬 ('The awkward situation of culture'). In Literary Criticism Editorial Department, (ed.) *Wo de wenxueguan* 我的文学观 (*My Literary Outlook*). *Wenxue pinglun bianjibu bian* 文艺评论编辑部编 Shanghai: Shanghai shehui kexueyuan chubanshe.

Liu, Lydia (1993) 'Translingual practice: the discourse of individualism between China and the West', *Position* 1(1), Spring.

Liu, Zhengqiang 刘正强 (1989) *Lun Zhongguo chuantong wenhua ji He Shang' de youhuan yishi* 论中国传统文化及"河殇"的忧患意识 ('On the anxiety of Chinese traditional culture and 'He Shang''), *Hainan shifan xueyuan xuebao* 海南师范学院学报, no. 2; reprinted in *Zhongguo renmin daxue shubao ziliao zhongxin* 中国人民大学书报资料中心. *Dianying dianshi yishu yanjiu* 电影电视艺术研究 no. 9, pp. 99–104.

Lyotard, Francois (1984) *The Postmodern Condition: A Report on Knowledge*. Minneapolis: University of Minnesota Press.

Mao, Zedong 毛泽东 (1971) *Jieshao yige hezuoshe* 介绍一个合作社 ('Introduction to a cooperative'). In Ding Wang 丁望 (ed.) *Mao Zedong xuanji buyi* 毛泽东选集 (*Collected Works of Mao Zedong: Appendix*), vol. 3. Hong Kong: Ming Bao Yuekanshe.

Marcus, George. E. and Fischer, Michael M.J. (1986) *Anthropology as Cultural*

Critique: An Experimental Moment in the Human Sciences. Chicago: University of Chicago Press.

Morgan, Lewis H. (1967) *Ancient Society, or Researches in the Lines of Human Progress from Savagery through Barbarism to Civilization*, Eleanor B. Leacock (ed.). NY: The World Publishing Co (1877).

Ong, Aihwa (1994a) 'Engendering Cantonese modernity: social imaginary and public culture in Southern China'. In *Gender, Social Regulation and Economic Restructuring in East Asia*. Diane Wolf, Cynthia Truelove and Tai-luk Lui (eds) (forthcoming).

—— (1994b) 'On the edge of empires', *Positions* 1(3).

Rofel, Lisa (1992) 'Rethinking modernity: space and factory discipline in China', *Cultural Anthropology* 7(1), pp. 93–114.

Said, Edward (1983) 'Traveling theory'. In *The World, the Text, and the Critic*. Cambridge: Harvard University Press.

Shi, Shuqing 施叔青 (1989) *Niao de chuanren: yu Hunan zuojia Han Shaogong duitan* 鸟的传人:与湖南作家韩少工对谈 ('The inheritors of the bird: a dialogue with Hunan writer Han Shaogong'), pp. 124–40, in *Wentan fansi yu qianzhan* 文坛反思与前瞻 (*Reflections and Expectations of the World of Literature*). Singapore: Ming Chuang chubanshe.

Siu, Helen (1990) 'Recycling rituals'. In Perry Link, Richard Madsen and Paul Pickowicz (eds) *Unofficial China*. Boulder: Westview Press.

Stalin, Josef (1940) *Dialectical and Historical Materialism*. New York: International Publishers.

Tong, Enzheng 童恩正 (1989) *Muoergen de muoshi yu Zhongguo de yuanshi shehui yanjiu* 魔尔根的模式与中国的原始社会研究 ('The Morgan Model and the study of primitive Chinese society'). In *Wenhua renleixue* 文化人类学 (*Cultural Anthropology*). Shanghai: Shanghai renmin chubanshe.

Wang, Jing (1994) 'Romancing the subject: utopian moments in the Chinese aesthetics of the 1980's', *Social Discourse* 6 (1–2).

Watson, Rubie S. (1991) 'Wives, concubines and maids: servitude and kinship in the Hong Kong Region, 1990-1940'. In *Marriage and Inequality in Chinese Society*. Berkeley: University of California Press.

Wu, Xiaoming 伍晓明 (1992) *Ershi shiji zhongguo wenhua zai xifang mianqian de ziwo yishi* 二十世纪中国文化在西方面前的自我意识 ('Cultural self-identity in the face of the West in twentieth century China'), *Ershiyi shiji* 二十一世纪 (*Twenty-first Century*), no. 14, December, pp. 102–12.

Yang, Mayfair Mei-hui (1988) 'The modernity of power in the Chinese socialist order', *Cultural Anthropology* 3(4), November, pp. 408–27.

—— (1994a) 'Using the past to negate the present: ritual ethics and state rationality in ancient China'. In *Politics and the Art of Social Exchange in China*. Ithaca: Cornell University Press.

—— (1994b) 'A sweep of red: state subjects and the cult of Mao in China'. In *Politics and the Art of Social Exchange in China*. Ithaca: Cornell University Press.

Zhang, Rulun 张汝伦 (1987) *Wenhua yanjiu san tiyi* 文化研究三提议 ('Three proposals for studying culture'). In Fudan University Journal editorial department (ed.) *Duanlie yu Jicheng* 断裂与继承 (*Rupture and Continuity*). Shanghai: Renmin chubanshe.

Chapter 6

Anthropology without tears

How a 'local' sees the 'local' and the 'global'

Wazir Jahan Karim

INTRODUCTION

The ambiguous relationship between indigenous anthropologists practising anthropology in the developing world and governments under which they live has something to do with the theory of knowledge generated from past and current anthropology. With the world system being what it is today, where military and economic supremacy continues to divide nations into leaders and followers, developing nations are not only wrestling with local experiences of colonialism but the global birth of the 'new world order' declared by Bush at the end of the Iraq war of 1991, when Iraq's attempt at self-promotion to the ranks of a world order nation failed. Asad (1973), Cohen (1989) and Rosaldo (1989) have previously described the colonial legacy of anthropology – how the production of ethnographic knowledge through participant observation was also a useful way for the British Colonial Office to get on with its job better – to rule colonies with the minimum amount of opposition and conflict. Today, local anthropologists who continue to study minorities through the ethnographic method are more or less accused of the opposite by their own governments. Anthropological research apparently stimulates opposition and conflict among indigenes, who would have otherwise gone along with mainstream development. On a continuum of social respectability, in the social sciences, local social anthropologists are possibly the least respectable and economists the most. Economics is modernity and progress, that part of the 'new world order' which developing nations aspire to promote, but anthropology is the whip of powerful nations against the weak (See Cohen 1989).[1] It helps them generate information about human rights, minorities and the environment, for these powerful nations to use as bargaining strategies for so-called multilateral economic cooperation. Hence local anthropologists are perceived as agents of the West and the 'new world order', who perpetuate the continuity of the colonial–colonized experience and directly and indirectly the global dominance of the European intellectual tradition; an issue which has earned Said the reputation of a popular critic and hero of the non-West (1979, 1993).

In this chapter, I shall be dealing with the issue of the contextual meaning of anthropology as the 'mother of all battles' of experts on social knowledge formation and application, both global and local, through the view of one who teaches anthropology in the field. In this discussion, three global faces of anthropology come to my attention.

First, in the context of its usefulness in institutions of higher learning in carving out the careers of many distinguished and less distinguished European and American scholars and providing degrees to the younger enthusiasts of culture to uphold its traditions, anthropology is concerned with the commercial reproduction of local knowledge into a global intellectual resource. Second, in the context of its European and American 'centricities', it serves to generate social knowledge for the consumption of a European and American audience; most anthropological knowledge is appropriated through an unknown or lesser-known language media and interpreted through English or a European language, then packaged through theories and paradigms understood only to those who subscribe to the network of information building of anthropology as a global intellectual resource. Third, in the context of the transferability of anthropological knowledge from theory to action, much of this has been in the form of generating new theories about the usefulness of social knowledge rather than concrete 'action-oriented methodologies' to help minorities who are now in considerable trouble with their governments. For those without the time and patience to wait for these perceptions to bear fruit, activism through existing movements concerned with the plight of minorities becomes popular and many of these seem to take place under the rubric of practices of human rights and peace groups, indigenous third world networks, environmental networks, minority ethnic associations and minority woman associations. The less active and more pensive may throw in an annual subscription of Cultural Survival International in good faith.

THE EARTH AS AN ONION STORY: APPLICATION OF MA' BETISE' SOCIAL THEORY ON THE TENSIONS WITHIN GLOBALISM AND THE 'NEW WORLD ORDER'

The distanciation of anthropologists of the developing world from the distinguished inner circle of practising social scientists in western Europe and the United States may be more simply explained through the Ma' Betise' world view of earth as an onion (See Karim 1981: 69). Earth, they state, is like an onion floating on water (See Table 1 and Karim 1981). It has seven layers of 'life', or worlds with different levels of civility and power, reflecting different degrees of human adaptation to natural and cultural life. The highest level of civility and power is the seventh world of powerful ancestral spirits (*moyang*) who command the state of the arts of the rest of earth. This seventh world, the first layer of the onion, houses ancestral spirits who are as powerful as the 'White European'. Through 'spirit-attacks' (*tenong*) they can defeat other human beings by casting injury, illness or death on those who do not honour or respect them. Significantly in modern 'global' languages, this world corresponds to the emerging 'new world order' of powerful nation states, sometimes described by its leaders as the 'world community' and also the Group Seven (G7) economic caucus under the leadership of the United States.[2] This is also the world where, with a few exceptions, those in power within the European Community murmur their approval each time the United States proposes military action against nation-states who defy the sanctions of the 'new world order'. This is also the world which has mastered the technology of modern warfare fought remote-control style in distant battlefields in the sixth world, the second onion layer. It is also a world where a little know-ledge goes a long way through satellite television, direct dial telephone, facsimile and electronic mail.[3] In this 'seventh' world, wars, riots, famines and the struggles of minorities for land and self-determination become global commercial resources in a matter of minutes.

This is also the world where the majority of western/European anthro-pologists live, where they learn to sort out field data, otherwise known as local knowledge, through the theoretical mode to which they are accustomed.

Table 1 Ma' Betise' world view of the earth as an onion

1 First World: dunia' lapi mui			
2 Second World: dunia' lapi ma dunia' hatek	UNDERWORLD minorities	endangered cultures	extinct
3 Third World: dunia' lapi empek			
4 Fourth World: dunia' lapi empat			
5 Fifth World: dunia lapi' limak			
6 Sixth World: dunia' lapi enam	WORLD	the South	newly independent minorities amidst nation- state major populations
7 Seventh World: dunia' lapi tuju	OVERWORLD	the North	world powers and the new world order

Source: Adapted from Karim (1981: 69)

As an intellectual community, they usually divorce themselves from their political leaders, often also dismissing popular knowledge of political, economic and social events as unrepresentative, ridiculous or boring. This interpretation of popular knowledge may be localized within the intellectual community, but others outside this western/European world who watch the way in which many local sources of data become global knowledge and listen to the popular responses of the western/European other about themselves, realize that their ethos of interpretation will always be different.

The second layer of the onion in Ma' Betise' world view represents the sixth world of humans, plants and animals living in tense coexistence amidst contradictory ideologies of naturalism – an assumption that humans can appropriate the natural resources of earth for personal happiness and wealth and another that humans have to coexist with plants and animals who have a right to a natural habitat of their own, to a share of the earth's resources of land, food and shelter (See Karim 1981). On another level, this world manifests a struggle between those with power and the power-less. The powerful, in the form of developers, investors and politicians, attempt to gain a larger share of natural resources, while the powerless among minorities, destitute peasants and workers try to retain whatever they have. Yet, in this attempt, they are constantly pushed back by the former, who may be ideologically or politically allied to the 'most powerful' in the seventh world. The economic realities of this world are such that ethnic minorities fight, not for development, modernity and change but for traditional rights over ownership of land and the use of natural resources which they are now being denied. Wars, famines, ecological crises and minority struggles will always occur in this world and not the seventh, since participants of this world will always try to turn the forces of naturalism to their advantage, with some gaining more resources and others less than their fair share.

In wider geopolitical terms, this world corresponds to the emerging nation-states of Asia and Eastern Europe, where governments cooperate or defy the seventh, and receive their share of reward and punishment accordingly. In this world of independent nation-states, concern for nation-building often converges with sentiments of nationalism and racism, resulting in land disputes and claims over natural resources, warfare, ethnic cleansing and genocide. Land and economic resources seem to be the preoccupation of leaders anxious to correct the errors of colonial history and to popularize their powers in concrete terms (See Vilas 1993).

In all fairness, moving away from Ma' Betise' interpretations of pre-colonial to colonial time, the sixth world was created by the seventh who a millennium earlier had decided on its boundaries, its population profile, the production of its natural resources, the markets of these resources and the prices and profits to be gained from this production. In post-colonial time, the sixth world is then the 'action' world generated from the powers of knowledge of the seventh. It is a world where the paradigms of distinction between global and local are preset by the seventh, where a nation-state may be admitted as a member of the seventh if it chooses to become worldly, globally conscious and environmentally friendly; that is to say, when it reproduces the metaphors of freedom, democracy and liberalism prescribed by the seventh, at any one moment in time. For those who do not try to design their governments and policies through the ideas of Plato, Mills, Ricardo and Smith, knowledge is persistently interpreted as local, parochial and savage, lacking in dignity and repute, undeserving of international aid, whether financial or military.

For the seventh world, the sixth world is also a strategic place in time to fabricate from the wealth of local knowledge, an 'enemy' (Esposito 1992). The invention of the 'enemy' is now pervasive in those Muslim nation-states where conformity to the prescriptive rule of social behaviour seems to be at its worse. Libya's Gaddaffi, Iran's Ayatullah, Palestine's Arafat, Iraq's Sadam, Somalia's Aidid, are all representations of the 'enemy' of the seventh world. Symbolically they also reaffirm the image of the enemy in European history and the need to obliterate from earth an impossible tongue-twister: the mad, Muslim Mullah who murder men and mothers in the name of Mohammed. Thus the sixth world is the playing-field of the seventh, the subject of enquiry of controversy and debate where western/European intellectuals indulge in the universalisms and pluralisms of theory-building for purposes of knowledge production as a global resource.

The Ma' Betise' fifth, fourth, third, second and first world corresponds to the underworld of lower beings, who attempt to struggle to the fifth through the creaks and crevasses of earth. These layers symbolically reaffirm the powerlessness of those who have not yet managed to secure a proper abode in the sixth world. If the ancestral spirits of the seventh world are godly and the powerful in the sixth are wealthy, these are hated and despised for what they represent (see Said's 'Ariel' and 'Caliban' metaphors of the new world order (1993)). It is obvious that these worlds correspond to a power hierarchy, with the seventh world grabbing the most and the fifth and lesser worlds the least in this scheme of civility and power. The least wealthy and greedy of the sixth world have adapted to an uneasy power distribution system which is cyclical, shared amongst all living things wanting similar resources. They continue to believe in the spirit of naturalism, with the uneasy knowledge that naturalism works against them in a world where others also believe in the accumulation of wealth and private property. For the Ma' Betise', their living conditions in the sixth world are closer to the fifth. Indeed, since the Ma' Betise' also believe in rebirth and the recycling of souls, a dormant fear is the possibility of being reborn into the fifth world as a lesser being, a Caliban deprived of the most basic forms of humanity. Indeed, if the current displacement of Ma' Betise' from land and forests continues, this might well become a reality in their future construction of local knowledge. Leaving aside Ma' Betise' pessimism about the future, the inner layers of the onion up to the fifth correspond to societies who fear their own extinction or the loss of their rightful place on earth – the Kintak, Kanak and Ma' Betise' of Malaysia, the Amerindians, the Muslim Bosnians, the Kurds, the Palestinians, and scores of other small societies now endangered by landlessness, deforestation, depopulation, famine, war and genocide. Many others like the Tiano Indians, Andaman Islanders and Tasmanian aborigines are already there – now in lifeless forms buried in the boiling cauldron of the first three worlds.

MALAYSIA: INTERNAL AND EXTERNAL TENSIONS IN GLOBALISM AND SOCIAL TRANSFORMATION

We now ask the question, what do we do with this social knowledge which we have created through the worlds we represent? Is anthropological knowledge generated to enrich the western intellectual tradition or destitute populations from which this knowledge was appropriated? Is it the anthropologist's responsibility to remove from the post-colonial world (the sixth) fabricated and imaginary images of smaller societies as backward and rebellious, necessitating mainstreaming, images which often destroy the people whom anthropologists have worked with? What does the future hold for the use of social knowledge of the kind produced by anthropology? On another level, what if the society that the anthropologist works in becomes a target of western/European propaganda against Islam or Communism – the 'enemy'? Should he or she address this issue in anthropological research or is it best ignored and left to political scientists to ponder upon? Should the observations of anthropologists be confined to the internal dynamics of power struggles, factionalisms and alliances within a nation-state or colony or should they also observe and address the wider global context of power relations in which these relationships are embedded? I would like to say that as an anthropologist of the sixth world, I am struggling to come to terms with these issues, which may have been raised before but which have come to bother me recently as I continue to publish research in the prescribed language of anthropology, ordered by my European *moyang* (ancestors) of seventh world anthropology. The political leaders of my nation-state of Malaysia have an opinion of anthropologists like me. We emulate the western tradition of using our subjects as our playing fields and in this neo-colonial encounter of so-called objective enquiry supposedly reject all development efforts at mainstreaming minorities, to enjoy the benefits of modernity and industrialization. We are supposedly afraid that we will become redundant as the economists take over the development of the Orang Aslis, our minority indigenes, our source of bread and butter. Indeed, our main concern is to help them remain museum pieces for the satisfaction of western minority-sensitive governments and tourists.

Malaysian national leaders are now as skilful in using Chomsky (1991) and Said as *surahs* from the *Qur'ān* to establish the fragile position of newly independent nation-states like Malaysia, struggling to rid itself of Euro-American domination and at the same time maintaining a Euro-American friendliness in foreign policy and trade to avoid being subjects of missiles and carpet bombs. After all, the Prime Minister has already six big Ms to his name – Mahathir bin Mohammed, the masculine Muslim Prime Minister of Malaysia. To ensure that Malaysia does not join the lower depths of Muslim nations who have become 'the enemy' who now enjoy prime time news coverage on satellite television, he has successfully created a government with a balanced policy towards ethnic pluralism, padded by metaphors of religious freedom and democracy. Through the rubrics of modern capitalism, everything seems to work well for everyone in Malaysia. The Malays hold special privileges, the Chinese dominate businesses and the Indians occasionally have a good bash at transport and energy, bringing things to a standstill and leaving the nation in total darkness to remind it of its inter-ethnic dependency. Religion is equated with progress and the development of a modern civil eastern society. Muslim women are heavily courted to join the workforce and pristine or Muslim charismatic movements are crushed even before the local anthropologist can convert them into data. The local anthropologist, as scholar or activist, is generally a pain in the neck to bureaucrats, economists and developers. He or she does not define development, to mean overcoming a quantum leap into industrialization while purring like a tiger, but instead talks of cultural resilience and innovativeness in adaptation to new technology. He or she talks of land and forest resources for minorities instead of calculating the amount of new jobs created for voters with every new licence issued to loggers and house developers. He or she is emotional rather than practical, and pessimistic rather than optimistic about the future.

Yet the ultimate trump card of the Prime Minister is in being a hero of the South, in his leadership over regional organizations like ASEAN and ZOPFAN and his ability to develop concepts like the East Asia Economic Caucus which challenge the priorities and privileges of the Group of Seven and NAFTA.[4] At a press conference in Hong Kong in 1992, when questioned about Malaysia's dubious stand on minorities and the environment agenda, he replied that the problem was that Malaysia's tropical timber fetched such low prices in the European market: 'Pay us more for our wood and we will chop down less trees', he said. As for preserving Malaysia's biosphere as a lung for the North, he suggested that the North should pay for Malaysia's oxygen if it was to be their source of life and longevity. Then Malaysia would be able to treat it as a commercially viable natural resource. When asked about world criticisms on its deforestation policy and how it has affected the Penans, he suggested that the North reviewed their development projects on golf-courses and created their own biosphere. Malaysia would be happy to supply the North with seeds and many varieties of insects and mosquitoes to make their eco-system complete. Obvious in this message was a note of advice to social scientists and other minority-sensitive organizations that nation-states like Malaysia are grappling with bigger issues with far-reaching implications for the future of minorities. Hence the kind of knowledge generated by anthropologists, which is local and pluralistic, cannot become a national agenda for public discussion since it is paradigmatically and semiotically associated with a discourse which is Euro- and Ameri-centric. The work of many activists, anthropologists or minority indigenes participating in action research projects is equally criticized since their grants are usually obtained from American or European sources. The fear of the 'new world order' reaching the last vestiges of civil life in the forests and mangroves of Malaysia is real, and a reaction has been to interpret the kind of social knowledge generated by anthropologists as history-good for the past, bad for the present and future and generally counterproductive in helping minorities advance along with the rest of society.

However, on the local level there are people who are unconcerned about the 'new world order' tensions and who make a living by enacting the drama of everyday life through Malaysia's fastest growing sector – tourism. Once it is known that the anthropologist is capable of generating a reservoir of social knowledge on the pluralistic formation of ethnic cultures, the metaphor of the indigene as a museum piece begins to take shape among curators, tour package operators, tourist guides and petty bureaucrats who then begin a profitable trade of selling culture. In recent years in Peninsular Malaysia, the Orang Asli or indigenous minorities have become associated with tourism, appearing in state and national exhibitions, carving spirits in museums and performing festival dances and shamanistic seances in tourist-packed centres.[5] The rewards for the Orang Asli are usually just compensation for the loss of earnings for the day, without any extra money for the previous day's labour put into the gathering and plaiting of wood or leaves to make up the exhibits and costumes. Many of the young girls involved, now physically conscious of their looks and committed to Avon and cover girl images of sophisticated beauty, hair frizzed and tarnished by peroxide, lips coated ruby red in high gloss, bodies fitted with tight Levis and white khaki shirts tucked in with brown leather belts, resent being turned into exhibits for tourists. They do it for their uncles or brothers who have become the local contacts of private and public agents of tourism. They are usually sulky and petulant before and after the show, complaining that they have had no time for sightseeing and have been herded back and forth like cows. The commissions obtained by the Orang Asli men who do this must be profitable for them to carry on with these ventures.

Another interesting source of tension has been the sudden disappearance of ritual and festive artefacts and their gradual reappearance in museums and tourist shops in Selangor. A Ma' Betise' who was asked to demostrate carving in a recently opened museum in Shah Alam, said that he saw my late field father's *genggong*, a piano-sized traditional xylophone constructed from pulae wood *(alstonia)* traditionally used in festive dances *(jooh)*. No one knew how it got there. My field mother was certainly not paid any money for it. Although I knew who the local Ma' Betise' cultural broker was, I was not prepared to put a bet on it, and obviously some other petty officials were involved in acquiring *objets d' art* from many Orang Asli groups. At the end of June 1993 an old drum made from goatskin disappeared and it will obviously share the same position of honour in the museum without the knowledge of the maker and owner.

I am trying to say here that cultural knowledge has both a local and global commercial value, in the field and beyond, in museums and institutions of higher learning. The way in which the local anthropologist has put it to use is no more justifiable than the way in which it is exhibited and sold to the general public, except that local governments encourage the latter.[6] Selling culture not only improves the local tourist industry, it actually enhances Malaysia's image globally. Here one finds modernity at its best – economic development with a distinct cultural heritage. In both instances the rewards to the participants of culture are minimal.

For more than five decades, anthropologists have been studying culture as an academic exercise, either advancing or applying western theories, concepts and methodologies without reference to the global–local dimensions of social realities. The discipline has also rigidly bound itself around obsolete notions of cultural 'objectivity' or 'objective' representations. In the study of minorities in particular, a humanistic committed approach may be more relevant, representative and helpful to minority groups which are now everywhere in considerable trouble with their governments. Participatory anthropology would be a positive direction of change and may give anthropology a better image and identity, not to mention a good kick in the backside. The appeal of the anthropologist is in the transferability of culture from the local to the global in the direction of 'high culture', while the appeal of the indigene is in the transferability of interest in culture from the global back to the local. The anthropologist, the petty cultural expert and the indigene are all 'cultural brokers', but of the three, it is the petty cultural expert which is rewarded with most success since he or she revitalizes local knowledge through mass media, under the rubrics of national identity and cultural pluralism. The petty cultural expert learns to be innovative in this revitalization and ready to embrace new forms of civility which emerge from the dying cinders of tradition. Indeed, he or she creates these forms and forces them to happen. The local anthropologist is less ready to do this and instead collects his or her brokerage fees from higher cultural forms in the academe. In doing so, he or she becomes symbolically dissociated from local processes of cultural reconstruction and invention. A favourite pastime of local anthropologists is to say that this metamorphosis cannot take off so smoothly. Bogged down by observations of numerous development ventures which seem to retard rather than advance the societies they study, they write instead of the heap of ashes that follows the dying cinders of tradition.

THE LOCAL ANTHROPOLOGIST AND CONCERN FOR ECONOMIC DEVELOPMENT IN ACTION

The projects that many local anthropologists are now concerned with are those that deal with social transformation, in particular the relationship between cultural life forms and the environment, how new forms of local knowledge and economic activity will be generated as the environment undergoes radical physical changes (Nandy 1992b). As an example in Malaysia, the draining of mud-flats in mangrove rainforests automatically prevents the Ma' Betise' and other locals from hunting and gathering bivalves, mangrove wood and leaves for thatching. It simply does not make any sense once this is done to develop the village into a tourist project, since the resources needed for such tourist activities to flourish have been virtually wiped out. It is also not very perceptive to introduce integrated land schemes of rubber and oil palms to hunters and gatherers who have no idea as to what these schemes entail in terms of management and labour. It makes them wait for cash coupons to be handed out, whereupon a hedonistic form of consumption of beer and food takes place among the men, thereby wiping out any possibilities of saving money for the months to come. Alcoholism among men and hunger among women and children is the end result. This is the observation of an anthropologist working with the Kensiu in North Malaysia (Suichi Nagata 1993, personal communication) but I was struck by a similar report of the Bushmen in Namibia recently. Under a project of the United Nations World Food Programme and the Lutheran Church, Bushmen are made to settle down into agriculture and integrate into the mainstream of life. Alex Meroro, the project manager for the Lutherans, was concerned that somehow, they could not 'jump stages of evolution' (*New York Times*, 2 July 1993). Banned from hunting and despondent in agriculture rendered more difficult by long droughts (their crops were a failure), the Bushmen sold their food to soldiers to buy alcohol in an attempt to drown their sorrows.

The marginalization of social knowledge as a development 'peripheral' and its conversion into commercial antiquity has a lot to do with the way an independent nation-state visualizes the usefulness of social theories of change. These theories threaten the smooth implementation of macro-economic policy which is unconcerned for a differentiated order of things and beings. Economists are indifferent to the application of local know-ledge into a vital resource in development policy and this makes the job of an anthropologist an extremely tiresome one. Culture is a peripheral of economics and economics is the main frame of society. This was casually stated by one of the editors of an important book published by the Malaysian Institute of Public Administration (INTAN), entitled *The Malaysian Development Experience* (1994). I asked her why they wanted me to write a chapter on traditional medicine. She said that the thrust was Malaysia's phenomenal economic development since independence in 1957 but along with this development there were other peripherals like culture, art, music and medicine. It would be nice to have these put in somewhere to show how successful Malaysia is in retaining its distinct identity despite its successful economic growth. The concern for economic development secures culture a unique place in history, which reminds people of its origins, heritage and identity. For local governments, the concern of the anthropologist is counter-productive since the culture of minorities has a historic value and nothing else beyond that. They are backward and primitive and the task of the government is to modernize them and keep them abreast with things on the global front. Ong (Chapter 4, this volume) also describes how women and minorities in China become the target groups for restructuring. By this definition, however, it also becomes convenient to remove them from their habitat which is contributing to their culture lag – a visible symbol of the past in the present. In Malaysia, the image of the Orang Asli or indigene as museum pieces is not only a reaction to the global campaign of minority rights but a demonstration that interpretation of local knowledge is different from the global. The position of not belonging to the world of advanced nations is further used to justify a different priority of concerns for indigenes. In this sense, the anthropologist will never be seen to be as effective as the economist in developing the defences of the nation against empowerment from the West.

THE GLOBALIZATION OF INDIGENES THROUGH RELIGIOUS CONVERSION

The selective interpretation of certain forms of social knowledge as history has also been a convenient strategy to advance religious ideals in a country where freedom of worship is legally endorsed in the Federal Constitution. Unfortunately, animism, now upgraded through 'naturalism' in the United Nation's environment campaign, has never been given its proper place in global and local definitions of religion except perhaps to the animists themselves. The conversion of animist Orang Asli indigenes to Christianity and Bahai have taken place over more than a century as a result of English, Dutch, Portuguese and American colonial rule in South-east Asia. In South-east Asian colonial history, Christianity has probably been most successful in equating animists with pagans and non-believers. In Malaysia, the conversion process continues through Muslim sectarian movements, government backed religious organizations and Islamic-based political organizations. Christian missions which are most successful are the Baptists, Lutherans and Methodists, although the Catholic Church has also recently joined the bandwagon of this ideological warfare.

The reason why the Orang Asli are a target is because as animists, they seem to contradict universal rules of orthodoxy and civility, to be devoid of culture and religion, a population perceived as socially impoverished with no store of local knowledge of their own other than anecdotal accounts of their wanderings in and out of the forest. In 'the earth as an onion' story, missions would place them in the fifth world of human depravity, pristine and barbaric, without any global vision to enter the civil society of the sixth and seventh worlds. Significantly, a variety of different approaches have been employed to convert them; Muslim missions build prayer houses *(surau, madrasah)* and send along religious teachers to teach them to read the *Qur'ān*. Christian missions bring in high-powered electronic equipment in the form of videos and cassette players and compact disks, blasting out evangelical songs in disco style. Bahais distribute pamphlets and state how much better they are since they have already incorporated Muslim and Christian principles into their religion. They are a world religion interested in uniting the world community in a brotherhood of peace and goodwill. All three groups appeal to the global vision of unity and progress which the Orang Asli sadly seem to lack. Significantly, of the three, the Christian missions have probably been most successful in converting whole villages and I suspect this has a lot to do with the image portrayed of Christianity as modern and western. The indigenes immediately think they are making a leap from the sixth to the seventh world. Western clothes are a big hit among the young and take precedence over the Muslim veil and *hijab*. Pop music, whatever its contents, is a great event not to be missed. Videos, compact disks and computers fascinate them more than *Fardu'ain* classes in Arabic. A prominent Semai Orang Asli leader, Anthony Williams Hunt jr (known more often as Bah Tony for his preference to assume his Semai rather than English ancestry), said that he was perplexed how after only a few months of exposure, whole Semai villages were converted to Baptists (1993). Girls would drag their boyfriends to Church and wives their husbands. This may not seem unusual. Women have been known to do this everywhere, but Bah Tony attributes this to the relative social isolation of Orang Asli women *vis-à-vis* their men (1993). Christianity becomes the *modus operandi* to globalism – modernity and an exciting new social life. The tolerance of these missions for idolatry was another factor. Spirit houses bearing figurines of guardian spirits become crowded with those of Jesus Christ and the Virgin Mary and animistic figurines are gradually removed to leave behind only the latter. This is all done between doses of paracetemol, food and disco music. The approach seems to be much more subtle and cheerful than the substitute of moral lessons for Islamic teachings in Orang Asli schools. Certainly, it is a foregone conclusion that state intervention in the spread of Islam increases the fear of participation in it. The state endorses Islam as a national religion and Muslim Malays have always enjoyed a hierarchically superior position to the Orang Aslis. Orang Asli experiences with them are entrenched in a long history of defeat in power politics and development priorities. Going back to the onion story, this local link between the fifth and sixth worlds fuses together a history of persecution, rendering an appeal for the seventh. So they reach out to the seventh world to embrace the global wisdom it can offer and in the process alienate the power centres of the sixth even more. Local emissaries are then produced from the power centres of Orang Asli villages in the form of village headmen or elders who stand to gain financially for every convert they bring, but they become associated with state processes of Islamization and many end up losing their credibility even after winning a few converts along the way. Significantly in many Orang Asli communities, only the headman and members of his family are Muslims.

PARADOXES IN LOCAL ANIMISM AND GLOBAL NATURALISM

The recent rediscovery of naturalism in animism and some worldly religions like Hinduism and Buddhism as a worthy global ideological tool for environmental preservation and sustainable development runs contrary to other local Muslim missions to run it underground, and the fact that locals are doing it alongside European/Christian missions with vast international funding explains the paradoxical interpretations between global and local systems of knowledge. Local Malay missions carry the global message of Islam – unite in a brotherhood of peace and goodwill and unite against westernization. In this context, naturalism in animism should clearly be destroyed. To European missions, the naturalism of animism is parochial and savage, devoid of the advantages of progress and modernity. Yet the European intellectual community tries to market naturalism as an ideology of sustainable development in the developing world. The global is always seen to be more advanced and progressive, regardless of what precedes the formations of its ideology. So if naturalists have to become Christians and Muslims and Christians and Muslims naturalists, would animists then have to learn about naturalism a decade after their better halves have mastered these new sources of knowledge and devised the right kinds of strategies to impart it to them? The conflicting status of animism as the new language of naturalism in environmental movements contrasts with its diminutive local role as an archaic system of knowledge. In all these formulations of the global, animists have little choice but to watch their belief system shift from the futuristic and universal to the particular and peripheral (see Nandy 1992b; Botkin 1992).

Those in positions of power within nations where this takes place are aware of the contradictions but feel that minorities have very little choice but to be appropriated. The recently retired Director-General of Orang Asli affairs in Malaysia was new to this game but even he knew what the answers and conclusions were. In a conversation with him about some of these issues, he was smiling, apologetic and apocalyptic. 'Sure, they will change, but doesn't everybody?' he said. 'Five hundred years ago, the Malays were Minang, Bugis, Javanese, Boyan, Rawa and Melayu. Now they are all Malays. Fifty years from now, we will have Kintaq, Kensiu, Ma' Betise', Jakun Malays and as Muslims they will be absorbed under the category of Melayu in censuses and maps.' 'But the difference between the Orang Asli and the Malay', I said, 'is that they will not be statistically accountable, indeed if they became Muslims and were numerated as Malays, there would be no Orang Asli. It would be easier to dismiss the variants of culture they have upheld for generations and easier to implement regional development programmes over their land if these remain unknown.' The Director-General smiled and said, 'Perhaps this is what the anthropologist is for, to explain to us what kinds of development are best for what kinds of people.'

I have used this illustration of conversion to show that the future of local knowledge is contextually dependent on its globalistic potential to generate new sources of knowledge from within. The anthropologist is probably more able to provide enrichment by appealing to the universal theme of pluralism and freedom but contrary forces, stemming from the transnational links between local and global, may bury many of these cultures deeper, below the fifth world. It becomes increasingly apparent that the future of the indigenes of the developing world depends on the reactions and responses of the wider national community of locals to the global, the power-makers of the sixth against the seventh who have constructed their policies in relation to the 'other'. In this kind of social dialectics a web of criss-crossing messages diverges in different directions and the fate of local knowledge depends very much on its representation in historic and futuristic terms. Both local and global agents of change are capable of doing this and both are able to enhance or destroy its potential. Can the anthropologist perform better?

RECONSTRUCTING ANTHROPOLOGY FROM THE FIELD AND NEW MYSTIFICATIONS THROUGH POST-MODERNISM

As the local anthropologist becomes self-critical of his or her empowerment through the field of knowledge generated by anthropology, the contributions of anthropology to the theory of knowledge is again examined. What is this global intellectual resource for? For whom is anthropology being developed now? Why is it that as the field of theoretical anthropology is enriched by every new discourse it adopts, the people of the world from which anthropology makes its name become culturally impoverished by the day? How 'nativized' is anthropology and how can its nativity lessen the shame of the nudity of poverty, extinction and genocide? Is there an alternative anthropology devoid of the theoretical discourses of the West which can address the popular rather than the elite community of scholars with whom it socializes? Can universals be re-established without losing track of their origins in diversity?

To regain its credibility in the developing world – and I speak here for nation-states which have not developed their own paradigms in social sciences as in India (see Nandy 1992a) – anthropology has to learn to demystify itself. The complaint of many readers of the developing world about anthropological writing is that it is awesome. Understanding peasant behaviour through Redfield and Wolfe's coveted abstraction of Marx and Weber was complicated enough but to bring in Nietzche and Kant to interpret the psyche of the local, post-savage is even more mystifying. An extreme case was a student who in his final year exam said that the Marx and Max brothers were concerned about the same thing, the relationship of the little to the great tradition, and no wonder, because the people in the little tradition were little, lived in little houses on little pieces of land and had very little income!

Although many of the themes in anthropology concern people in everyday life, most of these are constructed through the ideas of European theoreticians writing from observations of their own societies. It seems that this has to be done before anything can be said to be of any value in anthropology. Criticisms of classic colonial style ethnography of the kind written by Malinowski, Radcliffe-Brown, Raymond Firth and Evans Pritchard were that it did not address the problems of change and modernity, and field data now have to be processed through modern or post-modern theory in order to be meaningful to the people studied. But is it any more meaningful now than before? What anthropology does now is provide box office seats to the ghosts of such theoreticians as Aristotle, Kant, Hegel, Marx, Weber and Nietzche but does this separate anthropology from the rest of the social and human sciences as a discipline which is more self-conscious of its relationship with the people of the non-western world? At the heights of post-modernist theory, where even more mystifying concepts have been introduced than modernists had to offer, anthropology has never wavered from the western tradition it was founded in. One may ask, what else is there to use given that the societies studied have never attempted to develop their own theoretical discourses of the social sciences? In any case, to move from Euro-centrism to other kinds of centrism, Islamo-centrism for one (Said 1993: xx; xxiv), does not help to overcome the problem that ideological bias for societies is still being dressed up in yet another tradition which is both externalized and ethnocentric.[7] It is still the anthropologist looking at the indigene as a component of its own intellectual history, and even if the anthropologist is concerned for his or her own intellectual development which may be enlightened through observations of behaviour of people of other cultures, what interest is this to anybody else except possibly to a student of anthropology who will be wanting to do the same thing the moment the thesis is out of the way and a job is secured? From my own observations of teaching anthropology for twenty years in the Far East, the trend of writing in anthropology alienates many students in the social sciences. The brighter ones read. They even buy books which is a consolation to those of us who write them. One or two find it awesome and even want to go on to graduate studies to be able to write like the *moyang*, but in reality many sign up for anthropology because they believe it can help them find answers to issues that bother them like juvenile crime, the environment, minority rights, human rights, women's rights, North–South tensions, infanticide, rape, racism, ethnic cleansing and genocide. Many local anthropologists have constructed their courses around these subjects and in the process of doing so have come to rely more on works outside anthropology.

The conclusion of many Malaysian students at the end of combined courses in sociology and anthropology is that while the anthropological method for field research is still the most satisfying in terms of its ability to develop involvement, sensitization and conscientization, western social theory in anthropology falls short of a necessary objective – one of popular representation – of what people in the street are actually doing and thinking and how they are reacting to local state representations of global events, how globalized everything local is made to be, and reactions to those through the idiom of local culture.

POPULATION REPRESENTATION AND A PEOPLE'S ANTHROPOLOGY

By popular representation, I am more concerned for a kind of people's anthropology, an anthropology of informality, not only subaltern (Hobsbawn 1972, 1981; see also Scott 1985; Rosaldo 1989) but the kind of study which is concerned for the production of popular knowledge.[8] Popular anthropology may be more concerned with the ethnocentricities of nationalism and how this shapes the position of the actors and determines structures of the local in relation to the global; for example, the world view of Americans (outside its intellectual community) about the United States, and its distanciation from the viewpoints of most of the developing world about Americans (provoking a variety of strategies of support and opposition) but nevertheless unified in the opinion of their diminutive role, without military or economic power, within the world community. The current self-critical moment in post-paradigmatic theory, what Marcus and Fisher refer to as an experiment of innovative discourses and methodologies, no matter how self-critical, does not help us understand, in space and time, the continued predominance of a western world view which is seen as 'global' and the diversity of others which are defined as 'local'. For example, the dominant view of Americans about America as a champion of democracy and human rights supersedes the increasing pools of 'local' knowledge appearing in local media about America as a champion of international terrorism.[9] This so-called self-critical moment in the social sciences may be yet another stopgap intellectual exercise of reviewing theories and methods in western social theory which did not marry well with social realities – the pluralisms of culture, the diversities of knowledge, the contextual complexity of narratives and so on. This phase of self-criticism and self-indulgence is less meaningful to the participants of culture than it is to the western/European expert. It overlooks a populist concern in indigenous societies; one of self-representation – that the 'native' voice wants to speak through a post-colonial experience and wants the global community to correct its history of always being 'subject matter' – for the West. A good example of this is the March 1994 trade crisis between Britain and Malaysia; a crisis concerning Malaysia's trade boycott with the British Government. Although this was an issue linked to alleged corruption among Malaysian leaders in the Pergau Dam–British Development Aid Programme, which Malaysia denies was 'aid' but a soft 'loan', the latest local reporting of this issue as of March 1994 (Chin 1994) is that a country like Britain which pursued colonization for 200 years will never ever acknowledge their political and economic advantage in Development Aid over ex-colonies like Malaysia. The highlight of the commentary was a simple question. 'What about the hundreds, if not thousands of billions of pounds which the British had plundered from the then Malaya in the past 100 years?' (Chin 1994). Although Malaysians would have liked to have seen more evidence of this alleged corruption gaining momentum in *The Times*, they nevertheless remained solidly united behind the common experience of sharing a colonial history and of suffering under British ethnocentrism. Andrew Neil, then editor of the *Sunday Times*, which carried the report (20 February 1994), denied that the *Sunday Times* had claimed that Dr Mahathir had sought such a bribe or had been paid one (*The Times*, 3 March 1994). This denial and refusal to apologize seems to have maddened Malaysians even more. This was typical of the British, claimed many prominent Malaysians. They will apologize to a western power like the United States, France or Germany but not to an ex-colony like Malaysia. The question of whether Malaysian politicians were corrupt was lost as the colonial-post-colonial continuities of British spheres of dominance *vis-à-vis* its celebrated freedom of the press tradition became a point of debate.

It is this kind of popular discourse and popular activism through the media that anthropologists should be sensitized to. It reflects the complexities of social realities in people struggling with different levels of meaning and relationships in global knowledge – a concern with the relationship between international aid, international trade and corruption; a concern with the moral link between colonial and post-colonial situations and a concern for European/western/white meanings of ethnocentrism *vis-à-vis* indigenous forms of self-representation.

The post-modernist exercise in self-indulgence separates the humanistic ideals of social science even more from the public actors of culture, who in this age of modernity have come to accept racism as a natural extension of ethnocentricism and materialism as a natural extension of basic needs. If the purpose is one of better representation than partisan social science, which was unable to predict the rise of capitalistic and consumer ideals among citizens of socialist or Marxist governments, what better explanation can the post-modernist offer us about ourselves in the future except to say that modernity is in all of us? The power of essentialist and primordial explanations of human failure is that it is difficult to argue against, given the evidence in history that the same sort of barbarism and savagery is being continuously repeated, despite the development of civil society. However, what it does not explain is why these essentialist trends are selective – why some forms of violence and consumption are condoned and others condemned, and some marginalized as evil and others hailed as 'virtuous', immediately patented as a prototype for the unawakened native. To understand this, we have to examine the spheres of dominance of knowledge, economics and the military and the constellation of events in space and time which makes this happen. Of course, greed, violence and domination is a human tragedy that is global and transnational, but the reality is that at any one moment in history one can predict who the victims usually are – indigenous minorities rather than majority populations, women and children rather than men, the elderly rather than youth, workers rather than producers, destitute states rather than wealthy nations, the non-aligned Movement of 108 developing nations rather than the G7 and so on.[10] So the dynamics of global power relations criss-crosses local lines of least resistance, but selective global and local strategies of which to defend and which to ignore provides the ingredients of affirmative theory. One could come out with very interesting insights on the relationship between genocide and rape camps in Bosnia-Herzogovenia and link it to more natural devolutionary processes of extinction taking place among many hunting and gathering societies in Asia, where ecological displacement, early death and the shortage of women are some major factors leading to a diminishing birth rate. These are issues related to women's reproductive health and society's capacity to reproduce itself in the future, but the gender of genocide and extinction does not seem to be so earth-shaking to the world community as to require affirmative action (see Karim 1993).

The convergence of 'elite' and 'popular' views in developing countries about the state of relations of the 'local' to the 'global' (including representations from within through the nation-state) has forced 'local' intellectuals to look for alternative paradigms to the current alternative in social theory, but whatever it addresses may again be problematic if it is merely composed in defiant reaction against the other to opt out of the race, through fundamentalist theological theory or to 'beat them at their game', by establishing yet another kind of late post-modernism. My concern over some of the alternative world views now attracting an increasingly wide Asian audience is that the debunking of the West and western theories of democracy and liberalism is now indulged in with such passion that ethnocentrism and sexism in these home-grown theories may be legitimized and take firm root in the minds of Asia's political and intellectual elites. Islamization and Confucianism may oppose the individualism and egocentricities of the West, the former with its spiritual conscientization of a community of believers (*ummah*) in the eradication of poverty and social oppression (Syed Agil 1989; Ahmad 1991) and the latter with its practical concerns for prosperity and health through a cohesive network of primary social groupings (Smart and Smart 1993), but both thrive on ethnocentrism, contain essentialist views of women and hierarchical notions of gender. Of the two, Confucianism may be more steeped in ethnocentricities, given the preference for cultural homogeneity through birth in East Asia and the restlessness in Korea, Taiwan, Hong Kong, Singapore and now China to introduce yet other success stories of thriving capitalism amidst 'soft authoritarianism' (Fukuyama 1992; and see Ong, Chapter 4, this volume). In other words, the so-called economic miracles of East and South-east Asia are less miraculous if we examine the basis of their success – family control over capital and other resources, business networks contained within ethnic boundaries, marriage alliances coinciding with trade mergers and the regeneration of employment within clan and kinsmen, fusing primordial loyalties with industry. Islam officially bans ethnocentrism and racism (*kaumiah*) but the segmentation of the Muslim (*ummah*) today reconfirms the pervasive reality of its existence and power to divide.

Hence, whether capitalism is linked to western democracy, Islam or Confucianism, an important observation is that there are rigid social controls governing the redistribution of wealth and property and that these are of a sexist and ethnocentric kind. In the core or periphery of westernization, intellectuals (who advocate one ideal against another) may be indulging in a fantasy of altruism – to argue for a new set of ideals in defensive reaction against another which is 'too western', 'too Islamic' or 'too Chinese'. Ideally, a significant difference between Islam and Confucianism is that its redistributive principles of wealth transcend family and kinship affiliation but in reality Muslim nation-states share the realities of Confucist-based states in that both are ridden with social elites based in monarchies, the military or businesses. It remains doubtful if these redistributive strategies will be gender-undifferentiated or find their way out of these privileged groups by the end of this century.[11] However, if it does, it will be the miracle of the sixth world overtaking the seventh and bringing along with it the fifth world to enjoy the fruits of the new heaven.

Affirmative theory must be more autonomous than reactionary, and more humanistic than hermeneutical. A humanistic approach will come out with better strategies of self-involvement and participation in the struggles of indigenes for social equity, justice and empowerment while a hermeneutical approach will lead to the formulation of alternate paradigms which may be reactive and defensive more than useful to the participants of culture. Local intellectuals are now so active in addressing the issue of hegemonic social theory that a greater diversity of perspectives and contents of social knowledge may be constructed from many ethnocentric perspectives, blinding the intellectual vision of which affirmative theory best represents the public actors of culture. Tensions already exist among intellectuals operating from the borders of the global database as to the future role of the sixth world in the onion. For local intellectuals, this may be yet another attempt at self-criticism, to gain the status of the 'popular intellectual', now circulating madly on the western global frontier to present their own brand of self-therapy, but I remain stubborn of the opinion that the 'local' anthropologist including the variety types of the American and European 'home grown' may yet find a catharsis in popularizing anthropology, to best represent the public actors of culture.

What has been apparent is that anthropologists have not addressed or responded to the increasing alienation between East and West, North and South, or the 'earth as an onion' story; or how representative are these images of the developing world which are created through the globalization of knowledge and how distinctly different these are from the images that the developing world conceives of knowledge produced from Europe and the United States. To a fair extent, many Europeans would also deny they share the same pool of knowledge as the United States, and some

Europeans would also beg to differ, as would the English amongst them and so on. But on the other hand, there are popular universals (outside Europe's intellectual community) on who is the enemy and who is the ally and who is right and who is wrong.

Significantly, as this alienation process widens, global representations of social knowledge will render the knowledge of the developing world even more local. Since the same values and sentiments on friend, enemy, ally, world community and world order are increasingly split down the middle in binary style, less will be known of the side which does not control the media of satellite and electronic communication. There is no reason why anthropologists of the seventh world should be pushed out of its share of control, just because their feet are in the seventh and have their hearts in the sixth. One may say they are in the best of both worlds and may be the most competent people to balance notions of the local and global and bring it back to the people they have lived with, as a gift of reciprocity.

Hence anthropology should not only be demystified, it should be people-oriented and popular, representative and reciprocal. Its intellectual historicity should be integrative and relational and its sentiment human-itarian and messianic. Its method should be equitable and its objective commitment, equity. It may not be able to save the world from the chaos of today but it can at least put it in remission, like the ashes of Sai Baba on the palms of an ailing man. It must be brave, and express itself more clearly as to what its role is in the theory of the creation of knowledge. Books like Rosaldo's *Culture and Truth* (1989), Ashis Nandy's *Traditions, Tyranny and Utopias* (1992c) and *The Intimate Enemy* (1992a), and Said's *Culture and Imperialism* (1993) address an intellectual community beyond the confines of their restricted disciplines because they are concerned with the role of the intellectual community in global terms. Most anthropo-logical works, on the other hand, are written mainly to address an endogamous community of European or western anthropologists. They seldom address the people from which ethnographies were derived. They are particularly weak in theory-building relating to the universal concerns of social knowledge and issues in the social sciences; for example, greater sensitization and understanding of environmental conservation and sustainable development, inter-ethnic conflict, conflict resolution, racism, genocide or demographic and social mapping of cultural and physical extinction. To do so effectively, a differentiated concept of who is who in the local and global and whose definitions one may use becomes import-ant. It is imperative that ethnographies are recast and written for the overall objective of uplifting indigenous knowledge to the level of social theory – such as how animism has contributed profoundly to naturalism which is now advocated in theories of sustainable development, or how egalitarianism in small-scale societies may be closer to democracy than western capitalism. The recognition of 'native' intellectual activity as post-colonial rather than post-savage is a particularly important perspective of knowledge, in both the local and global. I would like to conclude on an optimistic note by saying that if there is any discipline in the social sciences which is capable of doing this, it is anthropology.

NOTES

1 On 14 March 1991 at New York, US Ambassador Thomas Pickering attributed success of the war to the United Nations saying that 'the co-operation it achieved gives us a strong basis for continuing to build what the U.S President calls a new world order – an order based on international collective security' (*Star*, 15 March 1991).

2 Other than the United States, membership of the G7 group includes Britain, Canada, Italy, France, Germany and Japan.

3 At war or in peace, modern technology now has the same functions – to subsume, capture, edit, interpret and screen. A member of the seventh world can partake in a war peacefully by supporting it through an opinion poll conducted by telephone, then watch it unfold itself on satellite television and immediately phone or fax a friend to express satisfaction or regret. Eventually, everything which is relayed through global networks will be sponsored and marketed commercially with military hardware in display or action capturing the highest bidder at prime-time news.

4 ASEAN refers to the Association of South-east Asian Nations, and ZOPFAN the concept of Zone of Peace, Freedom and Neutrality, in South-east Asia. The East Asian Economic Caucus concept developed to provide some autonomy to third world Nations struggling against the monopolistic control of world powers over global defence strategies and western trade blocks. NAFTA refers to the North American Free Trade Area, uniting the United States, Canada and Mexico in a powerful trade bloc.

5 Until 1994, the Department of Orang Asli Affairs was incorporated into the Ministry of Culture and Tourism. It is now part of the Ministry of National Unity and Social Development.

6 The latest university in Malaysia, the University of Malaysia in Sarawak (UNIMAS), does have a Faculty of Social Science but no specific programme for anthropology, although it is the most culturally diverse state in Malaysia. Other new universities, like Universiti Utara Malaysia (UUM), have also avoided developing faculties in social science or anthropology. Significantly, the University of Brunei has also not developed a faculty of social science, and anthropology is almost unknown.

7 The Association of Muslim Social Scientists and the International Institute of Islamic Thought publish the Journal, *The American Journal of Islamic Social Sciences*, based in Washington. Two recent articles of interest are Ibrahim Wagab's 'Islamic perspective on theory building in the social sciences' (1–22) and Louay Safi's 'The quest of Islamic methodology: the Islamisation of knowledge project in its second decade' (23–48), published in Vol. 10(1), Spring 1993.

8 See Rosaldo's discussion on subaltern analysis (1989: 186–95). Most of these studies (Fanon's was highlighted) are concerned with the dynamic interplay of culture and power and pinpoint the centres of dominance and the public's way of dealing with it in everyday life. These studies could be further widened to include the global dynamics of power relations and its articulations in public culture.

9 See the *New Straits Times*, reproduced from Gemini News, 'US Waging International Terrorism', 6 July 1993, p.14; also *The Economist* (America vs. Islam, 3 July 1993, pp.37–8).
10 The Non-Aligned Movement (NAM) is interested in a constructive North–South dialogue. It is currently headed by President Suharto of Indonesia who failed in his attempt to seek an audience with the G7 countries at Tokyo on 5 July 1993. Although he was denied access to the leaders of G7, Japan's Prime Minister Kiichi Miyazawa said that he would get leaders of the G7 countries to realize that their economic success partly depends on NAM members who provide them with markets and raw materials. See also the South Centre report (August 1992) on 'Non alignment in the 1990s: contributions to an economic agenda', 1–57.
11 Indeed, China's move towards capitalism does not take on the same dramatic proportions as Russia, but the reality of massive economic differences between the prosperous port cities and the countryside has been a contributory factor in its current economic reform.
Refer also to Yang, Chapter 4 in this volume, where she discusses China's move into modern capitalism and its impact in the countryside.

REFERENCES

Ahmad, Z. (1991) *Islam, Poverty and Income Distribution*. Leicester: The Islamic Foundation.
Anthony, W. H. Jr. (1993) 'Gender relations among the Semai and the perception of the "Self"'. Paper presented at the Seminar on *Reflexivity and Gender*, Women and Human Resource Studies Unit, Universiti Sains Malaysia.
Asad, T. (ed.) (1973) *Anthropology and the Colonial Encounter*. New York: Humanities Press.
Botkin, D. B. (1992) 'Rethinking the environment'. *Dialogue*, 2: 61–5.
Carter, D. C. (1993) 'Recognising traditional environment knowledge'. *Indigenous and Traditional Knowledge*, April, IDRC Reports 21(1): 10–12.
Chin, V. K. (1994) 'British government likely to retaliate', Comment, *Star*, p. 19.
Choong, Soon Kim (1990) 'The role of the non-western anthropologist reconsidered: illusion versus reality'. *Current Anthropology*, April, 31(2): 197–200.
Chomsky, N. (1991) 'US Gulf policy'. *Open Magazine* Pamphlet Series, New Jersey, 22 January, 1–17.
Cohen, R. (1989) 'Human rights and cultural relativism: the need for a new approach'. Commentaries, *American Anthropologist*, December, 91(4): 1014–17.
Esposito, J. (1992) *The Islamic Threat: Myth or Reality*. New York: Oxford University Press.
Fabian, J. (1983) *Time and the Other: How Anthropology Makes Its Object*. New York: Columbia University Press.
Fanon, F. (1968) *The Wretched of the Earth*, trans. C. Ferrington. New York: Grove. (First published 1961.)
Fukuyama, F. (1992) *The End of History and Last Man*. New York: The Free Press.
Giddens, A. (1990) *The Consequences of Modernity*. Cambridge: Polity Press.
Hobsbawn, E. J. (1972) 'Social bandits: a reply'. *Comparitive Studies in Society and History* 14: 503–5.
—— (1981) *Bandits*. New York: Pantheon Books. (First published 1972.)
Karim, W. J. (1981) *Ma' Betise' Concepts of Living Things*. New Jersey: Athlone Press, LSE Monographs in Social Anthropology, No. 54.

—— (1993) 'With Moyang Melur in Carey Island: more endangered, more engendered'. In D. Bell, P. Caplan and W.J. Karim (eds) *Gendered Fields: Women, Men and Ethnography*. London: Routledge.

Marcus, G. E. and Fischer, M. M. J. (1986) *Anthropology as Cultural Critique: An Experimental Moment in the Human Sciences*. Chicago: University of Chicago Press.

Morales-Gomez, D. A. (1993) 'Knowledge, change and the preservation of progress'. *Indigenous and Traditional Knowledge*, April, IDRC Reports 21(1): 4–5.

Mudimbe, V. Y. (1988) *The Invention of Africa: Gnosis, Philosophy and the Order of Knowledge*. Bloomington, IN: Indiana University Press.

Nandy, A. (1992a) *The Intimate Enemy: Loss and Recovery of Self Under Colonialism*. New Delhi: Oxford University Press. (First published 1983.)

—— (1992b) Proceedings of the International Seminar on 'The Environment and the Regeneration of Culture', 14–17 December, Key Note Address by the Governor of Penang, His Excellency Tun Dr Hamdan Sheikh Tahir.

—— (1992c) *Traditions, Tyranny and Utopias: Essays in the Politics of Awareness*. Delhi: Oxford University Press.

Rosaldo, R. (1989) *Culture and Truth: The Remaking of Social Analysis*. Boston, MA: Beacon Press.

Safi, L. (1993) 'The quest of Islamic methodology: the Islamisation of knowledge project in its second decade'. *The American Journal of Islamic Social Sciences* 10(1): 23–48.

Said, E. W. (1979) *Orientalism*. New York: Random House Inc. (First published 1978.)

—— (1993) *Culture and Imperialism*. New York: Alfred A. Knopf Inc.

Scott, J. C. (1985) *Weapons of the Weak: Everyday Forms of Resistance*. New Haven, CT: Yale University Press.

Smart, J. and Smart, A. (1993) 'Obligation and control: employment of kin in capitalist labour management in China'. *Critique of Anthropology*, March, 13(1): 7–31.

South Centre Report (1992) 'Non-alignment in the 1990's: contributions to an economic agenda', pp. 1-57.

Sunday Times (1994) 'Wimpey offered contract bribes to Malaysian Prime Minister', 20 February.

Syed Agil, S. O. (1989) 'Rationality in economic theory: a critical appraisal'. *Journal of Islamic Economics* 2(2): 79–94.

Vilas, C. M. (1993) 'Latin-American populism: a structural approach'. *Science and Society* 56(4): 389–420.

Wagab, I. (1993) 'Islamic perspective on theory building in the social sciences'. *The American Journal of Islamic Social Sciences* 10(1): 1–22.

Chapter 7

Chimpanzees, diamonds and war
The discourses of global environmental change and local violence on the Liberia–Sierra Leone border

Paul Richards

INTRODUCTION

Political and moral discourse in the societies of the Upper Guinean forests in West Africa has long been focused on the issue of how to strike a balance between two sets of values – those associated with collective survival in a harsh forest environment, and those that arise from, and facilitate, participation in international commerce (Richards 1996). In this chapter I describe and elucidate two local commentaries upon this balancing act. Both commentaries stem from rural communities in and around the Gola Forest (a boundary wilderness between Sierra Leone and Liberia). They reflect, respectively, the standpoint of rice-farming villagers and young diamond diggers operating on the forest edge. The terms in which these two commentaries are couched may, at first sight, appear odd, and perhaps troubling, to a wider audience. Some elements of these local discourses have been picked up and presented in an unsympathetic light in international press comment on the Liberian civil war (cf. Kaplan 1994). It is the purpose of my argument to demonstrate that when context is taken fully into account these discourses are (1) coherent and pertinent reflections upon practical dilemmas associated with human expansion in a West African forest environment, and (2) illuminate current patterns of resource exploitation and violence in the region.

The first commentary is, in essence, a discourse that addresses the issue of accountability of individuals to the group in 'egalitarian' forest edge rice-farming communities struggling to come to terms with the locally destabilizing consequences of international trade in forest products (ivory, rare animals, wild spices, kola nuts and latterly timber). But the same forest environment is important also for its reserves of precious minerals (principally diamonds, and some gold). The young men employed in digging these minerals in remote low-technology forest workings are troubled by a rather different set of global–local articulations. To them, the issue at stake is the ironic contrast between their present tenuous living conditions and the promises of security and permanence the outside world seeks in their environment. Diamonds are (supposedly) 'for ever'. Conservationists seek to rescue the rain forest for posterity. These hopes sit oddly with the reality of life on a rain forest diamond mine in the middle of a war fostered by external interests. New and strident voices from such unstable wilderness sites tell us that the world is a very different place from the way its international environmental managers conceive it to be.

FIGHTING FOR SURVIVAL: THE MORALITY OF TRADE IN FOREST PRODUCTS

Rice farmers and entrepreneurs

The Mende-speaking peoples of southern and eastern Sierra Leone and north-west Liberia live on the western edge of the Upper Guinean block of the rain forests of West Africa. For several centuries Mende forest edge village farming communities have been engaged in the labour-intensive task of reducing high forest to farm land suitable for dry land rice cultivated by bush fallowing methods. Rice is a short-season crop (typically maturing in 3–4 months), and requires considerable informal sharing of labour among household groups in order to deal with labour bottlenecks in planting, weeding and harvest (Richards 1986). Failure to mobilize timely labour results in cumulative inefficiencies in farming, and is the major cause of seasonal hunger. Seasonal hunger can be managed either by cooperation, or by resort to credit from village merchants. Egalitarianism in inter-household social relations (a feature of other rice-farming communities in the region, cf. Linares 1992) is strongly defended, but merchants provide crucial assistance when these cooperative arrangements fail (as they must in years in which general hunger prevails).

Merchants in forest edge villages typically trace their origins to communities in the Mande world of the Upper Niger basin (in Guinea and Mali). 'Mandingo' traders may first have contacted forest edge communities to establish regional trade in commodities such as salt and kola nuts directed towards the savanna. Taking up more permanent residence in forest communities and marrying locally, Mande merchants also quickly established trade in forest products (ivory, camwood and skins of rare animals, including leopard, chimpanzee and crocodile) with Europeans on the coast, from the fifteenth century onwards. In an apparent attempt to secure such trading interests along the Atlantic littoral one Manding group, the 'Mane' of Cape Mount, pursued a series of military campaigns in the Sierra Leone hinterland during the sixteenth century. These campaigns have become known to historians as the Mane Invasion (Rodney 1970). Linguistic evidence suggests that the Mane may have been mainly Vai (Hair 1964, 1967). Today, the Vai, a Mande-phone group noted for their mercantile activity, live astride the southernmost portion of the Sierra Leone–Liberia border.

From an early date, then, many rural communities in the Sierra Leone interior will have been familiar with the problems and political challenges that arise in the context of trying to strike a balance between egalitarian values associated with successful rice farming, and non-egalitarian values (a respect for both hierarchy and individualism) associated with the further extension of regional and international trade. The historical ethnography of the region contains a number of snapshots of political leaders seeking to balance the equation as best they might. The following two instances will suffice. Rodney (1970) notes that in the eighteenth century, when people were busy on their rice farms in the forests behind the Sherbro estuary, chiefs stepped in to close down trade in its entirety. The late eighteenth-century English merchant reformer, Henry Smeathman, was told by informants on the Sherbro coast that if he persisted with his technical innovation in rice agriculture, the sickle (a threat to the genetic integrity of planting material upon which the entire community depended), his agents would be brought to book via witchcraft ordeals (Richards 1996).

Evidence of the same balancing act is not hard to find in local politics to this day. Mende chiefs accused of inclining too much towards the interests of local merchants will often make public statements of commitment to egalitarian values, for example, by encouraging the building of village grain stores, or by ordering the clearing of community rice farms, or by advocating the formation of farm labour exchange groups. They might at the same time take a tough line against farmers who clear more land than they are eventually able to plant; this *de facto* indication of a breakdown in labour-sharing arrangements is an offence known in Mende as *lobai* (waste). Finally, where general hunger looms (due to poor or excessive rains), local by-laws forbidding merchants to purchase and export local rice during the hungry season will be pressed into service to ensure that rice is available for loan to local farming families (Richards 1986).

The attitude towards Mandingo merchants among Mende rice-farming households tends to vary from tolerance of a necessary evil to a more positive acceptance of those merchants who align themselves with local concerns through marriage. An in-marrying merchant has in effect signed up to participation in the local egalitarian networks of inter-family farm labour exchange, and thus has more than one route to loan recovery. Down on their luck, farmers welcome the extra flexibility to repay loans in labour as well as cash or kind, but they are not unaware that they pay dearly for the credit on offer. Merchants become too firmly enmeshed with the local domestic scene at the risk of losing their trading capital to family demands.

But the moral economy of credit is not the only source of ambiguity in the relationship between rice farmers and Mande traders. The record of participation in international trade, where networks peter out on the forest edge, is littered with misunderstandings, broken promises and unenforceable contracts, trickery and violence. The trade-related low-intensity conflicts now raging in this border region have only served to remind local communities of how much they lose by entering this economic vortex.

A sense of the despair caused by such developments is apparent in an elderly hunter's account of how the trade in forest products was first established in Sembehun on the western edge of the Gola Forest. This account, referring to events in the mid-nineteenth century, was recorded months before the onset of hostilities in the Liberian civil war, but there are striking similarities between the mid-nineteenth-century social catastrophe it describes and the events set to overwhelm the border region (Richards 1996).

The story tells how a group of merchants from Bopolu (a small Mandingo town now in south-west Liberia) established contracts with local hunters to supply ivory, leopards' teeth and skins in return for salt, guns and trade gin. Having fulfilled their side of the bargain, the Sembehun hunters then rounded up the young men of the community to head-load these items to the coast (probably at Cape Mount). The youths never returned. Plied with food and drink on board the ships of a Spanish (Cuban?) slaver at Cape Mount, the boys were promptly hijacked into slavery. Meanwhile, their passions inflamed with gin, local leaders began to quarrel over the division of the profits from the new trade. Soon they were plunged into war using the new weapons supplied by their Mandingo agents. The story ends on a pathetic note. Sugar, supplied by the chief broker of the trade in Bopolu, was divided up among the heads of household in the community, to assuage suspicions roused by the non-reappearance of the young men of the village. The sugar is presented as the first instalment on the fabulous riches the young men will soon remit to their parents from a better world overseas.

Bɔni hinda

The Smithsonian Institution in Washington possesses, in its archives, a strange collection of magical paraphernalia made out of chimpanzee skulls, collected in the forests of northern Liberia during the nineteenth century and labelled 'Mandingo' (an ethnonym applied in Liberia and Sierra Leone to the class of merchants involved, historically, with the spread of Islam and trade within the rain forest region of the western half of West Africa). The purpose of the following notes is to explain how and why this endangered forest primate has become a particular focus for the moral concerns of those forest-dwelling villagers who fear Margaret Thatcher may have been correct – that there is no such thing as society, only families and individuals. One strand of local opinion considers that it may have been the corrosive influence of trade in forest products, directed by the Mandingo, that first brought about this unhappy state of affairs.

In 1989 I organized a survey of the impact, on Mende villagers, of a number of slogans used by conservation programmes in Sierra Leone. One such slogan was a vehicle sticker designed by the Primate Society of Great Britain – 'primates, their future is our future'. Most interviewees inferred (correctly) that the slogan implied that humans and other primates had a common destiny. Several informants found this notion quite appalling. Their reasons were straightforward. Whenever real chimpanzees are abundant they provide 'cover' for a form of politically motivated sorcery known as *ngolo hinda* (literally 'chimpanzee business'). Allegedly, practitioners of 'chimpanzee business' carry out ritual murders while disguised as chimpanzees in order to boost their political charisma.

Ngolo hinda is one of the forms assumed by a set of beliefs, widespread among rural peoples in the Upper Guinean forests, to which the term 'cannibalism' has sometimes been applied, for example, in colonial legal documents (Kalous 1974). Similar practices of ritual murder supposedly involve the leopard and the Nile crocodile. There is no adequate English generic term, so it is better to follow the suggestion of the Mende historian Abraham (1975) and refer to this complex of ideas by the Mende terms untranslated (the most suitable label to cover all three cases is *bɔni hinda*).

Those who believe that *bɔni hinda* occurs have the notion that the perpetrators of the ritual murders disguise themselves in the skins of wild animals and murder their victims with special knives intended to simulate the attack of the animal in question, or (alternatively) that they prosecute such an attack by turning themselves into the desired animal by magical means (lycanthropy, cf. Jackson 1989). The aim of these murders is to acquire ingredients for a 'medicine' called *bɔfima* (a word Migeod (1926) claims to be of Mandingo origin, meaning 'black bag'). This medicine is said to be capable of 'refreshing' the political charisma of those who perpe-trate such murders. Possessing the medicine is thought to make the face of a person who aspires to political leadership 'shine' in a crowd and so compel attention and loyalty, for example, during the campaign meetings that precede chieftaincy elections and other local political contests.

It is an open question whether or not *bɔni hinda* murders actually take place, or are largely or mainly conjured up in the minds of those who fear the possibility. Cases occur in the legal records of the Colony and Protectorate of Sierra Leone from the early to mid-nineteenth century (Kalous 1974; Stanley 1919), and continue to arise from time to time today (e.g. nine persons from Kori Chiefdom in Kpa-Mende country were executed for alleged involvement in such activities in 1977). One of my key informants over a number of years of fieldwork had been accused of 'chimpanzee business' and arrested on four separate occasions during his lifetime (first in the 1940s and most recently in 1987). As a blacksmith, renowned for the quality of his hunting guns, he was always considered a frighteningly powerful 'loner', though very prominent in village politics. He was suspected of having attempted to murder a child born to one of his wives as the result of an affair. He had been unable to revenge himself directly, since the woman died shortly after the child was born and the father fled the village. Subsequently, whenever any child in the village took fright in the bush, perhaps disturbed by the sudden noises of real chimpanzees, a frequent crop-raiding pest in the area, this old accusation of *bɔni hinda* would rise up to haunt the man, and police investigations would recommence (only to be damped down by the subsequent payment of a substantial bribe).

Ethological models for *bɔni hinda*

Elsewhere I have reviewed the evidence that belief in *bɔni hinda* reflects known characteristics of the animal species in question (Richards 1993) and will only briefly summarize that material here. In all three cases it is the apparent element of deliberation – perhaps even premeditation – that marks out these three species as being different from other dangerous animals. Snakes, elephants, buffalo and bongo also sometimes kill humans but only attack when provoked (i.e. when cornered, or under attack from a hunter). Leopard, Nile crocodile and chimpanzee, by contrast, hunt and kill humans for food or sport. They are the only animals to do so in the Upper Guinean forest. Leopard and crocodile will apparently stalk and then eat their victims. The chimpanzee does worse; on occasion it will seize a sleeping baby left in shade at the edge of a forest farm while the parents are busy with farm work, or mug without apparent provocation a child on a forest path and proceed to mutilate its victim (damage to the genitals frequently results – primatologists agree that such attacks are possible, but some suggest that 'play' rather than 'attack' was intended, the animal not knowing its own strength).

Encroachment on the forest, and the elaboration of regional trade in forest resources, may have significantly changed people's experience of these dangerous animals. The Mende refer to the round-nose crocodile, found in the upper reaches of forest-zone rivers, as 'mother's brother' to the much more dangerous Nile crocodile. The latter species is restricted to the navigable reaches of rivers in the coastal zone, and up-country merchants would have discovered it as a hazard to life only through establishment of direct links with European merchants on the West African coast. Village chiefs, seeking to manage the potentially destabilizing effects of greatly increased trade in forest products via marriage alliances with Mandingo merchants, meanwhile found themselves, literally, 'mother's brother' to the village 'loan shark'. In the case of leopards and chimpanzees, violent attacks on humans reflect the pressure of human encroachment on the habitat of these animals. Mende hunters characterize human-eating leopards as being, typically, old males frequenting villages on the look-out for goats, perhaps unable to stalk more agile prey in the forest. Similarly, chimpanzees used to human presence are notorious among Mende farmers as raiders of tree-crop plantations around villages. Power (1992) – controversially – has argued that closely monitored chimp populations such as those at Gombe have developed a greater propensity for violence as a result of their familiarity with the presence of human observers (provision of 'food aid' to facilitate observation by researchers may cause conflict due to overcrowding, for example). Mende villagers have a not dissimilar idea that chimpanzee violence serves in some way as a distressing precedent for the kind of lapses in human moral values that intensification of forest resource exploitation provokes.

'Wild men of the woods': patrons who 'consume' their clients

Violence among real-life chimpanzees (now known to include cannibalism) sets a precedent for appalling possibility in human affairs, that of *bɔni hinda*. But *bɔni hinda* is an irregular feature of Mende rural life (cf. Gittins 1987 on the periodic moral panics in Mende communities that lead to the hiring of a witch-finder). Accusations arise only at particular moments of social tension, generally associated with power struggles among leaders. To grasp why Mende villagers are predisposed at these moments to fear 'cannibalistic' attacks on women and children it is necessary to examine the character of Mende village political institutions.

Mende rural political culture is strongly clientelistic, dominated by the needs and ambitions of *numuwaisia* (literally 'big people'). These are the village leaders who sit atop the various unstable patron–client formations that comprise, in alliance, the main structures of public life in Mende farming communities (Richards 1986). As is typical of such political formations, the rise and fall of individual *numuwaisia* is often quite unpredictable (Richards 1986), leading to considerable local speculation about the methods used to acquire and keep political power. Whenever the order of precedence among patrons is (relatively) settled, clients can estimate the consequences of their continued support for a given patron, and some degree of (albeit temporary) social harmony prevails. The Mende ideal is, as a proverb puts it, a social system in which everyone is 'for' or 'behind' someone else and no one can claim to be 'for' her/himself. But when rival *numuwaisia* lock horns in serious and often violent competition, their followers are reminded how insubstantial are the social agreements that bind together the different networks. There is understandable concern for the accountability of leaders when such struggles turn violently unstable.

What penalties will the winner exact from the supporters of the rival candidate in a chieftaincy contest fought with the passionate intensity described by Ferme (1992)? What stops a leader from exacting violent reprisals among his own supporters (allegedly the cause of the split between Liberian war-lords Charles Taylor and Prince Johnson)? In short, power struggles among *numuwaisia* provide a sobering reminder that the people at the top are not bound by the rules of the system. One Mende response to this worrying political discovery is moral critique based on ideas about *bɔni hinda*.

The 'culture theory' of Mary Douglas and colleagues provides a persuasive standpoint from which to probe the conceptual orientation of *bɔni hinda*. Douglas (1989) has argued that social institutions can be usefully characterized by the position they occupy within a classificatory 'space' defined by three main axes of organizational orientation: hierarchy, egalitarianism and individualism. Situating Mende village social groupings within this frame, it is clear that the ordinary followers of a 'big person' tend to place particular stress on egalitarian values when ordering relations among themselves. These egalitarian values are functional to the organization of labour in rice farming (the main subsistence activity) because labour bottlenecks sharply limit the productivity of individual farm enterprises unless there is flexible pooling of labour on a rotational basis (Richards 1986). By contrast, the ladder of patronage, basic to inter-village and inter-regional politics and trade, is strongly hierarchical. Anyone who aspires to act as a patron at the local level will be the client of some figure acting on the regional level, and so on up to apex of national politics, where 'cabinet government' is an uneasy coalition between the major political patrons within the national system. In times of political tranquillity, local 'big people' are 'under' regional patrons who are in turn 'behind' various national power brokers. From time to time, however, the rungs on the ladder become rotten. The ladder itself threatens to collapse under the weight of client demands or the pressures of external circumstances (e.g. the imposition of colonial rule, or a major shift in regional balance of trade). It is then that leaders switch (or appear to switch in the eyes of clients fearing abandonment and dreading potentially unstable outcomes) into a more individualistic mode of operation, as they urgently seek to reposition themselves and their followers in a rapidly changing world.

In the absence of ideological commitment to notions such as the 'hidden hand' of market forces, and the legacy of institutional investments that buffers such beliefs in the Western world, individualism may seem highly threatening, both to the carefully balanced egalitarianism among peers necessary to run subsistence agriculture, and to the continued effective functioning of both the monopsonistic networks of trade that 'drain' local products towards international markets and the 'reverse' networks of patronage that distribute political favours. These perceived threats to accountability of social actions within such weak institutional settings come into imaginative focus via the most dreadful form of individualism that the Mende can conceive – that of *bɔni hinda*: the seizing of political power through the mutilation and magical consumption of the vital organs of the most vulnerable members of society.

In her book *How Institutions Think* (1989), Mary Douglas discusses a hypothetical case in which a group of stranded explorers is faced with circumstances in which survival of the majority is only possible by practising cannibalism on one of the members of the party. She argues that groups dominated by egalitarian or hierarchical values, faced with this option, would be unable to pick a victim. Only groups dominated by individualism would have the requisite notions of social accountability to permit them to conceive of a *procedure* for the selection of a victim. It seems that rural Mende have arrived at a very similar set of conclusions with regard to the social circumstances under which 'cannibalism' is conceivable as a possible project. Fear of *bɔni hinda* arises precisely at the point where rampant individualism seems set to overwhelm other procedures of social accountability based on hierarchical and egalitarian principles.

FIGHTING FOR A FUTURE: CONSERVATION AND FORGOTTEN YOUTH

Clandestine diamond mining in the forest

In the foregoing example, *bɔni hinda* has been analysed as the discourse of farming versus trade (specifically, trade in hunted forest products). Within a political formation dominated by loose associations of patron–client networks it represents an attempt to work out some of the tensions that arise between distinct systems of production grounded in knowledge systems that operate on local and regional scales. But in addition to valuable rice-farming opportunities and animal products the forested regions of eastern Sierra Leone and neighbouring Liberia are rich in mineral resources, notably diamonds.

These can be mined with the simplest facilities and infrastructural support. Gangs of young men (tributors), sponsored by urban-based Lebanese or Mandingo merchants, or state officials (civil servants and officers in the police and army), camp in the forest for months at a time digging and sieving diamond-bearing alluvial gravels. Sponsors of operations on more accessible sites possess government operating licences. Diggings in the remote forest wildernesses on the Liberia–Sierra Leone border, however, are more often clandestine operations. This is certainly true of those in the gazetted forest reserves, where all mining activity is prohibited.

In forest operations the digging teams must head-load everything they need, and heavy items of equipment such as diesel-driven pumps are uncommon. Typical kit for a clandestine mining operation in the forest will be buckets, spades, sieves, a cutlass to make a shelter, a shotgun to supply meat, a few pots and pans, a ghetto-blaster and a supply of recreational drugs. Local back-up comes from the various isolated villages in the lightly populated enclaves in the border-zone boundary wilderness. These villages are sometimes beyond the reach of the modern state, and off-limits to all but the miners and their sponsors (known as 'supporters'). Supporters of clandestine mining operations may be considered to have only dubious loyalty to either Sierra Leonean or Liberian states. The miners themselves are young male school drop-outs (no women are allowed on diggings so as not to spoil the luck (*haija*) of the site). Some are voluntary exiles, for example, school drop-outs looking for excitement and quick cash, but many are more justly considered to be economic refugees from two state systems badly affected by economic mismanagement, international aid conditionalities and political turmoil.

Diamond diggings are often very violent places. The young miners keep each other under constant scrutiny, since a diamond is easily secreted and stolen. Sponsors can generally rely upon this self-policing to minimize losses, since a diamond without provenance sells for little more than the one-fifth of the local price that typically diamond diggers get as their share of the profits of the operation. At times, before the Liberian civil war closed the market, a gang of miners might be tempted by a big stone to head across the border to Monrovia, but sponsors generally would quickly get to hear about such thefts from informers, and sometimes violently take the law into their own hands.

Silent listeners in the forest

In March 1991 a small Libyan-trained guerrilla movement, the Revolutionary United Front (RUF), allied with, and modelled on, the National Patriotic Front of Liberia (NPFL), one of the major factions in the Liberian civil war, crossed the Sierra Leone border either side of the boundary wilderness comprising the Gola Forest reserves, and began to organize a rural rebellion intended to overthrow the All Peoples Congress (APC) government of President Joseph Saidu Momoh. The first priority of the RUF was to recruit and train an army of dissident youths to carry out the intended programme of rural destabilization. Isolated groups of diamond diggers on the border were soon swept up into the ranks of the RUF. Exploiting to the full the alienation of some of these young people from the state, the RUF sought to establish RENAMO-like bands capable of living for long periods off the land and of overcoming better-armed opposition through skilful use of ambush tactics.

It seems that many of the young recruits adapted quickly to an enforced existence as rebels. Their life may have been little different from pre-war life on a typical clandestine diamond mining site in the forest. Some were trained as guerrillas but still continued to dig for their new sponsors from time to time at intervals in the fighting. Others may have been conscripted and used primarily as *de facto* mine slaves (this phenomenon has since been reported from areas along the Liberian border controlled by other factions in the Liberian civil war). The proceeds from diamonds were needed to pay for the RUF war machine, and the diamonds were sold through trade channels opened up within NPFL-controlled territory in Liberia.

The spread of warfare throughout this forested borderland region was fuelled by a contradiction at the heart of the international community's new-found interest in tropical rain forest conservation, and one widely apparent to diamond-digging youth. Rain forests are supposed to be an evolutionary Eden, remnants of a natural world once wholly outside the human domain. But by reason of their remoteness and inaccessibility such forests also provide a zone of opportunity for clandestine activities 'beyond the pale'. Taking the rhetoric of the global free market at face value, diamond diggers might prefer to seek their fortunes overseas. But the western world applies free-market principles only to commodities, not to labour. The alternative for these youngsters, then, is to retreat into the West's evolutionary Eden and live off their wits, knowing full well that few outsiders will have the courage or knowledge to follow and scrutinize what they are doing. Preferring Rambo-style or Kung Fu dress, and cued into the modern world of media communications via radio, satellite television and telephone links, these youngsters are poles apart from the standard image of 'indigenous forest peoples'. Accordingly, they go about their business largely unseen. Considered of no account, these invisible listeners in the forest have felt free to parley their local knowledge with brokers of distinctly sinister intent.

Pandebu, 1989

To reach Pandebu our survey party left Lalehun, the Gola Project's base camp on the western edge of the Gola North Reserve, an hour before dawn. First we followed the old and overgrown track abandoned by the timber company when logging of the Gola North reserve proved too difficult and expensive in the 1970s. A mile or two later we picked up the smuggler's rocky footpath through unlogged forest that climbs the fifteen or so weary miles to the low but rugged summit of the Gendema Hills, before dropping sharply into the valley trench of the Moro River, the international border between Sierra Leone and Liberia. On the way we met a group of four Limba diamond diggers from the far north-west of

Sierra Leone. Sponsored in their mining activities by a senior civil servant from the northern provincial headquarters town of Makeni, they were returning home from Pandebu. Around midday we rested briefly at a point in the high forest marked by a large skull, the last remains of an elephant poached by a Liberian army officer in 1986. Elephants prefer to seek refuge during the dry season in the extensive swampy lowlands of the neighbouring Gola East reserve, venturing into the more rugged terrain of Gola North on foraging expeditions only from time to time. Even so, we passed a hollow close to the path with signs of recent elephant activity – one footprint judged to be perhaps two or three days old had neatly superimposed upon it the even fresher footprint of a large chimpanzee. Stopping only to note the number and strength of cartridge cases abandoned by hunters on the forest path, we arrived on the outskirts of Pandebu towards evening.

The first (and surprising) sign of human habitation was a lean-to mud shed housing the oven of the village bakery. Here, in one of Sierra Leone's least accessible villages, a Fula migrant from the Republic of Guinea kept satisfied his rural clientele's sophisticated taste for that excellent French innovation, the fresh baguette. Diamond diggers do not deprive themselves of life's little luxuries.

Entering the village we discovered ourselves in a settlement of perhaps 350 people, with numerous substantially built houses, a mosque and a number of *semei* (open-sided square buildings in which hammocks were slung for their owners' evening-time relaxation and conversation around a late rainy-season log fire). Several of these buildings were already relaying to all-comers the latest African news and comment courtesy of the BBC's *Focus on Africa* from large, well-endowed portable cassette-radios balanced on the *kakei* (the low walls of the hammock houses). Ears would prick up at any mention of Sierra Leone, Liberia or Guinea. Diamond miners may work hidden away in remote boundary wildernesses but they are in touch with the global telecommunications economy, making up their own minds about international debates concerning resources and development.

The latest pronouncements of world leaders concerning subjects of local interest – forest conservation and human rights in Africa, and the aid conditionalities that further limit educational and job prospects in a country like Sierra Leone – are greeted with cool and cynical appraisal. They know that the voices they hear addressing them on these matters are the polished products of a privileged education. One year's fees for a child at a private secondary school in Britain would be enough to run an entire rural primary school in Sierra Leone for a decade. Their own education blighted, these young miners find themselves digesting the fact that a minister in the APC government sent his daughter to be educated in a British school once attended by the British minister of overseas aid.

As likely as not to cite the Krio proverb *wɔl nɔ lɛvɛl* ('life's unfair'), their ironic detachment from good causes such as conservation seems quite understandable.

Our team's arrival in Pandebu that evening, dead beat and desperately in need of whatever resources Mende traditional hospitality could muster, caused considerable embarrassment. We were unannounced, but not for want of trying. During the previous two months our project had attempted to complete the formal procedures for a visit to Pandebu, a possible base from which to survey uses of forest resources on the eastern side of the Gola North reserve. A letter prepared by the Senior District Officer in Kenema requested the paramount chief of Nomo Chiefdom to offer assistance in our work. This proved hard to deliver. The chief was unavailable on several visits to his headquarters at Faama, and was called away at short notice from a meeting booked several days in advance. After several weeks of frustration, one of our research assistants, well known in Pandebu, offered a short-cut solution by hiking directly across the forest to deliver the letter from the authorities in Kenema to the town chief of Pandebu in person. But despite protracted negotiations the village authorities decided they must first consult with the paramount chief. No reply came. The forest survey programme was now seriously behind schedule, so we decided to chance an unannounced visit, hoping local standards of hospitality would prevail over political diffidence. Indeed this proved to be the case, and after some initial awkwardness we were given places to sleep.

A quick dash to the Moro river to wash that evening suggested the nature of the difficulties caused by our visit. Close to the river on the Sierra Leonean side we passed the workings of a group of Liberian diamond miners. When we arrived at the river a Liberian ferry-man was already half across the river, in his dug-out, to meet us, assuming we wished to enter Liberia using this totally unsupervised crossing. How many of these there are between the official border posts in Kailahun and at the Mano River bridge in the south is not known, but they are likely to be quite numerous. Even in the most thickly forested areas there are regular tracks through the reserves, and the upper portions of the Moro and Mano rivers are no great obstacles to passage except when in spate at the height of the rains. The splendid rapids on the Moro some five miles north of Pandebu are said to be fordable (with the river water constrained to deep niches in the rock outcrops) during the dry season.

Back in Pandebu later that evening we learned the basic facts of local transport geography. To reach Faama, the headquarters of Nomo Chiefdom, required an eight-hour trek on a rough track skirting the river. A rickety vehicle might or might not be available the next morning in Faama for the tedious, expensive and unreliable trip over forty miles of very poorly maintained dirt roads to Kenema. Onward travel to Freetown might take the best part of a third day. But by making the canoe trip across the Moro Pandebu, people could reach the road-head in Liberia after only three hours, and generally reckoned to be in Monrovia that same evening. Monrovia was the source of the Fula baker's flour and of the cement, corrugated roofing sheets and other heavy items used in building and equipping Pandebu's several substantial houses. Monrovia was also the place where many of the diamonds mined in Pandebu were sold. Some of the miners were of Liberian origin, and 'supported' by Monrovia-based business interests (Lebanese traders and others). But most Pandebu citizens seemed to have identity cards for both countries. In effect they were citizens of two states – or none.

The demands of hospitality met, it took several earnest discussions the following morning before we were able to convince the village authorities to allow us to stay for a few days and begin surveys. An interesting feature of these discussions was that they hinted at a considerable local contest between community power brokers keen to keep outsiders at arm's length in the interests of mining sponsors exploiting the recession-shrunk edges of the two state systems, and the ordinary Pandebu citizenry – heavily migrant in origin, and (as noted) sophisticated in its understanding of global as well as local political and cultural trends – keen to be a recognized part of this wider world. In the end the second body of opinion prevailed, and we were permitted to stay, specifically on the understanding that our surveys would help put Pandebu back on the map. The absence of a primary school was the thing most keenly felt in this community otherwise wealthy by the standards of much of rural Sierra Leone. Our proposal to undertake household censuses met with strong approval because it would make evident the number of school-age children resident in the village not receiving any kind of formal education. Might our report, we were asked, not then state the case for a second local development priority without which a school would be insupportable – a road? How, without it, would the materials to build a school be transported? What kind of teacher would ever agree to come and settle in a place so far off the beaten track, without the chance to leave it from time to time?

When compiling the socio-economic recommendations stemming from the Gola Study, I tried to keep faith with these commitments in two ways: first, by suggesting to the special ministerial adviser to the President that a road to connect the villages on the far side of Gola North was an urgent priority if these places were not to be lost, *de facto*, to the Liberian sphere, and second, by making the case (in the final report on the Gola study (Davies and Richards 1991)) for school and road as part of a linked development and conservation package for the region. The first approach was politely discounted; the second brought forth the strong objections of the conservationists interested in the future of Gola (including a written request by the joint-author of the report that he be specifically disassociated from any such recommendation: Davies 1991, personal communication).

But now the issue is academic. Pandebu is no more. It was taken over by the RUF early in the rebellion, and is reported to have been totally destroyed in subsequent fighting between RUF and military forces of ULIMO and the Sierra Leone government. The survivors are displaced persons in Lalehun and other villages on the western side of the forest, or have been taken by the retreating rebels into Liberia. A window of opportunity was opened for the rebels by the failure of the Sierra Leone state to secure its frontiers in a region that had become a refuge not just for wild animals and rare plant species but also for young people blocked in their hopes of more conventional progress. These potential recruits were a magnet for the RUF. There can be debate about whether the RUF was propelled, in this strategic ambition, by Libyan youth revolutionary ideology or by concern to secure monopoly control over rich diamond deposits and forest resources (Richards 1995). But the local clamour for a school and a road must now be seen as a last cry for conventional help before a more deadly form of external 'assistance' arrived. Pandebu has now paid for its privacy in full.

CONCLUSION

This chapter has described two struggles to debate the morality of forest conversion in part of the Upper Guinean forest block in West Africa. An older discourse attempts to lift the lid on the way in which wild animals – and chimpanzees in particular – provided 'cover' for unbridled individualism in forest resource exploitation; a discourse that might validly be considered a way of trying to secure a better balance between local and regional knowledge systems and interests. In the second case the point at issue is the *lack* of articulation between global and local viewpoints, as expressed in the failure of the outside world to interest itself in the educational needs of remote communities of forest diamond diggers, fully aware, through their media links, of what they are missing.

Bɔni-hinda is a commentary that enfolds within its moral and ethical concerns feedback on the process of deforestation and its problematic consequences for the people of the region. That such beliefs are simply written off by the rest of the world as 'barbarous misunderstandings' of reality is testimony to the distance that outsiders have yet to travel to gain any insight into the real dilemmas of collective human survival at nature's expense. At least the Mende have some sense of the magnitude of the problem this poses (in contrast to the glib sentiments sometimes expressed by rich country supporters of international conservation), even if (like the rest of us) they lack answers concerning how to live in harmony with nature while meeting human material needs and ethical commitments.

In the second case it is not chimpanzees in the wild but the 'naturalism' of the conservationists – the naive assumption that a *laisser-faire* approach is nature's best or most adequate defence – that has provided some of the 'cover' behind which war-lord individualism on the Liberia–Sierra Leone border has taken shape, feeding off a global over-supply of recreational drugs, videos of violence, cheap automatic rifles and political hypocrisy. Will the world be able to count on local intellectual imagination to invent for a second time a moral discourse capable of forging effective links between local knowledge (in this case the knowledge of diamond diggers) and global concerns (this time the agenda of the conservationists) sufficient to constrain the individualistic excesses that otherwise threaten to consume Africa's remaining wilderness areas?

REFERENCES

Abraham, A. (1975) 'Cannibalism and African historiography'. In A. Abraham (ed.) *Topics in Sierra Leone History: A Counter-colonial Interpretation.* Freetown, Sierra Leone: Leone Publishers.
Davies, A. G. and Richards, P. (1991) *Rain Forest in Mende Life: Resources & Subsistence Strategies in Rural Communities Around the Gola North Forest Reserve (Sierra Leone).* Report to the UK Overseas Development Administration: Department of Anthropology, University College London.
Douglas, M. (1989) *How institutions think.* London: Routledge.
Ferme, M. C. (1992) *'Hammocks Belong to Men, Stools to Women': Constructing and Contesting Gender Domains in a Mende Village (Sierra Leone, West Africa).* Ph.D. dissertation, University of Chicago.
Gittins, A. J. (1987) *Mende Religion: Aspects of Belief and Thought in Sierra Leone.* Studia Instituti Anthropos 41. Nettetal, Germany: Steyler Verlag.
Hair, P. (1964) 'An early seventeenth-century vocabulary of Vai', *African Studies* 23(3/4): 129–39.
—— (1967) 'Ethnolinguistic continuity on the Guinea Coast', *Journal of African History* 8(2): 247–68.
Jackson, M. (1989) 'The man who could turn into an elephant'. *Paths towards a clearing: radical empiricism and ethnographic enquiry.* Bloomington, IN: Indiana University Press.
Kalous, M. (1974) *Cannibals and Tongo Players of Sierra Leone.* Privately published: Auckland.
Kaplan, R. (1994) 'The coming anarchy', *Atlantic Monthly*, February.
Linares, O. (1992) *Power, Prayer and Production: The Jola of Casamance, Senegal.* Cambridge: Cambridge University Press.
Migeod, F. W. H. (1926) *A View of Sierra Leone.* London: Kegan Paul, Trench, Trubner.
Power, M. (1992) *The Egalitarians, Human and Chimpanzee: An Anthropological View of Social Organization.* Cambridge: Cambridge University press.
Richards, P. (1986) *Coping with Hunger: Hazard and Experiment in a West African Farming System.* London: Allen & Unwin.

—— (1993) 'Natural symbols and natural history: chimpanzees, elephants and experiments in Mende thought.' In K. Milton (ed.) *Environmentalism: The View from Anthropology*, ASA Monograph 32. London: Routledge.

—— (1995) 'Rebellion in Liberia and Sierra Leone: a crisis of youth'. In O. W. Furley (ed.) *Conflict in Africa*. London: I. B. Taurus.

—— (1996) *Fighting for the Rain Forest: Youth, Resources and War in West Africa*. London: James Cuorcy.

Rodney, W. (1970) *A History of the Upper Guinea Coast*. Oxford: Clarendon Press.

Stanley, W. B. (1919) 'Carnivorous apes in Sierra Leone', *Sierra Leone Studies* (old series), March.

Afterword

Affirmative theory: voice and counter-voice at the Oxford decennial

Peter Harries-Jones

A sense of uneasiness pervaded the Oxford decennial, some of which will find its way into the published papers, but most of which could only be caught in the dynamics of the conference itself. The conference registered its uneasiness in verbal comments from the conference floor, and, in a much less expected and far more dramatic way, in a structural tension between the first three panels of the conference and the fourth panel, some papers of which are published here. The opening session of the conference was labelled 'Shifting contexts' (see also Strathern 1993). Whether the shift was to be towards encouraging cultural critique through use of experimental writing in anthropology (Marcus and Fischer 1986) or whether the shift was to be towards greater social relevance, was never clear. 'Crisis' in anthropology is an overworked term but the fourth decennial conference seemed throughout the week to be poised between a 'crisis of relevance' and a 'crisis of representation' in anthropology.

By design or by accident – and the evidence suggests that the organizers had a hand in this risky but successful tactic – our panel, 'What is social knowledge for?' was a turning point. The panel re-framed themes in 'Shifting contexts' and from its opening moments evoked a dialectic between the conference's dominant voice and a counter-voice. The dominant voice of the conference was theoretical, descriptive and individualistic in orientation. The counter-voice, on the other hand, presumed there was an intimate linkage between social purposes and anthropology which required activism.

One clash was over the issue of technoscience. The dominant voice seemed bent on evolving a post-modern dialectic between local and global – taking descriptions of globalized forms of culture as a point for departure. The counter-voice replied that instead of taking the pervasiveness of mass communications for granted, anthropologists should be active in explicating local cultures and 'situated knowledge'. It argued that 'situated knowledge', or its synonyms, always runs counter to knowledge in its technical form, unmasks the hidden power of the latter and thereby limits its effects.[1]

Another clash occurred over the purposes of theory. The counter-voice suggested that anthropology should do more than simply engage in theory for theory's sake. The counter-voice was insistent that the concerns of anthropology and the concerns of social equity were congruent. The position of the counter-voice was admirably summarized in Karim's paper, 'Anthropology without tears'. Karim poses the question of why the situating of ethnographic projects has rarely been acknowledged as a major problem in anthropology. The ethnographic question – why this group rather than another, why this locale rather than another – seems to be dictated by personal opportunity, rather than by any broader aim of ethnographic research.[2]

Karim claimed that the limitations of this conventional academic approach were now evident, for the discipline displays inattention and inaction on pressing global issues. Specifically, anthropologists seem unwilling to take up the subject of the perverse uses of western knowledge. Most western anthropologists seem totally unconcerned with the shape that dominant forms of western knowledge take in an international context. The powerful combination of western economics plus military strategy creates a constellation of events in time and space which perpetuate greed, violence and transnational tragedy. Yet the discipline is not only unwilling to take up the critique, but in ignoring these issues gives no relief to the native world from which it draws – and does little to lessen the shame of poverty, extinction and genocide which are that world's recurrent features.

Does this inaction derive from a lack of conscious knowledge about the perverse uses of western knowledge, or from pathologies in the construction of anthropological theory? Karim gives no answer. Instead, she suggests the need for an 'affirmative theory' in anthropology. In this chapter I want to spell out Karim's idea more concretely, since her paper mentions 'affirmative theory' only in passing. After probing for some clues as to anthropology's inaction, I wish to put her concept into the broader literature on social knowledge and social advocacy and finally to draw some conclusions about voice and counter-voice at the decennial conference.

AFFIRMATIVE THEORY

Any affirmative stance confirms and assents to a set of propositions about social equity or social equality. If it does not directly raise a call for action, the concept certainly implies rejection of inaction on social equity and social equality issues. This is also true of any advocacy approach. Karim's paper contains three suggestions or pointers towards the introduction of an affirmative theory. The first concerns current theory. To regain any credibility in the developing world, anthropology has to learn to demystify itself theoretically, and back away from the elite community that it currently socializes with its knowledge, Karim says. The field of theoretical anthropology in the West is enriched by every new discourse it adopts, but the people of the world from which anthropology draws its insights gain little in return (see also Yang, Chapter 5; and Ong, Chapter 4, this volume). Instead of increasing the distance of the inner circle of practising social scientists in West Europe and the United States from anthropologists of the developing world, the discipline should transform itself into a field of enquiry that is popular and representative, and reciprocal.

The second point concerns anthropological practice. Anthropology must take on the ethnocentricities of nationalism, not avoid them. It must refute the argument of those popular actors who in this age of modernity continue to make use of the combination of ethnocentrism and materialism in order to create their own versions of racism. The dynamics of global power currently criss-cross the lines of least resistance and are selective. One can easily predict who its victims are – indigenous minorities rather than majority populations, women and children rather than men, the elderly rather than youth, workers rather than producers, destitute states rather than the wealthy. Anthropology should, but does not, consider why some forms of ethnocentric violence are condoned by the West while other forms are marginalized as 'evil'.

The third is a point about style, and concords with other literature in recent years examining 'the crisis of representation' in anthropology. Anthropology's intellectual endeavours should be addressed to popular scholars of culture rather than continuing as a social science whose primary aim is to give an objective account of the ethnographic 'other'. Karim argues that the conclusion of many Malaysian students at the end of combined courses in sociology and anthropology is that while anthropological method for field research is still the most satisfying in terms of its ability to build involvement and conscientization, the interrelation of ethnography and theory in anthropology falls far short of necessary social objectives.

Karim states that anthropology's message should be 'integrative and relational, humanitarian and messianic' and from her point of view the teachers of that message, anthropologists, should frame their discipline with this in mind. It is clear therefore that affirmative theory implies 'consciousness-raising' and 'empowerment', or something similar. Both terms are dubious constructs in anthropology. 'Empowerment,' though it has the benefit of being a well-known human experience, is not a well-defined social process in the anthropological literature. This is in distinct contrast to participatory action research (PAR) or almost any other counter-discourse initiated in the third world, where the process is central to discussion of the socio-political aspects of knowledge (Fals-Borda 1990). Empowerment, like 'consciousness-raising', the older of the two terms, has received very unequal treatment in the two traditions – positivist and Marxist – which have dominated the sociology of knowledge over the last century. Perhaps here, in the literature of the sociology of knowledge, we may find some clues as to why modern anthropology holds the two notions in low regard, but reciprocally seems to lack capacities for its own auto-critique and epistemological correction, a trend which Karim finds so disturbing.

PRISONERS OF THEORY?

In the Marxist tradition consciousness-raising was a process tied mainly to the issues of social class dominance and of the 'oppressive elements of reality'. Though Marxists had general rules about how thinking and ideas developed together with human activity and how consciousness developed as human needs developed, they tended to link consciousness very specifically to class-consciousness and the understanding of political programmes. In Latin America the Spanish term for consciousness-raising is *conciéncia*, the Portuguese term *conscientizaçao*, 'learning to perceive social, political and economic contradictions and to take action against oppressive elements of reality' (Freire 1970: 19). As Paulo Freire put it:

> consciousness is in essence a 'way towards' something apart from itself, outside itself, which surrounds it and which it apprehends by means of its ideational capacity. Consciousness is thus by definition a method, in the most general sense of the word.
>
> (Friere 1970: 56)

In the Marxist explanation, 'social being' precedes consciousness, not the other way around. It is fundamental to Marxist understanding of social empowerment that empowerment is a process through which 'subjects', those who know and act, transform an object, 'concrete reality', both through dialectics and through 'authentic praxis'. A perception of reality not followed by critical intervention in the relationship of oppressor to oppressed 'will not lead to a transformation of objective reality – precisely because it is not a true perception' (Freire 1970: 37).

Clearly there is a need for a focus on the context of domination in any discussion of consciousness-raising, but is it justifiable to categorize any perception as being false or deluded if not framed in terms of the relations of political dominance and/or class relations? Surely power and ideology are not *global attributes* of human consciousness; put another way, human consciousness cannot be reduced to 'authentic praxis'. This mistakes the relation between reflection and action, for while a focus upon intentionality and praxis may be part of political empowerment, it is not the whole process of empowerment. Human action, like human consciousness, relies also on imagination, and on non-purposive social interaction ('play') and cultural predispositions. The neglect of these in a Marxist discussion of empowerment is a serious weakness and is perhaps a reason for its limited use in anthropology.[3]

On the other hand, positivists and many phenomenologists have made the question of consciousness-raising non-problematic in their discussion of the sociology of knowledge. A sociology of positivism could ill-afford to admit to obscurity in states of human consciousness. Berger and Luckmann who tried to take sociology beyond its positivist frames in the 1960s note that the sociology of knowledge originated as an enquiry of intellectuals about intellectuals and their own position in the twentieth-century state. As might be imagined, this examination produced and embedded an elite perspective of knowledge. Berger and Luckmann, writing at approximately the same time as Freire, tried to alter the direction of this discussion by turning the sociology of knowledge towards a sociology of everyday events. Their focus is the realm of 'common-sense knowledge', for it is '[common-sense] knowledge that constitutes the fabric of meanings without which no society could exist' (Berger and Luckmann 1967: 15).

I take Berger and Luckmann as an example for they are still cited in the social sciences as authoritative in this field of enquiry. Reviewing the Berger and Luckmann arguments a quarter of a century after publication, not only is it evident that some of their major suppositions about common-sense knowledge require re-thinking, but that they more or less ban provision for study of consciousness-raising in their social construction of knowledge. They suppose that the acquisition of social knowledge is derived through 'the identification of the self with the objective sense of the action of interaction'. This, I think, is no longer tenable because it renders too large a gap, a dualism, between the subject and the processes of interaction. Berger and Luckmann argue that the painful conflict between rules, and awareness of alternatives to rules, is in the end subordinated to social processes which generate objectified knowledge. Thus 'by virtue of the roles he plays the individual is inducted into specific areas of socially objectivated knowledge' (Berger and Luckmann 1967: 76).[4] Missing from their discussion are questions of reflectiveness, the details of a dialectic between identification of self by others which most anthropologists and sociologists would today find necessary. It is unsurprising that in their discussion of processes of socialization, Berger and Luckmann transpose forms of social dissent into 'problems' of abnormality, deviance and unsuccessful socialization (Berger and Luckmann 1967: 167–73).

If questions of self-identification are put 'beyond the purposes of discussion' (Berger and Luckmann 1967: 132), so too are possibilities for new action patterns inducing learning which, in turn, brings about epistemological change. To discuss such possibilities requires an understanding of double-loop reflectiveness, and Berger and Luckmann have no comprehension of this – as in their example of sociologists considering the sociology of knowledge. They argue that 'To include epistemological questions concerning the validity of sociological knowledge in the sociology of [common-sense] knowledge is like trying to push a bus in which one is riding' (Berger and Luckmann 1967: 13). The epistemological questions Berger and Luckmann rule out, though they may be self-referential, are crucial.[5] The problem for Berger and Luckmann lies in their image of the relationship of passengers to their bus. Theirs is an image of a school bus trundling along a country lane, or a bus full of holiday-makers moving along the expressway from town to seaside. But what if the bus was taking prisoners from gaol to the site of a prison labour project? Or what if the bus turned out to be Derrida's bus containing self-imprisoned epistemologists? In the latter instance 'the bus in which one is riding' assumes a very different form.

The Derrida analogy resembles the situation in which Karim made the presentation on 'affirmative theory' to the Oxford decennial conference. I was reminded of a similar paradoxical situation, that of social advocacy research in Canadian sociology. In Canada there has been a decrease in the theoretical opposition to social advocacy mainly because of the rise in the number of social movements, but this increase in the activity of advocacy has occurred without a corresponding increase in the practice of social advocacy in the university system. Spencer argues that the avoidance of advocacy research on the part of Canadian sociologists springs from constant reaffirmation of traditional values in academic research. Marxists might argue that academics are responding to the ideological demands of their capitalist masters, but Spencer believes that the position is more complex. Academics seem to be monitoring themselves in the research review process, and although research could include social advocacy they are obeying the umpires that they themselves have chosen. Canadian sociologists have themselves to blame for becoming prisoners of theoretical positions which are devoid of engagement on the unsettled issues of knowledge and interests: 'Just as lesser mortals, sociologists are prisoners of their own beliefs. And they, too, deserve liberation' (Spencer 1991: 213).

SOCIAL MOVEMENTS

An advocacy approach is intended to alter both perceptions and conceptions of knowledge and in this sense goes beyond a purely factual cognitive domain to encompass 'consciousness-raising' and 'empowerment'. Because advocacy addresses percepts as well as concepts, is active rather than passive, is experiential in addition to being cognitive, advocacy has a variety of reflexive forms. One useful result of social advocacy may be to remove deeply embedded patterns of communication which hinder appropriate construction of knowledge. In short, advocacy is a type of 'applied epistemology' covering a range of issues about how information is constructed into 'facts', which are then taken as being 'objective knowledge' and lead to denial or refusal to consider alternatives.

In my own work I link the analysis of social advocacy to the formation of social movements. This link helps me to understand how existential conditions of social advocacy – these abstract notions of consciousness-raising and empowerment – fit social processes constructing knowledge and contribute to 'historicity' (see p. 165). It also provides a very broad canvas for an anthropologist, a canvas which must be global in scope if it is to tackle the urgent problems of our day – economic, environmental and military. Any sociologist or anthropologist who is to grapple with these issues requires theories matched to a praxis that encompasses a global reach.

Social movements provide such a linkage between theoretical ideas and global reach. They provide a particularly compelling link when the problem at hand combines political and social research, advocacy and the 'authoritative knowledge' of natural science. One example from my own experience occurred in the early 1980s, when it appeared that Ronald Reagan, then President of the United States, was taking seriously the possibility of using nuclear weapons in his confrontation with the USSR. Fortunately, at a time when tensions between the two nations were at their height, it became known that military research on the effects of nuclear exchange was tragically incomplete. While the US military had many studies on blast and radiation damage resulting from nuclear exchange, it had neglected to undertake research on dust, particulates and soot thrown up into the atmosphere as a result of the vortex created by nuclear blasts. The horrific aspects of this neglect of a broader perspective of the effects of nuclear exchange became known as 'nuclear winter'. The nuclear winter hypothesis proposed that the dust and soot clouds thrown up in an atomic exchange between the two superpowers – even in an exchange of minimal proportions compared with the number of warheads available – would cool the earth's atmosphere to the point that most of the world's nations would be unable to produce food for several seasons. In other words, nuclear exchange between the USA and the USSR would affect most of the world's non-combatant nations by causing a global famine. The peace movement's response to this information about 'nuclear winter' was to bring people out on the streets in demonstrations throughout Europe and North America, and in doing so, the movement contributed vitally, I believe, to the de-escalation of the nuclear threat.

A significant aspect of the nuclear winter hypothesis – and it always remained a hypothesis – was that the initial research on the question was locally based and concerned quite disparate issues; an investigation by German researches into the atmospheric effects of forest fires in Scandinavia; a theoretical exercise conducted in the USSR by members of the academy of computer scientists on a precise simulation of weather patterns in Siberia during a single winter month, from which they drew a notion of albedo effects; renewed investigation by paleo-anthropologists on the theory of meteorite impact causing the sudden disappearance of dinosaurs; and research undertaken by NASA scientists on dust storms on Mars gathered during their probe of the Martian atmosphere (Harries-Jones 1985).[6] These disparate local studies and their probable interrelationships galvanized the international scientific community. Regardless of scientists' ideological beliefs, of their political attitude towards the peace movement, or even of their status as citizens of the two hostile nations, the combination of scientific theoretical modelling and social movement praxis around nuclear winter produced a compelling example of what can be done, and how catastrophe in human history may be averted.

Of course, not all social movements have global reach, nor are all engaged in a response to a perceived threat of immanent extinction of the human species. The definition of a social movement is varied; the term may be used to designate very small groups, such as the urban movements characteristic of many cities of the Third World, or it may refer to the new social movements encompassing human rights, the women's movement, environmentalism and peace. Any anthropologist studying social advocacy and placing the study in the context of social movements must proceed with due caution about the range of reference. Nevertheless, there is a persistent attempt to divert attention from their global characteristics. In the United States, social movements are referred to as private interest groups and are nearly always placed in the same category as lobbyists funded by private corporate interests. This arises because the United States currently fashions public interest as the same, or even of lesser moral worth, than private interest and permits an undifferentiated lobbying process among respective 'interests', whether corporate, public or personal, to generate its legislative activity. In Great Britain social movements are nearly always called 'lobbyists', as if they were peripherals on a national political stage dominated by British political parties, a tactic which diverts attention away from their transnational standing. Canada retains the term 'advocacy groups', but here too, the term 'special interest groups' is frequently substituted, even though the so-called 'special interest' is usually a 'collective interest'.

The position of advocacy groups and social movements in Canada is somewhat different from either the United States or Great Britain in that the Canadian Federal Government funds a select number. It offers both annual sustaining grants as well as funding their presence at specific hearings. For example, a recent House of Commons committee hearing on ways and means of reducing spending on social programmes gave The National Association of Women and the Law, one of several women's advocacy groups, £40,000 to prepare its brief.[7] In addition, the Federal Government contributes approximately £200,000 to this organization as a sustaining annual grant. Not all advocacy groups are financially blessed in this manner, but these figures are representative of those that are. From one perspective the figures show that a number of Canadian advocacy groups have little grass-roots support and are financially dependent on the Federal Government for their continuation. From another perspective, this represents a flowering of the social advocacy process in Canada which has important consequences for the political health of the country as a whole.

As to why Canada has embedded social advocacy groups into its political process, so that the government actually pays the representatives of social collectivities to oppose them, is an interesting question that goes beyond the issues in this chapter. But it is significant that the development of this phenomenon is closely tied to a range of constitutional questions, including the perennial question of the Francophone majority presence in Quebec and minority presence of First Nations, or aboriginal peoples in Quebec and elsewhere in Canadian provinces. It is also tied to the recent creation of civil liberties in Canada by means of a formal constitutional instrument, the Canadian Charter of Rights and Freedoms which came into existence in 1982. And it is tied to the support of multiculturalism as a national policy in Canada, a policy stemming from the early 1970s.

Cleveland (1991) has suggested that in each of the cases listed above, liberalism's political idea of 'equality of opportunity', a definition which pervades Canadian politics no matter which party is in power, finds itself incapacitated. The liberal position conceptualizes equality of opportunity for abstract individuals but does not, and cannot, guarantee equality of conditions for concrete individuals. Since concrete individuals, as distinct from abstract individuals, are defined by their social relations with collectivities, liberals are unable to secure the interests of specific social groups. This situation is doubly ambiguous if specific social groups call for state intervention on their behalf when social group activity might harm the interests of another group. Such a situation has arisen with the political claims of the women's movement (Cleveland 1991: 193) but can be extended to many other instances from small ethnic groups living in Canada to that amorphous 'class interest' called environmentalists.

In any event, Canada has been a leader in this political innovation over the last two decades and it was no surprise that Canada took a lead in establishing non-governmental organization (NGO) involvement in the Earth Summit at Rio de Janeiro in 1992. The Canadian government is most likely to fund NGOs within its borders to take the lead once again in organizing a successor to Rio, a second global environmental conference.

For social theorists, a flowering of NGO and advocacy group presence in a nation-state has both theoretical and methodological implications. In the first place it is possible to see, in a very concrete manner, how modern nation-states utilize what Alain Touraine refers to as the reflective capacity of human societies to generate their own 'self-production'. 'Self-production', stressing as it does the recursive aspects of social formation and reproduction, is a concept alien to both Durkheimian and Marxist traditions. The term emphasizes all societies' 'ability to turn in on themselves, to work upon themselves by creating a *symbolic representation* of experience ... and by representing this production of themselves in the form of *cultural legitimation* of their self-generating activity' (Touraine 1981: 59).

Touraine's analysis of social movements is one of the very few that links social action to recursive formation of social knowledge.[8] His central notion of 'historicity' also builds on this. Historicity is at the very centre of cultural contestation between dominant groups and those social movements which oppose the dominant elite's cultural perspective:

> The sociology of social movements cannot be separated from a representation of a society as a system of social forces competing for control of a cultural field ... this sociology of action ceases to believe that conduct must be a response to a situation, and claims rather that the situation is merely the changing and unstable result of the relations between the actors who, through their social conflicts and via their cultural orientations, produce society.
>
> (Touraine 1981: 30)

Compared with Berger and Luckmann, Touraine is a 'radical constructivist' who regards the evident conflict generated by social movements less as a form of deviancy, as is the case in mainstream North American sociology, and more as an exemplification of an overall pattern of cultural action characteristic in the tensions of 'programmed society'.[9] And in the post-industrial or 'programmed society', Touraine argues, it is that fraction of *professionals* who perform the role that used to be played by artisan workers in industrial society. These professionals of the programmed society 'speak in the name of knowledge against an apparatus that seeks to subject knowledge to its own interests, and they ally themselves with those who are forced to the sidelines by a central apparatus and submitted to its power' (Touraine 1981: 22).

In short, Touraine finds a new place for the sociologist and/or anthropologist that is no longer entirely centred within academe. The professional researcher is not merely a rapporteur of social movements to other academics, nor a disinterested commentator about social movements' cultural orientation. Rather the researcher can become an active intervener in the birth of a social movement's epistemology and engage actively in its cultural critique.

METHOD IN SOCIAL ADVOCACY

By definition, the position of the professional researcher in affirmative theory, as in social advocacy, becomes attached to 'interested knowledge' and if researchers form part of the situation which they have to interpret, this conflict between participant activism and objectivity is supposed to endanger the value of their conclusions. The issue of 'value neutrality' has always been presented as being methodologically necessary because it supposedly guaranteed the truth of observation. Yet, according to Morgan, the assumptions of 'value neutrality' hide two doubtful propositions. They assume that the researcher is independent of the world and, reciprocally, that the world is external to the observer. In fact, the minds of researchers are never separable from the 'real objects' they observe, and this situation becomes readily apparent when the experience of scientists themselves is evoked. According to Morgan, the paths of scientific endeavour reveal a form of commitment and engagement to scientific problems not unlike the situation in which social advocates place themselves. The development of science occurs in community-specific situations in which a particular set of problems among a particular group of people interested in a particular issue produces new insights and knowledge. Morgan's position is that since all science is a process of engagement between scientists and that which they study, then assumptions of universal scientific discourse and 'value neutrality' paraded in textbooks need to be worked over again.

In Morgan's view an object gains in objectivity through comprehending the many ways in which the object is observed. We need to take into account the whole process of observation and interaction which leads to classification of evidence as objective knowledge, and to be especially wary if the claim to objectivity is made on the grounds that there is only a single method through which objective generalization can be derived. There are many different ways that appropriate generalization can be drawn, each resulting from engaging the object of study in different ways. Morgan argues that critical re-framing is the most important form of generalization that a social advocate can undertake. By challenging the basic definition of the problem at hand it is possible for social advocates to re-frame the contexts in which the issue first arose, and begin to reshape in a clear and systematic manner the outcomes likely to result from that re-framing. At the same time the advocate must apply 'systematic doubt' as a defence against dogmatism:

> In adopting the kind of scientific attitude which encourages us to identify both facts and counter-facts, arguments and counter-arguments, it is possible to build a rich and changing picture of the problems at hand, and to guard against the traps that often accompany the advocate's strong value orientation.

(Morgan 1991: 226)

Morgan's arguments have been used to good effect in defining the relationship of anthropology to environmentalism and the environmental movement (Milton 1993: 6,7,14). The global issues of a degraded environment are unlikely to be resolved through a single overarching method, Milton points out. Rather environmentalism is a form of transcultural discourse in which valid generalizations flowing from local and personal knowledge, the sort of cultural knowledge with which anthropologists are most familiar, interleave with the kinds of expert knowledge typical of natural science, which in turn interleaves with critical re-framing of issues – the knowledge most associated with advocacy groups and social movements. In my view the brief but spectacular history of the nuclear winter hypothesis provides a suitable model for this trend of interwoven references. And while distinction of levels of reference must always be taken into account, I believe such a model of interleaved references would be crucial for an affirmative theory.

THE CONFERENCE

Now let me return to the conference and draw some conclusions. As I have said, the dominant voice undertook a literal reading of 'shifting contexts' and several of the papers' authors were content to evoke images of anthropologists as neutral observers of a shift towards global cultural formation. For example, several papers were devoted to discussing varieties of commodity consumption and its effect on the 'creolization' of culture.[10] According to our counter-voice, the very example of creolization of culture, and its accompanying commodity forms, was an instance of the way in which 'the human' has become re-focused through the lens of technocracy. To insist that anthropologists remain neutral observers of this context was, in fact, to take an intellectual position about globalization, and allows little room for critique of the process by which commoditized forms of culture are disembedded from their social matrix and marketed through simulations of cultural performance.

Whether we like it or not, said our counter-voice, we have all been subjected to the implosions of technoscience. So, when we are undertaking research about culture, we should move from the framework of technocracy towards deriving new 'situated knowledge'. To quote Haraway, a member of our panel: 'Commitment after the implosions of technoscience requires immersion in the work of materializing new tropes in an always contingent practice of grounding or worlding.' Instead of being a 'modest witness to the extensive gains of technocracy', Haraway argued, we should stand as another sort of witness, uncovering sets of relations that the 'miscegenation of technoscience, always in a commoditized form, can never take into account'. We must consider how to cast our lot for some ways of life, and not for others. All knowledge-making technologies must be made visible and open to critical intervention in a relentless manner. We must be committed to knowing about the people and positions from which knowledge can come and at which it is targeted. Such a stance of critical reflectivity creates 'strong objectivity' quite distinct from the rather weaker, but common scientific notion of 'objectivity' where 'subjects and objects [are] exempt from the permanent finitude of engaged interpretation'.[11]

The positions of Yang, Ong and Martin are included in this volume and therefore do not need to be repeated. Each in their respective ways elaborated problems associated with the pre-articulated character of western knowledge and its cultural consequences. Yang and Ong both stressed that nothing will be changed until anthropologists begin to consider 'non-western societies' as equal producers of cultural knowledge. In resonance, Richards discarded his written paper and asked the audience to help him fund a conference which would refute the long accepted viewpoint that violence in Africa stems from primordial ethnic loyalties. The resemblances in tactics and world view of 'ethnic' groups such as Renamo in Mozambique, the RUF in Sierra Leone, the Khmer Rouge in Cambodia and Shining Path in Peru are troubling, and must be explained. (Two years later, we can add genocide in Rwanda to Richards' macabre list.) Are these violent social movements local refractions of global processes, with coordinate technological and cultural underpinnings, he asked? For the remote areas of rural Africa have not experienced cultural 'creolization' as a neutral cultural innovation; a whole generation of youth in Africa have known little but a state of 'permanent rebellion'. Truth for this generation is little more than a fact to be grasped about the AK47 assault rifle. The possessors of modern scientific knowledge should organize their technology, especially communications technology, so that its transfer empowers this present generation of rural youth, rather than continues to promote such a violent rebellion, Richards said.

CONCLUSION

As I have mentioned, any discussion about empowerment and social movements must also include the question of universities as a locus for anthropological research. The mainstream in anthropology, certainly as represented by Raymond Firth at the Oxford conference – where he once again insisted on this point – has never really questioned the academy as the central place from which the 'objective' observation of culture is undertaken and analysed. With autonomy guaranteed by an institutional structure, academic ethnographers are licensed, with very little constraints upon them, to make abstractions from 'cultural reality' and to reconstruct 'social facts' in the name of anthropological theory and of social science in general. But the universities themselves seem to be suffering shifts in context, both as key institutions of the nation-state and as key contributors to a fund of knowledge on which any nation-state draws.

A sea change in public opinion – driven by financial constraints – about the nature of knowledge and about the autonomy of universities with regard to distribution of knowledge has occurred in Britain, Australia, Canada and, to some extent, the United States. It is clear that the sea change has been exacerbated by protestations from the private sector, which during the last decade or so has had the ear of neo-conservative governments. As the wealth of industrial nation-states becomes more closely aligned with the production and distribution of *technical knowledge*, so in the opinion of businessmen and economists and bureaucrats, universities must be more firmly a part of technical production. Together, these 'others' demand that universities become the technical agencies of the state – specifically by splitting research from teaching functions and by directing research to strategic technical ends.

There appears to be an undermining of two axioms of post-secondary education which were almost unquestioned during the era of high industrialization. The first axiom holds that there is a realm of 'objective knowledge' and 'recognized truths' which academics disseminate. This epistemological axiom has a sociological corollary – that 'objective knowledge' is most effectively maintained in educational institutions that are relatively autonomous, and whose faculty enjoys the freedoms of comparative autonomy (Barnett 1990). Until now anthropology has insisted that it is able to produce objective knowledge about the characteristics of local culture, though it may have its own polemical arguments as to what 'facts' constitute that objective knowledge.

Perhaps the post-modern argument about the objectivity of knowledge has had its own reverberations and these reverberations have produced an unexpected loop between 'the passengers on the bus' and 'the bus', i.e. the university itself. In any event, the undermining of both axioms at the level of the university as an institution presents very real problems for anthropology, the more so in that both the locus of observation, the university, and the target reference, 'culture', are increasingly becoming subjected to the global spread of markets, commodities and consumerism. Surely the first counterpoint is to reorient the direction of the theoretical towards the boundaries that exist, the interface between university and other agencies for social action. As Karim states, activisim concerned with the plight of minorities seems to take place via social movements under the rubric of human rights and peace groups – not in anthropology.

Beginning with the assumption that all knowledge is 'interested knowledge', one set of links which most anthropology departments could pursue is reciprocal research with NGOs; and beyond this, departments could help strengthen the global position of NGO activity. Such a move is already being undertaken through the United Nations University's Programme on

Multilateralism. Here a number of alternatives are being considered to the usual ideas of multilateralism as diplomatic interactions between 'regimes'. The United Nations University programme is focusing on long-term structural change which privileges the interests of the less powerful, while not ignoring the constraints imposed by the more powerful. Their programme on the 'new multilateralism' (Cox 1992) is paying particular attention to transnational social movements.

When social advocacy is intimately connected with social action, when methods of 'systematic doubt' are enhanced so that advocacy claims can be better evaluated, when an affirmative theory in anthropology is wedded to a 'new multilateralism', the outcomes not only renew anthropological concern about the human condition but promote disciplinary necessities. For 'shifting contexts' this programme of the counter-voice of the Oxford decennial is the most viable strategy we have available.

NOTES

1 As Moore states (Chapter 1, this volume), 'Anthropologists for all their concern with local understandings and specificities do not habitually view the people they work with as producers of social science theory as opposed to producers of local knowledge. This is connected to the lack of politicization of knowledge production with the discipline of anthropology as a whole ... western social science repositions itself as the originary point of comparative and generalizing theory'.
2 The same point is made by Marcus and Fischer (1986: 93 and 184), who go on to suggest that this issue becomes increasingly evident the further one moves back into the history of anthropology. Of those notable exceptions cited by Marcus and Fischer, one was the plan put together in the 1940s by Max Gluckman for the Rhodes-Livingstone Institute in Zambia.
3 Nowhere is an alternative to this point about the relation between 'consciousness' and 'being' better put than in Vaclav Havel's statement before the United States Congress in 1990: 'the salvation of this human world lies nowhere else than in the human heart, in the human power to reflect, in human meekness and in human responsibility. ... Without a global revolution in the sphere of human consciousness, nothing will change for better in the sphere of our [social] Being as humans, and the catastrophe toward which this world is headed, be it ecological, social, demographic, or a general breakdown of civilization will be unavoidable.' When Havel, a leader of a human rights movement, found himself through a sudden political transformation occupying the top position in a former communist state, he felt the need to turn inside out this aspect of Marxist philosophy (Havel 1990: 2).
4 Roles represent a reflection of the institutional order (Berger and Luckmann 1967: 74) and, just like legitimation and institutionalization, occur as concomitant of the construction of objectified knowledge: 'the representation of an institution in and by roles is thus the representation par excellence on which all other representations are dependent' (Berger and Luckmann 1967: 75).
5 Moore argues (Chapter 1, this volume) that anthropological writing about local knowledge often implies that they constitute closed systems, and are

therefore incapable of self-reflection and auto-critique; in fact this has long been thought to be one of the criteria which distinguishes traditional from modern societies. This is true, but as I am arguing here, self-reflection and auto-critique require taking into account a whole pattern of reflective loops in order to account for the possibility of blocked reflectiveness. The only anthropologist I know who considered this issue is Gregory Bateson (see Harries-Jones 1995).

6 My own part in these events was, initially, fortuitous. I was at an international scientific conference in Helsinki discussing issues surrounding technological intrusion into the biosphere at the precise moment (September 1983) that a political crisis emerged between the superpowers over the shooting down of the Korean Airliner 007. All international scientific conferences became closed, except ours, where Russian scientists presented their version of the nuclear winter hypothesis. This release of research information occurred six weeks before a similar but rather larger conference on nuclear winter by the Americans in Washington. The Helsinki conference asked me to be their Recorder, so I was given the task of issuing some of the first press releases on nuclear winter.

7 The recent House of Commons standing committee from which these figures are drawn heard the briefs of 165 advocacy groups.

8 Others include Giddens (1984) and Melucci (1989). Gregory Bateson has a great deal to say about recursion, but does not link his discussion of the recursive forms of cultural life to social movements (Harries-Jones 1995).

9 There is a formal underpinning to 'radical constructivism', of which Touraine shares the primary proposition, namely that 'knowledge does not reflect an "objective" ontological reality, but [is] exclusively an ordering and organization of a world constituted by our experience' (von Glasersfeld 1984: 24). A radical constructivist is one who emphasizes an epistemology of fittedness among dynamic constraints. For a radical constructivist, the central issue is a 'study of *how* intelligence operates, of the ways and means it employs to construct a relatively [constrained or] *regular* world out of the flow of experience' (von Glasersfeld 1984: 32). The flow of experience becomes regular, 'fitted' and viable. Finally, the relation between action and 'fit' is reflective, a fitting of an understanding of constraints into performance. Radical constructivism is, however, primarily concerned with cognition and holds that any viable cognitive structure, or any lasting evaluation of knowledge is fitted to the experience we have of constraints. To this Touraine would add that such constraints are necessarily derived from the contestations of social action.

10 A quote from the paper of Daniel Miller is indicative: 'the media is now the locale of localities. The consumer of the media is de-localized by taking in products from elsewhere while localizing the acts of consumption. What sustains product distinctiveness? Not just the immediate use the consumers make of it but the construction of cultural milieux – symbolic labour as the work of (re) signification' (Miller 1993).

11 Haraway termed the latter 'the flaccid objectivity of the patriarchy.' In her formal presentation (not published here) Haraway stated that the great divide between man and nature and its gendered corollary, which anthropology has always used to distinguish the boundaries of culture from the boundaries of the natural, has been breached by global technoscience. The characteristics of this breach are so fundamental that they require an intensive search for other forms of contrast and comparison.

REFERENCES

Barnett, Ronald (1990) *The Idea of Higher Education*. Buckingham: The Society for Research in Higher Education and Open University Press.

Berger, Peter L. and Luckmann, Thomas (1967) *The Social Construction of Reality: A Treatise on the Sociology of Knowledge*. Garden City, New York: Anchor Books.

Cleveland, John (1991) 'Why is the feminist movement still politically marginal?', pp. 182–202 in Peter Harries-Jones (ed.) *Making Knowledge Count: Advocacy and Social Science*. Montreal and Kingston: McGill-Queen's University Press.

Cox, Robert W. (1992) 'Multilateralism and world order'. *Review of International Studies* 18: 161–80.

Fals-Borda, O. (1990) 'The application of participatory-action research in Latin America', pp. 79–97 in Martin Albrow and Elizabeth King (eds) *Globalization, Knowledge and Society*. Newbury Park: Sage.

Freire, Paulo (1970) *Pedagogy of the Oppressed*. New York: Seabury Press.

Giddens, Anthony (1984) *The Constitution of Society*. Berkeley, CA and Los Angeles, CA: University of California Press.

Glasersfeld, Ernst von (1984) 'An introduction to radical constructivism,' pp. 17–40 in Paul Watzlawick (ed.) *The Invented Reality*. New York: Norton.

Harries-Jones, Peter (1985) 'The nuclear winter hypothesis: a broadened definition,' pp. 374–82 in F. Kenneth Hare (ed.) *Nuclear Winter and Associated Effects: A Canadian Appraisal of the Environmental Impact of Nuclear War*. Ottawa: The Royal Society of Canada,.

—— (1995) *A Recursive Vision: Ecological Understanding and Gregory Bateson*. Toronto: University of Toronto Press.

Havel, Vaclav (1990) Extract from a speech (21 February 1990) to a combined session of the Congress of the United States quoted in *OCUFA Forum* 6(21): 2.

Marcus, George and Fischer, Michael M.J. (1986) *Anthropology as Cultural Critique*. Chicago: Chicago University Press.

Melucci, Alberto (1989) *Nomads of the Present: Social Movements and Individual Needs in Contemporary Society*. Philadelphia, PA: Temple University Press.

Miller, Daniel (1993) 'Introduction' to 'Embodiment and consumption'. Paper presented to *The Uses of Knowledge, Local and Global Relations*.

Milton, Kay (ed.) (1993) 'Introduction: environmentalism and anthropology', in *Environmentalism: the View from Anthropology*. London and New York: Routledge, ASA Monographs 32, 1–17.

Morgan, Gareth (1991) 'Advocacy as a social science', pp. 223–31 in Peter Harries-Jones (ed.) *Making Knowledge Count: Advocacy and Social Science*. Montreal and Kingston: McGill-Queen's University Press.

Spencer, Metta (1991) 'Advocating peace', pp. 209–22 in Peter Harries-Jones (ed.) *Making Knowledge Count: Advocacy and Social Science*. Montreal and Kingston: McGill-Queen's University Press.

Strathern, Marilyn (1993) 'Introduction' to 'Shifting contexts'. Paper presented to *The Uses of Knowledge, Local and Global Relations*.

Touraine, Alain (1981) *The Voice and the Eye: An Analysis of Social Movements*. Cambridge: Cambridge University Press and Paris: Editions de la Maison des Sciences de l'Homme.

Name index

A Cheng 101, 102–3, 108–9
Abraham, A. 143
Ahmad, Z. 133
Aidid, General 119
Anagnost, A. 68, 100, 104
Anderson, B. 65
Anderson, P. 43
Appadurai, A. 43, 44, 62, 63
Appelbaum, R. P. 79
Arafat, Yasser 119
Arce, A. 41, 51, 57
Asad, T. 115

Barlow, T. 84
Barnett, R. 169
Berger, P. L. 160–1
Berman, M. 99
Bloch, M. 97
Bodanis, D. 18
Bodunrin, P. O. 5
Botkin, D. B. 128
Boyle, R. 20
Burgess, J. 18
Bush, George 115

Callaway, H. 61
Cambrosia, A. 20
Cao, W. 108
Chang, K-C. 102
Chao, W. 96
Chatterjee, P. 64, 83
Chen Shisi 99
Chin, V. K. 131
Chomsky, N. 121
Chow, T-t. 67, 101
Chun, A. 80
Cleveland, J. 164
Clifford, J. 61, 63, 107
Cohen, P. A. 66

Cohen, R. 115
Cohn, B. 30
Comaroff, Jean 61
Comaroff, John 61
Corrigan, P. 30
Cox, R. W. 170
Crossley, P. 67

Davies, A. G. 152
Dean, K. 100
Deleuze, G. 9
DeLillo, D. 16, 33
Deng, X. 65–6
Derrida, J. 161
Devan, J. 80
Dikotter, F. 67, 78
Dirks, N. 101, 105
Dirlik, A. 64, 85
Douglas, M. 146, 147
Duara, P. 84, 100

Edelman, G. 18
Engels, F. 97
Esposito, J. 119
Evans Pritchard, E. 129

Fals-Borda, O. 158
Featherstone, M. 43
Feld, S. 71
Ferme, M. C. 146
Firth, R. 129, 168
Fischer, M. 61, 107, 131, 156
Foucault, M. 10–12, 53, 101
Fox, R. 62
Freire, P. 159
Friedman, E. 64, 71
Friedman, J. 102
Fukuyama, F. 37, 80, 133

Subject index

ACT UP 17
affirmative theory 133, 134, 157–9
Africa 19, 168; African philosophy 3–6;
    interpretations of technology 8
agrarian development 51–8
'agrarian structure' 52–3
agriculture: agricultural knowledge
    56–8; failure of enforced 124;
    farmers' organizations 41;
    globalizing and localizing processes
    46–50; rice farming versus trade
    140–2
alienation: of global groups 134–5; and
    micrograph images 29–30
American Indians 98
Ancient Society (Morgan) 96, 97
animism 125–6; and naturalism 127–8
Anthropology as Cultural Critique
    (Marcus and Fischer) 61, 107
ASEAN 121
Asia 118, 133; modernity 78–84
authoritarianism, and Chinese
    modernity 79–81

Bahai 126
Bemba political control 10–11
'bio-politics' 12
Biology as Ideology (Lewontin) 16
bɔni hinda (ritual killing) 142–7, 153
Bosnia-Herzegovina 133
'break the three irons' campaign 68–9
Britain: colonialism 30, 60, 83; dairy
    farmers 48; export quotas 41;
    Pergau Dam crisis 131–3; social
    movements 163
bronze, use in early China 102
Buddhism 95, 100, 127
Bushmen (Namibia) 124

Canada: attitude to American Indians
    98; social advocacy research 161;
    social movements 163–4
cancer 21, 25, 28, 32
capitalism 64, 66, 68–9, 78, 94–5, 97,
    104–5, 110, 121, 134; *guanxi*-based
    73, 79, 80, 82, 83
chimpanzees: attacks on humans
    144–5; and *bɔni hinda* 143–4
China 133: modernity and tradition
    93–110; state and popular
    modernity 64–86
Chinese in Malaysia 121
Christianity 5, 99, 100, 126–7
citizenship 44–6
colonialism: 5, 30, 60, 61–2, 78–9, 104–5,
    118; legacy of anthropology 115
commoditization: and 'creolization'
    167; and social identity 55–6
communication media 156; and cultural
    flow 43; use in Liberia–Sierra Leone
    border 149, 150
Communism 120
Communist Party 95, 100, 101
Communist Revolution 94
Confucianism 69–70, 78–84, 97;
    ethnocentricities of 133–4
consciousness-raising: neglect by
    anthropology 158–9; and sociology
    of knowledge 159–61
conservation: impact of slogans on
    Mende villagers 143; and Liberian
    youth 147–53, 154
consumerism, China 69
consumers' associations 41
consumption, as definition of
    citizenship 46
contrapuntal anthropology 84–6